IMPROVING
SCHOOL PUBLIC
RELATIONS

IMPROVING
SCHOOL PUBLIC
RELATIONS

ROBERT P. HILLDRUP

Allyn and Bacon, Inc.

Boston   London   Sydney   Toronto

Library of Congress Cataloging in Publication Data
Hilldrup, Robert P., 1933–
      Improving school public relations.
      1. Public relations—United States—Schools.
I. Title.
LB2847·H53   659·2'937101'0973   81–22828
ISBN 0–205–07738–2   AACR2

Printed in the United States of America

10 9 8 7 6 5 4 3 2 1   86 85 84 83 82

CONTENTS

"Planned public relations is usually a stepchild of conflict"—Kinsey M. Robinson, as quoted by Dr. Laurence J. Peter in *Peter's Quotations*, (William Morrow and Company, 1977).

"Let advertisers spend the same amount of money improving their product that they do on advertising and they wouldn't have to advertise it. Will rogers, *op. cit.*

Preface

To say that the American public today is fully committed to an anti-public education posture is as inaccurate and as dangerous as saying that public education and its leadership could do no wrong; that the public would stand for anything.

Still, the fact must be faced that even where a legitimate and long-standing honeymoon has existed between public education and its public, malaise has appeared and divorce may be in the works. This book is addressed to principals, superintendents, public relations personnel, and school board members in those communities and in communities where open warfare has broken out between the education community and the public it is supposed to serve.

The thesis here, quite simply, is that most of the problems ravaging the public schools today are at their core problems of public relations: missed signals, poor planning, muddled thinking, and, sadly, inept leadership or, at best, leadership that has not been trained. These problems are, for the most part, both predictable and preventable. Where they occur, they occur because education managers—boards, superintendents, principals, even leaders of teacher unions and parent groups—have either lost, or never developed a sense of place, purpose, and perspective which the public at large expects.

Many of these management errors bring immediate, negative results. Of even greater concern, however, is the "mind bent" which leads to a repetition of such errors, particularly those with delayed but devastating effects.

The intent of my words is positive. If the book seems to deal excessively with the warts on the face of public education, the high blood pressure, giddiness, and other symptoms of disease, the approach is only the one the health professional takes. For it is not the things that are going right, functioning normally, doing the jobs for which nature created them that concern the physician. The physician's concern is the lifestyle, the symptoms, and the disease which may threaten the survival of the patient. What caused these problems and how to prevent or correct them is the issue, although the treatment can be more painful than the practice which set things wrong in the first place.

Not everything in this book applies equally to every school, community, or school district. Sex education, for example, may not be an issue in a liberal, urban system, while the contents of a single library book (which most of the complainants usually haven't read) can tear a small district to pieces. In both areas, however, the caliber of instruction in reading and math is apt to be a highly explosive issue.

Further, a forty-mile bus ride in Utah each day may be accepted as the normal way to get to and from school, but a four-mile ride in Indiana, if ordered by a federal judge, can be a major educational and community crisis. Let either transporation system be run by an incompetent and the issue becomes worse, no matter how long the ride, who ordered it, or what state it's in.

The term "public relations" as used in this book should not be misconstrued. As used here, it has little or nothing to do with advertising, market research, sales techniques, better breath, the support that lifts and separates, or any other attempt to persuade anyone to buy, borrow, or steal that which he doesn't want and certainly doesn't need. The term as used here means exactly what Webster said it did before Madison Avenue discovered it: relations—successful I hope—with the public in its various forms.

If much of what is said seems to touch on the problems of racial minorities in the schools, the white minority included, it is because I am convinced that this problem affects every school district in the nation, even those with no integration problems or, indeed, no racial minorities. The establishment of stable, integrated schools of high quality is still the main problem in many urban and suburban schools in the United States. It is required by law and it is morally right to the extent that the rights of all are protected. It is a public relations problems of the first magnitude and it is addressed here with what I trust will be recognized as constructive candor.

In preparing this book, I have drawn on my own experience as parent, teacher, PTA president, school administrator, education editor, and public information director for an urban school system. Some of the experiences which led me to my conclusions were funny, many infuriating, a few were tragic. But enough were also rewarding to make me believe that public education, its potential, not its problems, is still probably the best thing the United States ever developed.

Portions of this book appeared earlier in somewhat different form in *The American School Board Journal,* the *Journal of Educational Communication, The PTA Magazine,* the *Indiana School Boards Association Journal,* and *The New York Times.*

Robert P. Hilldrup

ACKNOWLEDGMENTS

A WORD ABOUT THE SUPPORTING CAST

This is a disclaimer, because it is not possible to thank all who helped in the preparation of this book or to chastise those who made the effort more difficult than necessary. Those who have experienced a breech birth in either body or spirit will know what I am talking about.

Special recognition, however, must go to my wife, Jo Ann, and to our sons, Lee, Frank, and Mark who, though they hadn't the foggiest idea what daddy was growling and writing about, always tried to be supportive.

And finally, a special word of dedication to the late Dr. Robert L. Hilldrup, Professor and Chairman of the departments of history and political science, Mary Washington College of the University of Virginia, who many years ago dedicated his first book to his son.

Management for Public Acceptance

If those who must run the public schools have reached a state of continuing paranoia today, one can hardly blame them. To paraphrase the late Sir Winston Churchill, they have much to be paranoid about. Something *is* after them. And that something can be found almost anywhere in the professional lives of the school board members and administrators to whom law and public policy have given this awesome responsibility.

The sources of these problems are as diverse as the problems of school management themselves. Is it curriculum? Indeed. Either the implementation, or the lack thereof; the degree to which curriculum has grown and multiplied can cause grave problems. Or, conversely, the degree to which it has not done so may create crises just as grave.

Is it personnel? Of course. It is promotions and transfers, training and demotions, employment and retirements and mandated reductions in staff; unions and contracts; lifestyles and living conditions, even the matter of sexual preference in both personal life and on the job.

Is it money? By all means. It is what you have and what you don't, what you've spent and what you haven't—and how. It is what steps have been taken to obtain additional funds, and from what source, and, indeed, whether the step should have been taken in the first place.

Discipline? Safety? No matters are dearer to the hearts of parents—and teachers—although the raging disorders which occasionally flash through classrooms and cafeterias and across campuses may have knowingly or unknowingly been aided by the parents and teachers themselves.

The school manager has only to look around at the politics; buildings; plans or lack of plans; parent groups or even the absence of such groups; and the press. *Everything that a school manager does or does not do has a public relations impact on his professional life and that of the institution for which he is responsible.* To avoid disaster this must be recognized.

Some of the problems become exceedingly complex when they touch many or all of the categories just listed. An element of the problem that cannot be overemphasized is that schools today touch far more receptors —publics, if you will—than we have stopped to realize. It is only when this realization is forced upon school managers, frequently as a result of a crisis, that some attempts are hurriedly made to adopt a strategy of action or reaction. Too often, this type of management by crisis simply ensures that public relations problems will not just continue, they will grow. It is not enough to recognize that public education is more complex, more expensive, more entangled in law and litigation than ever before. An operational commitment that sees sound and sensible goals and recognizes the public relations implications in attaining them must exist.

Vulnerability of Leadership

One of the things that makes superintendents of schools leap up from a sound sleep in the middle of the night and rush about checking the doors and windows is the realization of just how vulnerable they are to sloppy staff work. Sometimes, of course, it's the superintendent's own fault, he having appointed an incompetent to a position of trust in the first place. But all new superintendents are entitled to at least a short grace period, and the public, in most cases, will grant it to them.

In the following example, a new superintendent almost got his administration in trouble right from the start by looking only at the potential profits of a public relations situation without considering the perils.

This superintendent was both headstrong and overly cautious, the kind who forms blue-ribbon committees to make decisions on issues and actions primarily to leave him free to act immediately on matters that should be left alone. This time, however, he wasn't entirely to blame.

The superintendent had come up with a basically sound idea: to enlist one of the city's major department stores to sponsor an annual luncheon for the top scholars from the city's high schools. In his letter to the students selected, the superintendent wrote, "You are being honored as one of the top seven students, chosen on the basis of academic records, from the graduating classes of each of our high schools."

However, a principal, concerned that he might be criticized because all seven of his top students were of one race even though his school was fully desegregated, decided to take the matter to an assistant superintendent. The assistant superintendent agreed: change the rules from the academic basis the superintendent had specified and juggle the invitations to bring in some students of a different race.

All this might have been fine except that everyone in the school, as well as the parents, knew exactly who ranked where among the top students, because each was already scheduled for special recognition at graduation. The result was perfectly predictable. The father of a student removed from the luncheon list to make room for a student of another race called the superintendent on the day of the banquet to voice his angry complaint. He threatened to complain to the news media and to the board. Such an action would cause negative publicity not only for the superintendent and his school system, but also for the sponsoring store, the mayor, and the state superintendent of public instruction, who were also participating, and whose support was necessary to the new superintendent.

Only the fact that the superintendent was new—and that he promised the angry parent that action would be taken against his racist subordinates—kept the matter quiet. The luncheon went off without a hitch. Angers faded into summer. No actions were taken by anyone, including the superintendent, and the incident blew over.

It would be pleasant to report that everyone involved learned a lesson in public relations, to say nothing of honesty and integrity. This was not the case. The superintendent should have learned how vulnerable he was to staff errors, and that good administration and good public relations planning could help head off errors such as these. But most of all, he could have learned that the problems, and the solutions, frequently begin and end with top educational management.

The Need for Analysis

This example is fairly typical of an administrative action that needs public relations analysis. What can be learned from this example? What public relations opportunities were seized? Which were missed?

First, of course, was bad staff work, the insertion of a racial issue through the disregarding of the superintendent's express criteria for student recognition. A better superintendent, and a better staff, would have been alert to the racial implications of student selection *before* specifying and deciding upon the selection criteria. If the criteria were fair, and a school was to be represented by students of only one race, the superintendent should have known it ahead of time, and been prepared to accept that fact honestly and openly. If the criteria were unfair, they should not have been used in the first place.

The basic idea of student recognition, however, was excellent. An analysis of the program reveals several excellent opportunities to capitalize on student achievement and obtain positive support therefrom for the schools. Here are some examples:

1. Involving the business community, which in some areas in recent years has grown more and more suspicious of the cost/productivity factor in public education, was a wise step. This involvement provided the superintendent with an opportunity to display good graduates and let the business community see something positive it was getting for its tax dollars. This also represented a means by which the new superintendent could establish communication with appropriate business leaders.

2. The involvement of the political segment of the community (the mayor) was simple common sense and an opportunity to publicly ally the mayor with a successful school program. In addition, the event provided a good chance for media coverage for the mayor.

3. Involving the state superintendent of public instruction was a shrewd move with positive potential. All state superintendents like to be shown the accomplishments of local school systems, particularly when those accomplishments can be included in budget presentations to state legislatures, which can understand and relate to parental pride far easier than some more obscure, but very pressing, educational need.

4. Parents provide our first

KEY CONCERN FOR SCHOOL PR: *Never overlook a chance to let parents bask in the glow of public honor which their children have received for academic work. Nothing a school administrator can do has more potential for long-term positive results than that which implies the parents were just as responsible as the schools for the child's success.*

---

5. The superintendent had created a first-time media event, the kind that only informed, aggressive journalists are apt to question at other than face value. In this case, the publicity was positive, and extensive.

6. The recognition of the students by their peers was a subsidiary goal, and one not emphasized. Still, the youngsters got a chance to get out of class, had a trip downtown, and got a free meal.

What were the actual results? Points 1, 2, and 3, those involving the business community, the local political establishment, and the state educational authority were achieved. The objective in point 4 was lost, at least in the high school where parents knew that the most qualified students did not receive the invitations to the luncheon. Point 5 has to be considered a success also. The event got good print and broadcast coverage; the unhappy father did not speak out; and the media, left to its own initiative, did not bother to probe the matter by questioning the selection process. The success of point 6 is questionable. The students, for all their scholarship, probably took things more in stride than anyone else, the way young people often do, enjoying the event and the limelight, even those who had been in schools where racial factors had been introduced into the selection process.

In sum, the superintendent came off quite well. His good idea, however, almost aborted at a time when he was most anxious to make a good impression. That he was fortunate can hardly be questioned, but worst of all were the indications from his later administrative actions that he had not learned how fortunate he had been.

As an older superintendent on the verge of retirement after a successful, if stormy, career once observed, "I always made it a practice to ride with the devil himself—as long as he was going my way." Knowing how to utilize opportunities and events for public relations benefit is a judgment factor that is difficult to develop and does not always come with experience. Educational managers must know not only where they are going, but why, and anticipate not only the potential achievements, but the possible problems which are likely to accompany even the brightest of ideas. It is for the latter reason that the wise superintendent will have a loyal scout on staff. Such a person is not unlike the robot on the old television show "Lost in Space," whose primary function was to keep its human "family" out of trouble by screaming "warning, warning" every time danger approached. Such a staff member, if a superintendent will utilize him, will not serve as an impediment to progessive school management, but an insurer thereof.

There can be no more important understanding among school managers, therefore, than this

---

KEY CONCERN FOR SCHOOL PR: *Everything a school system or its officials does has some potential for gain and much potential for disaster.*

The Selection of Staff

How, then, does a superintendent choose good staff, men and women who understand the public relations implications of their acts and who are unlikely to cause, or aggravate, an exceptional number of problems?

The superintendent who is seriously concerned with this problem has taken a major step simply by recognizing it. For when things go wrong consistently—when the public always seems to be surly, if not downright violent—it takes an exceptional educational manager to admit that the reason may lie in his or her own organization and not with the public. And when those reasons do lie outside school management—an irascible and un-enlightened city council, for example—educational managers' understanding of PR implications can at least reduce the damage done by those outside the direct control of the school administration.

The superintendent in the illustration at the beginning of this chapter had a good idea, but then ran perilously close to wrecking it, because he had not had time to appraise the lack of judgment among key staff. To his credit, he was able to placate the parent, a tactic which is frequently necessary and occasionally justifiable.

Yet choosing the staff is still the issue. On-the-job training, while favored by some, is a dangerous tactic at best. Staff selection is an art, not just a science that can be governed by professional courses and certification. Knowing how to practice this art is a key for any top educational manager.

To begin with, as noted, there is no danger in having staff members who are smarter than the superintendent in their respective areas of oper-ation, provided, of course, that the staff are professional and loyal. Tests and measurements, being essentially scientific devices, are relatively poor indi-cators of leadership and judgment, to say nothing of loyalty, and although tests have a valuable place in analyzing pupil potential and achievement, they are of questionable worth in designating administrative managers.

One of the causes of poor communications and poor public relations, in my experience, is a simple one: *too much staff*. That, of course, is heresy to most educational managers, and to any other governmental bureaucracy as well.

Many managers honestly believe they need more staff, and sometimes they do. But the fact remains that each layer of administrative personnel carries with it a mathematically increasing danger of fouled communications and public relations blunders.

For some reason, layers of educational management tend to increase in direct proportion to a decline in numbers of pupils and teachers. This creates its own public relations problem on a variety of fronts, not the least of which is the teachers' union, which tends to look with narrowed and suspicious eyes on a growing management when its own membership is losing jobs.

For example, a school system of my acquaintance had an enrollment of more than 50,000 in 1960. The central administration included a super-intendent, an administrative aide, and two assistant superintendents. The instructional program was run, under one of the assistant superintendents, with the help of a research director, a director of instruction, and half a dozen subject and grade supervisors.

Eighteen years later, however, when enrollment had declined almost 40 percent, the same central administration required, *in part,* a super-intendent, a deputy superintendent, three assistant superintendents, a management "intern," and a three-member "community and government re-lations" team headed by a former music teacher to "handle" PR. The one-member research staff had grown to sixteen. Lower levels of adminis-tration had multiplied accordingly. And during the same eighteen-year pe-riod, pupil performance had plummeted and violence in the schools had soared. The position of director of instruction had been abandoned, it should be noted. Of course, it had been replaced, in part, by a director of secondary administration, a director of secondary instruction, an administrator of sec-ondary education, a director of elementary administration, a director of elementary instruction, and an administrator of elementary education.

Is it any wonder that no one in the organization could figure out what was going on? This certainly raises a

---

KEY CONCERN FOR SCHOOL PR: *If we cannot communicate with-in our own organization, how can we keep our public relations straight?*

We can't, of course, when we allow bodies to so clutter up the or-ganization that quantity is the only thing we can find when the public—and the schools themselves—see the need for quality staff.

To be sure, the years between 1960 and 1978 saw a considerable growth in the role of federal and state governments and in their direct involvement with local schools. This reasoning is frequently cited as the cause of the growth in the *quantity* of local school management (as well as a diminution in the quality). But the very school systems which have most greatly in-creased their central administrative staffs have also made certain that they added separate legal staffs and federal programs departments to handle much of the additional paperwork and *grantsmanship* that has proliferated from the growth of the state and federal educational bureaucracies. In sum, therefore, quantity of educational management alone is never an answer and, sooner or later, is bound to become a negative public relations factor in itself.

There are, of course, ways to get the mushrooming monster of school administration under control, and to make positive points with the public for doing so. It takes a courageous educational manager, however, to seize the opportunity, because many educational managers see their first allegiance not to the public, but to their own clique, their own administrative or-ganization. This, of course, is not loyalty. It is closer to pandering.

Yet the manager who does not make a careful review of staff to deter-mine how, ethically, he can get more work from fewer people runs the risk that staff cuts will be arbitrarily imposed by a cost-conscious board, which, in turn, is responding to legitimate citizen pressure and concern. There are many ways and places and people where these savings can be implemented without human hardship, if the manager will but plan ahead. Where such

a program is put into effect, administrative personnel may come to understand that their productivity will be a measure not just for promotion, but for
retention as well. The example cited just previously of the way one administration has grown despite declining enrollment is fairly typical of most urban
and suburban school systems.

Where should the manager who is concerned over the public relations
effects of a bloated staff look? The manager's immediate entourage is one
place. Because the staff is apt to have a high visibility, it also will attract
public concern if it is thought to be too large. The approach sometimes
known as differentiated staffing can be used. In effect, no department of the
educational bureaucracy can add a person unless that person assumes the
duties of, or replaces, someone already in the structure whose departure has
created a vacancy. Simple as this sounds, it means management can no
longer hire two people to do a job formerly filled by one. It also means that,
in particularly bloated situations, managers may have to choose whether to
fill a single position at a salary of $20,000 per year, or two positions at $10,000
each.

The effects of staff inflation are not just confined to central administration. Personnel services to students are another good place to look for
padding, simply because no one wants to deny students anything. As a result,
the schools are in many cases *over* staffed with guidance counselors, psychologists, job placement specialists, and, naturally, their clerical assistants.
Each position of this type should be carefully reviewed to see what specific
service it is delivering and how many children are *specifically* benefiting
thereby.

Limiting Staff Growth

Here is one way in which the growth of non-teaching staff can be
curtailed without deleterious effect on students and with a positive public
relations result:

Among the most criticized administrators in the school systems of
North America are guidance counselors. Counselors seem generally inacces-
sible to children in need and are almost always considered by teachers to be
contributors to classroom problems rather than problem-solvers. Part of this
may be because counselors seem always to be attending meetings or rushing
about to attend to some matter which does not involve direct work with
children or teachers. *Why* such conditions and attitudes obtain is an internal
public relations problem in itself; overall, it represents an area in which
correction can be accomplished.

Throughout my career in education, for example, I have heard weak
and ineffective teachers brag repeatedly about their plans to "pick up" a
cheap, quick master's degree in guidance and counseling as a means to: (1)
escape from the classroom, (2) get a private office, and (3) obtain a foothold

on the career ladder leading to other administrative jobs which demand even less in talent and ability. All too often, these teachers succeed.

All this shucking and jiving takes place in and around schools. Schools have children, and children are not unlike army enlistees. They know, instinctively, which of their caretakers and leaders are putting them on and which are ripping them off. Word gets around, and quickly, that Counselor Jones and Sgt. Smith are too busy promoting their own careers to have any real interest in the problems or the welfare of the troops.

In almost any school, particularly at the secondary level, students can tell you quickly and precisely who among the staff is accessible, has sound judgment, good advice, and can be trusted to offer help in either career guidance or a matter of crisis. Most often, in my experience at least, the staff member pupils would designate with such an accolade would be a classroom teacher rather than a guidance counselor or other established member of the administrative hierarchy. Thus, these suggestions:

1. In secondary schools, poll the out-going classes to determine which teachers are most respected for their advice, counsel, and willingness to help.
2. Relieve the two or three teachers so designated of at least 50 to 75 percent of their classes and make them available in a commons area for either appointments or drop-in counseling.
3. Retain one regular guidance counselor as a *go-fer*, to keep track of vocational and collegiate guidance materials and to make social service, medical, and other professional appointments as needed.

Such an approach would help to keep under control the growing clique of quasi-administrators to which the counselor so fervently attempts to belong; establish more intimate, trustworthy, and student-valued services; and provide a healthier organizational posture for all. It might even lead to one of the greatest public relations steps of them all—the regular teaching by *all* administrators of one or more classes in their areas of expertise, an event unlikely to be suggested by the administrators, you can be sure.

The problem with teacher guidance as a solution to over-administration is that really good teachers see guidance as a routine part of their job and do not want to "escape" from the life of the classroom into something else unless money, or the lack thereof, forces them to do so.

A Technique for Selection

The superintendent who wishes to hire or promote staff with good public relations judgment may find an impromptu type of interview valuable. Once you have established that the staff member knows a reasonable amount about the field (business administration, for example, in a candidate for an assistant superintendency in school business affairs), two questions, asked without warning during the interview, usually provide good indices. The questions are:

1. What have you read?
2. What do you think?

The candidate usually will respond to the first question by citing some material in the field of training, and should be asked to cite and comment upon something outside of that.

To the second question, most candidates will reply with a question of their own: "Think about what?" The candidate should then be directed to choose some topic outside the professional field.

The value of this technique, which, I might add, should be used in selecting teachers as well as administrative managers, is that it determines rather quickly: 1) if the candidates have any active interest outside their own field and 2) how well they can react to the unexpected or unanticipated. It is hardly reasonable to expect many Renaissance men in public education today, but the narrowness which has been in-bred into too many educational managers may contribute substantially to their inability to understand the broad implications of public relations in their jobs. In addition, candidates who cannot respond reasonably and lucidly to the unexpected question without the appearance of waffling or brain damage are unlikely to be comfortable when some segment of the public hits them with a question or challenge that was not covered in their professional training.

How the candidate responds to unexpected questions is almost as important as what is said. The time when the educational manager's success was measured by the degree to which the answer was couched in jargon so obscure that anyone's interpretation was correct is gone. The public still may not know what an educational manager is saying, but it has become smart enough to know that whatever it is, it is not worth listening to, or paying for, if it is not intelligible. These travesties of the malady known as Educator's Tongue-Tie will be discussed in grimmer detail in Chapter 5. Specific answers, delivered in English, generally are indicative not of oversimplification, as many educators would contend, but of clear thinking and well thought-out goals.

What is my job? What do I intend to accomplish? Why am I doing what I'm doing? How do I intend to achieve this goal? In what specific way will *everyone but me*, students and taxpayers particularly, be better off if I achieve this goal? None of these questions is difficult for an educational manager who has given some sensible thought, in perspective, to what he is about. And the manager who can answer sensibly is the manager least likely to have major public relations problems.

The ability to answer simply and directly, as the questions suggested earlier would demonstrate, indicates that the individual is staying well enough abreast of the world to have an intelligent opinion and information about it. An educational manager who does not take the time to read the morning paper before coming to work can expect to be blind-sided sooner or later when it's discovered that the rest of the world is talking about something affecting him that he did not even know had happened. We all may be dumb in some ways, but there is no need being any dumber than God intended.

I once suggested to a superintendent that this course of action would be a good one for him to follow. "Oh," he said, "I don't have time. I'm a 'selective' reader."

Well, a President of the United States may be able to afford that attitude, but a local superintendent or principal or any other educational manager who tries it will get badly burned sooner or later.

The Problem of Outside Advice

In the process of selecting educational managers for major staff positions, particularly those of a specialized nature, there is a public relations advantage to be gained by adding to the selection committee an *appropriate* representative from outside the school system.

The involvement of community groups in the selection process for superintendents has become increasingly common in many localities. This practice has grown out of the well-intentioned but carelessly thought-out attempts to "democratize" school leadership. The result has been rather like assembling a superintendent with a leg from the teachers' union, an arm from the PTA, and the heart of a banker. Each part could function fairly well in its original place, but assembled into one it seldom has the brain or blood or viscera to work.

A more sensible approach, at least when the superintendent is choosing a staff, is to add that representative from outside who brings specific, unemotional *knowledge or expertise* to the interview sessions. When that is done, a public relations plus can be gained in that the community is *sensibly* represented and involved. Of equal or greater importance, such an addition brings an evaluative perspective that neither the superintendent nor other educators who participate in the interviews may have.

For example, an accountant or finance director from a private firm can participate in the interview of candidates for the position of chief fiscal officer of the school system; a city editor or other middle-management person from the newspaper can assist in interviews for the director of public information for the schools; the school lunch director can be chosen with the help of the director of restaurants for a hotel chain.

Taking this tack will help all involved determine whether the candidates have in-depth knowledge of their fields, and whether they can communicate accordingly.

Training for Decision Making

One of the better documents illustrating how broadly public relations is involved in everything an educational manager does is the "Rolling Hills High School In-Basket," which was developed for, and distributed by, the National Association of Secondary School Principals in 1975.[1]

The "In-Basket" is a folder containing twenty-three communications of the types a principal might be expected to receive, plus a sheet or two on which to indicate the action taken in disposing of each. Each communication represents a problem. Some are routine personnel matters—time off to take a graduate course, relationships with the new building representative of the teachers' union. Others, however, deal with such things as grading, the contents of the student newspaper, behavior of a teacher off campus, confidentiality of student records, and the administraton of funds for male and female activities to comply with Title IX of the Education Amendments of 1972.

Nowhere, however, is there any guidance about how to resolve the problems. Nor is anything said about the implications. At least 75 percent, however, have overt public relations implications of the kind many managers do not easily recognize.

Too often, managers think of public relations as simply a relationship with the media or with public actions, events, or appearances. Nothing could be further from the truth. Successful public relations, when dealing with negative factors, frequently involves taking the proper action to keep a seemingly simple internal problem from blowing up into a community issue.

Take the examples cited from the "In-Basket." If grading inequities have developed, isn't it better to settle them quickly and quietly before some parent goes to the school board and/or the press? Isn't the same true about observing Title IX? Or counseling a teacher before he gets arrested for drinking or other misdemeanors?

Do it right and do it now. This approach can head off *negative* public relations and *that* is just as important as trying to develop the positive.

A Case Study in Mistakes—and Success

The effect of positive educational management in the face of public relations disasters can be little short of phenomenal. Here is an actual case:

---

[1] The problem-solving approach advocated by the "In-Basket" is one of the best examples of its kind developed for school administrators. It does not provide panaceas, but it does warn administrators what they have coming. Developing the "In-Basket" were Kenneth E. McIntyre (chairman), professor of educational administration, University of Texas; Walter F. Beckman, professor of educational administration, Califor-

There once was an urban middle school that was little short of a public relations horror, to say nothing of being an educational cesspool. Every time a vigorous public information program in the superintendent's office succeeded in calling media attention to an achievement by other schools, some act of violence would occur among pupils at this particular school to offset and undo any positive PR which had been otherwise achieved. The level of learning in the school in question was abysmal. Middle-class parents whose children were assigned there under a rezoning plan were particularly angered.

It would be nice to say that some aggressive, positive leadership was applied at this school and that things improved. It didn't happen. Students continued to roam the halls, pull fire alarms, and attack teachers and each other with a variety of weapons. When these same students finished the eighth grade, however, they went on to a high school quite close by, a school surrounded by many of the same negative influences, such as public housing.

Yet, at the same high school the situation was reversed almost entirely. Academic performance improved. Behavioral problems almost disappeared. It was the only high school in the city in which a visitor could expect a student to open the door, greet the guest cordially, and ask to be of assistance. But probably the most striking thing was that the middle-class minority clung to this high school with a fierce loyalty, even though it was far outside the area in which most of them lived. Why?

Critics and supporters of the system agreed that the success of this particular school, even with the influx of malcontents from what was generally considered the worst middle school in the system, was due to the personality and the leadership of one person—the principal. How was he able to take children from a school that was a public relations disaster and turn them into members of a school that could get positive, front-page coverage in *The New York Times*? It was the *art* of leadership, the *art* of discipline, the *art* of setting reasonable goals and making sure everyone worked toward them. There was no science to it. If there had been, some charlatan would have tried to bottle it for quite a few other educational managers to rub on themselves like hair tonic.

Looking back at this principal and how he managed to make a public relations gem, and a sound educational institution, out of his school, one fact in particular is striking, and it accounts for both successes. This principal succeeded because he had specific goals and expectations for himself, his staff, and his students. He knew what his job was: to lead. He made sure that his staff understood that their job was to teach and that the students understood that theirs was to learn. Each was reminded constantly that

nia State University, Fullerton; Larry L. Smiley, assistant professor of education, University of North Dakota; and Scott D. Thomson, associate secretary for research, National Association of Secondary School Principals, Reston, Virginia.

achieving these goals: 1) was worthy of the effort; 2) required discipline, whether from within or without; and 3) was frequently difficult to achieve.

No one in that school had any doubt about where he or she fit and what his or her responsibility was, to him- or herself and to others, because the principal did not confuse himself about his own responsibilities—and would not let others do it either.

This is a significant attitude, because it digresses to a very large degree from what is normally taught in schools of education about the principal's role and responsibility as a leader. It is not just teachers of educational administration and supervision who would dissent from the objective approach of this principal. Even authorities in "school-community relations" take a differing view. Gordon McCloskey, in a volume widely quoted at the time, *Education and Public Understanding* (Harper and Row, 1967), had this to say about what is still the traditional educational attitude—one which would not conform to the actions of the principal in question:

> Development of voluntary group thought and consent is the element which distinguishes the democratic concept of leadership from authoritarian concepts. . . . research and experiment also indicate that group thought and voluntary response result in better work plans, more work of high quality, more satisfaction within a group, more cooperation, less dissension . . .[2]

The record of the public schools in recent years would indicate otherwise. Voluntary response is indeed nice, as McCloskey indicates. It can even be more pleasant. But schools today are in crisis, a leadership and a management crisis, and much of this crisis, particularly the crisis of confidence the public is showing toward the schools, comes from just such situations as McCloskey and others advocate. Put another way, the committee approach to management decisions, and management action, has proven no more successful in developing the leadership necessary to run today's schools than in determining how to dock a ship while it sails into a harbor in rough weather.

Let me emphasize: *it is not undemocratic for society to expect its agents (school board, superintendent, principal) to exercise the authority they are given, to choose competent subordinates, and to carry out specific objectives in accordance with law and in observance of human rights.*

Take the high school principal we have been citing. This was no contemporary Mussolini dedicated to getting the trains to run on time regardless of who got trampled in the process. He was not one to allow

---

[2] In evaluating administrative growth, it is wise to remember that advocates of professional school public relations, as represented by McCloskey *et al.*, are not immune to the bigger-is-better syndrome. This is a form of self-preservation. Everyone in public school administration today is quoting whatever source he or she can find on behalf of more "participation, input, interaction, etc." the better to make their empires and departments appear indispensable.

himself to be sidetracked, as Emerson warned, into that "foolish consistency" which becomes "the hobgoblin of little minds . . . ."[3] Rather, he was able to make staff and students alike see that purposeful self-discipline was not only more desirable than that which could be externally applied, but that self-discipline was in itself a positive lifestyle much to be preferred to the external discipline which could easily and lawfully be applied as necessary. Of course, he was never totally successful with all pupils—or staff. But those who did not succeed or adjust through lack of their own effort at least did not find themselves deified as is so often the case today in weak, purposeless schools.

In almost every instance, this principal led by specific example, working toward a positive goal that was simply stated to his school and which had value the community could easily recognize. His rules were few, but like his goals they were easy to understand. Their enforcement was uniform and fair.

All teachers, for example, were expected to stand monitorial duty in the halls near their classrooms as classes changed. Some objected, on grounds that this was not *instructional* and that they were not responsible for the behavior of students not assigned to their particular classes.

"I am responsible for the behavior of all our pupils," the principal replied, "and I will be standing hall monitorial duty between classes. I don't think it unreasonable to expect the same from you." He got it.

Because of this understanding of objectives, this principal was in a strong position to make sure that any problem that arose within his school would be handled promptly and not turned into a public *cause celebre*.

In one instance, which I observed, a prospective patron, suspicious about the school since it was not one to which he would have sent his children except for redistricting, dropped in on the principal and asked for a tour of the building.

"I can't go with you right this minute," the principal said, "so why don't you just wander around on your own." He reached into his pocket. "I'll lend you my master key," he added. "If you come to a room that's locked and you want to look inside, use it. I don't think you'll find anything wrong, but if you do, I'm sure you'll tell me about it."

That's confidence. It's also pretty good evidence that leadership and public relations had been carefully developed in that school. For as Emerson also observed in the same essay in which he warned against "foolish consistency," an "institution is the lengthened shadow of one man."[4]

Yet this case is the ultimate proof that leadership is not scientifically quantifiable. For this principal was charged one night with sodomy with another adult. And though he proclaimed his innocence, he pleaded guilty to a reduced charge and was removed from his principalship.

---

[3] Emerson's *Essays* (First Series: Self-Reliance).
[4] Emerson, *op. cit.*

The strange thing about the public relations effect of the principal's arrest is that there seemed to be none, even among those of us who still consider homosexuals to be emotionally disordered no matter what the American Psychological Association decides by putting the matter to a popular vote.[5] Considering the substantial number of parents, black and white, well-to-do and poor, who wanted to find some way to save the principal's job, as opposed to none who indicated they wanted him to lose it, can there be any doubt as to the positive public support that comes from simply doing a job well?

Given the paucity of educational leadership in so many schools, as shown by the public's current discontent, it becomes easier to understand President Lincoln's tacit endorsement of the drunkenness of his successful commander, General U. S. Grant. "Find out his brand," Lincoln is alleged to have said, "and send a keg to my other generals."[6]

Although this should not be interpreted as an endorsement of homosexuality as a prerequisite for a successful principal, it does show that successful leadership consists primarily of getting a necessary job done. The public relations can then begin to take care of themselves. Conversely, failure to achieve clearly stated goals which take into consideration traditional values will sooner or later damn the schools and cost them the support they must have to survive, whether the fault is the superintendent's or the staff's.

On the other hand, public esteem for school administrators is not always as high as in the incident just related. In 1978, during a Democratic primary in New York, a former school administrator ran against a candidate who admitted that he had solicited sex from a sixteen-year-old boy. The school administrator lost.[7]

From Where Does Discontent Come?

In any analysis, it is necessary to determine whether the discontent being demonstrated is with the people in charge or with the institution itself. More often than not, the problem is with people. American discontent today is not necessarily with our system of government, but with how the people

[5] One can only hope that the American Medical Association does not decide to follow the scatter-brained leadership of the psychologists and decide, by popular vote, that cancer is no longer a disease with life-threatening characteristics.

[6] It is questionable that Lincoln ever said this. Given the record of most of his generals, he certainly should have thought it. Which may be one reason a really good school manager cannot be blamed for thinking it either.

[7] News reports of this event were widely circulated, not just by The New York Times, but by syndicates and news services. Needless to say, this did nothing for the image of school administration, although it does seem to show that in politics, a good organization surely does help. (Richmond (Va.) Times-Dispatch, September 13, 1978)

in charge have tried to make it a private domain. This is the reason laymen, unsure of the "correct" ways of getting things done, are voting meat-ax cuts in budgets as the only way to get the attention of those in government. This situation has been a long time a-building, which is one reason the crisis of confidence in leadership and its public postures and actions is not apt to disappear over night or by way of a new soft sell.

As long ago as 1973, for example, the distinguished pollster, Louis Harris, writing in *The Anguish of Change* (W. W. Norton & Company, Inc.) noted that the percentage of the public with a "great deal" of confidence in educators had dropped from 61 to 33 between 1966 and 1973, a decline of 28 percentage points. No other group experienced a higher percentage of decline. Even the percentage of decline for the military was less, *and this was during the heart of the Vietnam War.*

Harris wrote:

> People were less critical of the key institutions than they were of the men who were at their helm. It is almost as though the public felt that, if it took a man 15 to 20 years to rise to an important position of leadership, he had been so busy clawing his way to the top, that when he finally arrived his understanding of the public he was serving and his values might be 15 to 20 years out of date.[8]

It is not, therefore, that public education or, for that matter, business, labor, medicine, the courts, or the church are inherently bad. But, the public seems to be saying, "God save us from the people who are running them."

---

[8] By 1978, in a poll by the National Opinion Research Center of the University of Chicago, as reported by the National School Public Relations Association, the percentage of respondents with "a great deal of confidence" in the people running the public schools was down to 28.4, the lowest level in history. And yet administrator after administrator continues to glibly proclaim that the problems of the schools are simply those of image, not performance.

CHAPTER 2

The Press: Its Function And Dysfunction

There's good news and bad news in the relations of North America's public schools with the news media. The good news—in the eyes of some, at least—is that the media are not pestering the schools with quite as much attention as they have at certain times in the past. The bad news is that the nasty questions the media tend to ask seem somehow to be getting even nastier. But the worst news of all is that the schools are increasingly finding themselves ignored on the important, constructive issues, while the attention they get on the negative issues seems not to diminish, at least in the eyes of many school managers.

Balanced Coverage

Ken Muir, a past president of the National School Public Relations Association, tells a story that effectively illustrates the problem and at the same time indicts *The Washington Post*, one of the few genuinely great newspapers in the nation and one that, as a rule, gives exceptional coverage to local issues despite its responsibilities to national and international affairs. Muir, who is director of information for the Montgomery County (Maryland) public schools, one of the nation's wealthier systems and a bedroom suburb for Washington, pointed out that the *Post* had declined to report the release of a school budget involving hundreds of millions of dollars, but at the same time had given prominent coverage to the opinions of some thirty students at one high school on the matter of cheating. An isolated example? Perhaps. But not always, not everywhere.

What has happened, of course, is that the fad has flown from public education. What began as a hot item in the late 1950s in the post-Sputnik panic to catch up with the Russians—if indeed we were ever really behind them—slowly degenerated into a soap opera saga of busing, backlash, teacher strikes, Johnny's-Can't-Read, and miscellaneous articles on vandalism, violence, and general disorder.

Part of this problem can be illustrated by a congenital form of behavior among the press. Stewart Alsop, the noted Washington columnist, put it this way in his book *The Center* (Harper & Row, 1968):

> Although there are strays and nonconformists, the . . . press tends to travel in a pack (like beagles) . . .
> The beagle is a highly competitive dog, but he is always ready to follow uncritically any other beagle who claims to have smelled a rabbit. When one beagle gives tongue, all the others instantly join in, and off the whole pack scurries, each beagle yelping like mad in order to convince the onlookers that he was really the first to pick up the scent. Sometimes the scent is actually that of a rabbit, but quite often the beagles, as they chase each other around in circles, giving tongue lustily, are simply smelling each other.[1]

That this is so can be both advantageous and dangerous to a proper management posture toward the media. It is one reason that when a positive news story can be placed in one medium, other media follow suit. This is particularly true in the hundreds of medium-sized American cities where radio and television stations have neither the staff nor the competence to compete with the press, and thus must look to the latter for a sense of direction.

Educational managers need to understand, also, that the electronic media are required by their licensing to provide a minimum amount of news and public affairs programming. When they do not have the staff to do it, they are ripe to pick up a copy of the daily paper and use it as their

---

[1] Edward Behr, a noted foreign correspondent, tells this tale of press myopia in his autobiography *Bearings* (Viking 1978): Behr was stationed in Paris shortly after World War II when Mistinguett, the famous cabaret and musical comedy star of the era died. The next morning Behr received a cable from his editors at Time-Life: "Our information is that she had no pubic hair. Please check soonest and advise." In the space of two hours, an ancient paramour was located. " 'She had some, but very little,' he said with more than a hint of slobbering nostalgia, coupled with amazement that anyone would want to know." Alas, one of the prime functions of editors is to compel reporters to ask questions, the answers to which are unlikely to be used, and all involved know it.

source. If the story is good, it creates a ripple effect. Unfortunately, a negative story does the same.

The Role of the EWA and the NSPRA

These points are well understood by most members of the Education Writers Association (EWA), a national organization made up primarily of writers from daily papers across the nation. The EWA, under the direction of G. K. Hodenfield, became a major organization of influence in the 1960s, with Cabinet members and White House representatives anxious to participate in EWA conferences. Lately, the organization has lost prestige along with the accompanying decline in the public's interest in conventional education stories *per se*. Chick Harrison, the current executive secretary, however, has made some strong steps to arrest its decline.

The other major organization of national influence, besides the media themselves, is the National School Public Relations Association (NSPRA). Any school system with at least a thousand in enrollment should have at least one of its management people as a member.

The NSPRA membership is comprised primarily of those school employees whose duty it is to deal with the media, comfort the superintendent, try to keep principals' feet out of their mouth, and have instantaneous answers to everything. It is, by and large, a fairly impressive group. Many of its members have a broad background in both public education and the media. They, too, are paranoid these days, because more and more school systems seem not to realize that the success or failure of their public relations is something over which PR people have very, very little control.

School boards and superintendents too often do not understand what good PR people in education can and cannot do. Consequently, they have created the myth of the media magician—or court jester, or entertainer, or miracle worker.

Boards and superintendents must remember that PR people are caught at what educators love to call the "interface." That is where the public's interest in its school and the schools' interest in themselves come together. Being caught in the middle is something like having one arm tied to a porcupine and the other to a horned toad. Neither is apt to do much damage to the other, but God help the one in between.

The stresses of PR work are demonstrated in a study reported from Tennessee by the National School Public Relations Association. The study, undertaken by the National Institute of Occupational Safety and Health, listed PR as the 6th most likely occupation to produce mental disorders. By contrast, teaching was 47th and being a principal, 104th. Nothing was said about superintendents or school boards, so you can draw your own conclusions about where, and how, they might fit.[2]

A Sense of Misdirection

Now I am not, mind you, suggesting that all my hard working compatriots in the school PR business be summarily put out of business like so many Watergate burglars, whether they are half-crazy, completely crazy, or just being driven that way. But I am aware that the flack is coming to the flacks, as PR people are known by those in the news media who have not been able to land PR jobs themselves.

The line goes something like this:

Superintendent: "What happened to the public? Why does everyone hate us? Why is everyone trying to cut our budget?"

Superintendent's Yes-Man: "It's our image. Nobody knows what a good job we're doing."

Superintendent: "You're right. Let's fire the PR man and hire an imagemaker."

As Vonnegut would say, "And so it goes . . ."

Or does it? The school boards and school superintendents who are practicing this line of thinking—and they are many—are forgetting a variety of things, not the least of which was stated recently by Robert A. Marston, president of Robert Marston and Associates Inc. of New York. Said he:

> Professional public relations does not consist of turning a negative impression into a positive one by misrepresenting the facts in order to alter the image. . . . it is especially a fundamental understanding that, in all communications, honesty and candor must prevail.[3]

And so, the answer is not found in firing your current PR person who has not buffed the schoolhouse image sufficiently (for image, after all, as Plato pointed out, is by no means reality), and in hiring one who will buff away without regard for facts or reality.

---

[2] If a school district is not large enough to have a designated public information officer, then the superintendent should take it upon himself to at least be a member of the NSPRA. This will ensure that he receives much pertinent information, although of late the NSPRA seems to have lost some of its focus and has developed a lamentable hustle of its own to sell various curriculum materials. Part of this decrease in effective leadership may lie in a loss of objectivity and awareness of the fact that the most effective public relations can be conducted with a whisper instead of a bang.

[3] Marston's comment was part of a lament over the lack of integrity in the public relations operations of Richard Nixon's last administration. It was contained in a statement written for United Press International and distributed in 1974.

What Can One Expect?

The answer I submit from experience on both sides of this fence is to understand what public relations can do for a school system and, even more important, *what it cannot.* In other words, school systems should kill their media magicians for they are their own creations; they do not exist in reality. Public relations cannot fool the public indefinitely if the basic philosophy and accomplishments of the school system are not in line with what the community thinks it has a right to for its tax dollar.

Public relations cannot make the media go away by refusing to answer their questions, or denying access to top administrators. The media are going to ask hard questions. That is their job and no brave new world of PR people, brochures, and slide-tape presentations extolling the beauty of the new curriculum lab is going to deter a good reporter from zeroing in on the facts and reducing them to English. Simply stated, PR people cannot do the job the boards and superintendents themselves can and should be doing and requiring that other staff do too.

Take the shibboleth of "individualized instruction" or "open education" or any of the dozen other so-called innovations which are today's answer—but only until tomorrow's tough questions get here. Here's how it works:

A decision is made that this latest innovation is good. Who made that decision is never immediately clear. If it works—and few of them have, so far—those willing to take credit abound. If it does not, as is often the case, then something far removed, such as the state department of education, the state university, or "Washington" gets the blame for this bastard progeny.

Meanwhile, the PR person is set to work beating the tom-tom of attention for individualized ed, open ed, career ed, etc., an act which, by coincidence, may very well draw public attention away from some perfectly newsworthly but mundane accomplishment, or some very critical situation elsewhere in the school system.

And what happens when this latest so-called innovation collapses and an out-of-town villain on which to blame it all cannot be found? Why, give it to the PR person to bury, and while he's digging the hole, be sure to push him in and cover him up too. After all, it would have succeeded if he'd just "sold" it, right?

Leadership, in this case, must begin with the board. Does the board itself understand what its superintendent is proposing, and the implications thereof? If not, then that is where it had better begin.

A particularly good beginning is to insist that the superintendent deliver programs, proposals, and aspirations in English. School boards, made up as they are of educational laymen, are often prone to defer to those in public education management, particularly when they should not do so. And when the superintendent, as I have heard one do, says, "Your support is requested in facilitating . . ." instead of "Please," too many school boards tend simply to swallow it. Like children back in the classroom, many members are afraid to speak up and say that they do not understand in the misbegotten notion that they are the only ones in the dark.[4]

There are exceptions to the rule that boards should demand that their superintendents speak English, and it is only fair to state one. If your superintendent chooses to address you in Latin, give him a series of stars, a raise in pay, and hire yourself a translator. You may now be responsible for protecting an endangered species—the superintendent who is also a scholar.

Once the superintendent is persuaded that the board means business, the resulting improvement in staff communications will be downright amazing and there will be no need for a resident media magician to untangle the syntax.

The result is predictable. For the first time, the PR person can do his job (presuming that he knew how, in the first place). Because if the board insists that the superintendent and all the rest of the hired help (research department, curriculum people, and principals in particular) deliver their comments in the mother tongue, a strange thing will happen.

The public, it is true, will now know that a project flopped rather than "from a standpoint of optimization achieved only general portions of that which had been prioritized." But your PR person will not have to worry any longer about finding out where the good things are hidden in the school system, either. Because that's a tragedy of inarticulation that's often overlooked. The achievements of a school system, as well as the dead cats, can be buried under the same kind of internal goobledygook. Get rid of that, and your PR person may at last be free to do his job.

Keeping a Sense of Humor and Perspective

An exacerbating factor is that public educators, in my experience, have less sense of humor than almost any other single group of people when it comes to their own profession. It's true, I guess, that physicians and surgeons do not find jokes about medicine very funny unless they come from fellow professionals, so maybe it is not a failing just of educators.

The point of this, though, is one that is often overlooked: the devastating public relations impact that comes when people start to laugh at you. *At,* mind you, not *with.* Any time you put on your professional mien, and

---

[4] The quality of graduate degrees—and the training leading thereto—is still a very sore spot since masters and doctorates in education require less academically than master of arts, master of science, and doctor of philosophy degrees in the arts, sciences, and humanities. The public is also becoming very much aware of this issue, as will be noted in Chapter 4.

present a proposal, and find that the people who pay the bill, or provide the children, or determine the support, think you are so dumb it's funny, then you are in trouble. Ridicule can be a far more devastating opponent than anger.

A couple of years ago, Mike Royko, the syndicated columnist of the late *Chicago Daily News*, came across an announcement of vacancies for teacher-nurses at Walt Disney School in Chicago (the name of the school did not help any, obviously). Said the announcement:

> These positions will provide teacher-nurses with an opportunity to participate in self-renewal activities culminating in a professional renascence which will determine for those teacher-nurses their personal desire to pursue their reborn skills within the Disney setting or to elect to carry on those newly-acquired skills in a setting other than Disney.[5]

If you have been around education very long, you may be puzzled. What is the matter with that, you ask? And that, of course, is the problem.

Royko, with a narrow-mindedness educators never seem able to comprehend, thought it would be nice to get an English translation. The result, naturally, was a column that stopped just short of saying, but managed to imply, that if western civilization survives this type of professional lunacy, we'll all be lucky. I am sure lots of folks got a laugh out of that column. I hope some educators did, but I doubt it. Of course there is no excuse for that kind of pompous writing, particularly when the public gets hold of it. For certain, public support for "teacher-nurses" did not go up any in Chicago's version of Disneyland. A proper management attitude—and a little vigilance and action—could have aborted this whole negative column.

But do the media bear no responsibility for the current public relations plight of the schools? Of course they do. Stewart Alsop's comment about reporters and beagles is truth, not jest. And whereas the problem, and the solution, are essentially something for the schools to control, the media's current attitude does not make it any easier.

What Americans Want

In the post-Sputnik bloom of interest, schools may have come under a closer, harder scrutiny than ever before, but at least there was positive motivation behind it. Americans *wanted* to believe that their schools were essentially good, essentially sound, and fully capable of meeting all that

---

[5] Royko's comments were widely distributed by the NSPRA. There is considerable evidence that many school districts paid no attention at all.

Pandora's box of "needs" that got loose in the frantic search to scare up ways to catch the Russians.

Prior to the Sputnik launch in October 1957, the school beat for the daily press had consisted mostly of PTA news, the school lunch menu, sports, an occasional personnel change, and laments of the teacher shortage. The reporter assigned to school board meetings—when one was assigned at all—was frequently an older woman from the women's department. The cub reporter just graduated from obits was sometimes sent and the local government reporter sat in when he or she could.

There were exceptions. *The New York Times*, with its great gray thoroughness, was giving education serious coverage in the 30s and 40s. That was the exception, however.

With Sputnik beeping away, however, a mad rush was on. Education was suddenly news, hard news. Media management began looking for first-rate reporters to assign to education and first-rate reporters sought out the assignment. The result was a period of sound, in-depth reporting, stories that brought the public up to date on what was needed, what was being accomplished, and how to make things better. Writers such as Martin Buskin of *Newsday;* Ron Moskowitz of the *San Francisco Chronicle;* Fred M. Hechinger of *The New York Times* are merely representative of those who were writing about education in the past two decades. It is no coincidence that each played a substantial role in the growth of the Education Writer's Association.

Part of this age of journalistic enlightenment, of course, came from the credibility given to education as a spillover from the school desegregation decisions that began only three years before Sputnik. Court reporters, who had ranked somewhat higher in the journalism pecking order, had made it respectable to write about education.

It is difficult, if not impossible, to specify just when and how the media's commitment to sound education coverage began to collapse. Certainly, it did not happen all at once and, in some areas, it has not happened yet.

As the issue of busing spread out of the South into the inner cities and suburbs of the North and West, attention turned from learning to sociology—not that the two are inseparable. Miscellaneous assaults and robberies were reported with vigor, when the opponents were of different races. This created the spectre of a crime wave. Although the crisis of criminality in the schools was becoming very real, and will be dealt with as a separate public relations problem in a later chapter, the issue was not—as the media made it appear—a situation that arose only with desegregation. Students had robbed and fought and occasionally injured one another all along—albeit to a much lesser degree—but with the exception of the most glaring examples, these incidents had never been reported until desegregation came along.

Combine this with schools' frantic efforts to spend the mushrooming flow of federal dollars on every conceivable scheme, most of them bad; the emphasis on keeping everyone in school for as long as possible, the "democritization" and resulting diminution of the education process, the outrage over taxation and teacher militancy and public education was in bad trouble with its media friends.

Changing Media Practices

Once the school story became part of either the purely political arena, as in fiscal fights with county boards and city councils, a police beat story (criminal incidents), a courts story all over again (redistricting and busing), there was precious little room or reason in the media mind for continuing hard coverage of purely educational developments. Combine that with the head-in-the-sand attitude of educational managers ("If I don't talk to him, he can't quote me") and it is little wonder that the school beat was soon being assigned to re-treads, cubs, women's page feature writers, and whomever else the city editor could grab for assignment as his staff dispersed to cover other news. The space once given over to serious coverage of education needs and achievements became reserved for the medical columnist discussing the care and cure of athlete's foot.

Another reason for the decline of newspaper interest in, and support for, public education, particularly in the urban area is found in an understanding of the nature of the two. The press, with a few notable exceptions such as the *Washington Post* and *The New York Times,* is more hidebound in its conservatism than bankers and almost as bad as physicians. (Look at the percentage of newspapers that supported Barry Goldwater in 1964 when the Republican conservative was a landslide loser to Lyndon Johnson.)[6] The constituency of these newspapers is the middle class, particularly the white middle class. As long as this class and race make up a significant proportion of the public schools, and seem to be satisfied, even the most conservative paper will generally give good coverage and at least grudging editorial support.

But let a public school system become mostly poor and mostly black, and support from conservative papers vanishes proportionately. The poor do not buy all that many newspapers anyway, so why not?

Of course all this is ethically deplorable, but it is still a fact. Watch for it. The implications for public schools are significant.

As for radio and television, the former can seldom offer anything in the way of hard news other than what it has ripped out of the paper to read

---

[6] Given the malignant absorption of more and more independent newspapers by chains and monopolies, plus the fact that most cities with two newspapers are already one-owner towns, we may be closer than we think to having editorial stands on local issues such as education dictated by an owner far removed from where her or his words are read. For one of the few accounts of this dangerous and unethical situation, see the works of the late A. J. Leibling, the distinguished journalist.

on the air. The latter too often does the same, with the exception that it has to have color, movement, and light to photograph. Given those criteria, the addition of Shakespeare himself to the faculty would not make television, and radio would be left trying to drop his shortest sonnet into twenty seconds between the traffic fatalities and the noon commercial.

So much for the record. The media are not making the public relations problems of the schools easier or better. The temptation is great for educational managers to blame their public relations problems on the press. But the press, for all its failing, is not the one to blame, and the wise manager will recognize it and adjust his strategy accordingly.

Making the Hard Analysis Yourself

So what can the conscientious school manager do today to preserve both himself and his system from a media alternately disinterested and vindictive?

1. Look first at whether your system really is doing the job the public wants.
2. Make sure you have good PR advice and take it. (Superintendents have everything to gain and nothing to lose from staff which is smarter than they are—as long as the staff is loyal. The staff can do the work and the superintendent can take the credit).
3. Do not duck the press, but have your head screwed on straight when you talk with them. Remember that the press does not have all day for you to appoint a committee to draft a statement. If you cannot handle the press in a relaxed, conversational manner, you probably should not be superintendent.
4. There is nothing wrong with saying, "I don't know" or "That was probably a mistake," as long as you choose carefully when to say it and do not say it too often. It may enhance your credibility and gain you support. There is also nothing wrong in saying nothing, if you are on sound ground, but say it like this: "I'm not free to answer that question now, but I'll answer it just as completely as I can as soon as possible." A snappy "no comment," though saying the same thing, simply makes the press more churlish.
5. Make sure your staff, your principals, have some training in media relations; how to get good coverage and minimize bad.

And finally, reread number 1: If you do not have a good school system (and just because you think it is good does not make it so), do not get angry because your coverage is bad. Change the quality of what is being covered, and things will pick up all around.

Choosing the Public Information Head

But what if you, as an educational manager, have already done most of the things recommended herein by way of preparing to live with the press. How do you get someone to actually do the dirty work?

The staff selection procedures outlined in Chapter 1 come into play here. Of course, there will be a limit to how much you can spend to establish a public information system. Generally speaking, however, all school systems, with the possible exception of the very smallest, should have at least one staff member trained in public information techniques. In the smaller districts—and, desirably, even in the largest—the super-intendent can and should carry some, if not all, of this responsibility.

Before beginning such a program there is one pitfall that appears periodically like a highway pothole during the spring thaw. That is the natural antipathy of the public to pay good tax dollars to someone to sell it something it has paid for already, namely the schools.

A survey by United Press International in 1978 of government public relations programs at the federal level indicated that the federal government was spending "at least $1 billion a year solely to promote, communicate and sell its programs and sometimes itself to the American people." The trend, the study noted, was to more of the same.

The Department of Health, Education, and Welfare, for example, had Washington's largest PR department in terms of expenditures. This consisted of a public affairs staff of 459, including 96 media information specialists, 57 speech writers, 90 who worked full-time on HEW publications, and 44 who handled film and broadcast projects. Total salaries for the 459 amounted to $25.4 million per year.

People seem to have natural antipathy to being sold something they are suspicious of in the first place, particularly when they are paying both for the project and the guy who is selling it to them.

Some educational managers, as a result, have taken to hiding their PR people under a variety of fulsome titles. This is a questionable process. If a case can be made for a good public information program, and such a case can be made, then call it by the right name so neither it nor the public will be confused as to its role. Therefore, the title *Public Relations Officer* or *Director of Public Relations* should be avoided. The increasingly popular title *Director of School-Community Relations* should also be avoided because of the ambiguity of "school-community." *Director of Communications* is acceptable, but by far the best is *Director of Public Information*.

In districts of 20,000 pupils or fewer, one competent person can frequently handle most of this operation if given adequate clerical support, and can draw on funds and personnel in the event of an unexpected crisis of a long-range nature. A budget of 1 percent of the total operating cost of the school district is more than adequate. In truth, great sums of money are not needed for a good school public information program, because public information responsibility is an *attitude* as much as it is a program. If educational managers do not recognize their personal responsibility for a good public information program, the director of public information cannot do the job for them. Of course, where such undeveloped attitudes exist, it becomes part of the public information director's responsibility to help develop them. One rude secretary in a key position can neutralize the best of public relations efforts from the public information office.

The person selected to be director of public information should be chosen with almost as much care as the superintendent or the assistant superintendent for instruction. Indeed, many systems feel that the public information position should carry assistant superintendent's rank. In my judgment, a director level post is adequate, if solid backing comes from the superintendent. Whatever the title, however, the person in the information job must report directly to the superintendent, have instant access to him, and enjoy a level of confidentiality and communication with the superintendent second to none anywhere else in the system.

Although good information directors can be developed from within the ranks of public education—and I have seen a few—the best come from outside, primarily from newspapers. Radio and television, as mentioned earlier, are essentially entertainment media, particularly in the smaller cities, and do not have the staff or the expertise to develop the skills necessary for a good information director. An information director will work under many of the same deadline pressures faced in the newsroom. He must be a skilled and rapid writer. He must make sense out of jargon (where possible). He must know a considerable amount about many things in and out of the system. Above all, he must have news sense.

This latter characteristic will enable him to ferret out from the verbiage of the system those developments which he, as a reporter, would have wanted to turn into positive page one stories or features. Of equal importance, however, he will recognize the potential PR disaster in other developing situations and be able to warn the superintendent and others away from them (see an example cited in Chapter 7).

A good information director will be skilled enough with language to be an excellent public speaker and, at the same time, have sense enough to lie neither to the public nor the media. This means he will occasionally have to choose words with such care that he gives a satisfactory answer without appearing to waffle.

An ideal director will also have had public school teaching experience, or have spent time as an education reporter on a newspaper of some size or reputation. In addition, he should *like* public education and believe in it. This does not mean that he should be an apologist, or an uncritical advocate. If this person likes it and believes in it as he should, and carries the sound code of ethics which, presumably, make a good and fair reporter, he'll not be inclined to gloss over the shortcomings of the schools, but will present them in a light which leads people to believe they are worth correcting.

Duties and Responsibilities

The duties assigned the director will vary, of necessity, from district to district, but the director of public information should not be allowed to clutter his time when he should be flexible enough to meet the changing demands that swamp the schools so often. An adequate staff for a system of 60,000 would *ideally* include two professional assistants, one of whom should have photographic skills. One should be generally responsible for internal communications, the other for communications outside the system. The director should have first-line responsibility for media response and contact and should also be the official or unofficial ombudsman for the district.

In addition to press releases, the director should be responsible for arranging radio and television interviews, including regular programs and public service announcements, which the Federal Communications Commission requires the station to carry; and should establish a Code-A-Phone, or other recorded message system which will provide direct feeds twenty-four hours a day to radio, and also give the general public an opportunity to call for school board agendas, board actions, and the like. The Code-A-Phone should be changed daily if possible. A hot line on which callers can record messages for the director, the superintendent, or any other staff member, and which also can be used to receive complaints, is also an asset.

Further, where such events as busing to comply with a court order, substantial reassignment of pupils due to redistricting or school closing, or other major issues of long-term interest are likely, the director should have the funds and the labor to establish a telephone bank, which may be staffed by volunteers, to receive and disperse information.

From a publications standpoint, the director should see that newsletters which follow accepted journalistic practice are available at least once each month to all staff, including teachers, and also to the public at large. These should not be allowed to become vehicles for self-congratulation for employees seeking to build their empires or gild their lilies.

Although there is frequently demand for many publications of various types, a single general-purpose newsletter should be the primary source. The information therein should be of interest to both teacher and patron. Special purpose publications such as a speaker's directory, and a guide to the school system for new patrons are obviously needed.

In fact, given the proliferation of useless publications in most systems, the director should be required to review, and prohibit, those staff newsletters and the like which are duplicative, self-congratulatory, and which waste endless amounts of money, secretarial time, and the time of administrators who should be in the schools working more directly with staff there.

If a school-community relations department has been established in the district, as has been the case in many areas which have received large sums in federal aid, that department should also be made answerable to the director of public information. There is little evidence to indicate that these departments have succeeded to any substantial degree where they have been left under the control of the federal programs office. Frequently, they become a place to assign teachers and others who are not good enough to keep in any job worth doing and who will be too much trouble to fire.

One of the tactics the information director needs to keep in mind, however—and which is at times difficult to explain to the superintendent— is the need to avoid reliance on the printed word. This may seem a strange recommendation, given the stress just placed on ensuring that the information director has a sound newspaper background. However, particularly in the older, less affluent communities, the reading and comprehension level of the public you are trying to reach may not be much better than that of the pupils themselves.

Personal contact, with accurate information, with large numbers of people, either individually or in groups, is often more effective than printing thousands of newsletters and brochures which are not going to be read. Afternoon newspapers throughout the country are increasingly aware of this problem as their circulation declines and reliance on television and radio provide the high spots of the news increases.

The advantage of the printed word is that it can at least be kept until a later time, and if one does not wish to read it now, perhaps one will change his mind later. In addition, superintendents and boards like to see lots of colorful material and brochures as evidence that they are getting their value from the public information director. Keeping a sound balance in this regard may turn out to be one of the director's larger internal problems.

The responsibility for dispensing accurate information about the public schools is probably as crucial and as poorly understood as any within the framework of educational management. It is a responsibility that crosses and embraces all internal lines of structure, organization, and command. It reaches into all facets of the community, from the individual parent with a simple question concerning one child, to matters of policy, economics, and politics which may affect the school and the community for generations. It is a job that breeds paranoia, for it means a never-changing, no-win series of situations. For every question that is answered, there is another that must be dealt with; for every time the same answer is given, another source will be back with the same question (sometimes the same person who asked the same question just the day before).

Public education is not as stagnant as some today think. It may be convulsed, and it may be convoluted. It is certainly out of the channel in which it should be flowing, not so much because of flood as because it has just plain lost its way. It is the job of the educational manager to get it back where it belongs and to see that it stays there, and it is the job of every such manager, but the one in charge of public information most of all, to see that the facts and the information stay straight and move rapidly. This is a lonely job, and it makes for lonely feelings, particularly when the one most charged with information dissemination sees continuing evidence that those for and with whom he is trying to work and to help in education and in the press are most to blame for the informational disasters that occur.

Fortunately, as books such as this may indicate, those in educational management are at least beginning to appreciate the responsibility they have for their own public relations crises and for the corrections in their management information systems and practices necessary to set things aright.

One View from the Press

And there is a glimmer, no matter how faint, of recognition on the part of the press that their coverage of education has been sporadic, incomplete, subject to hysteria, and, occasionally, outrightly prejudiced. Haynes Johnson, the Pulitzer Prize winning Washington columnist, made some observations in this vein in the Martin Buskin Memorial Lecture to the Education Writers Association in 1978.

Said Johnson, in part:

> I'm a child of the Thirties, and I grew up in the area of progressive education. It looks to me as I look back that we have gone through nothing but fad after fad. We are always discovering something new and then rejecting it for something else. We have gone from the progressive period through the war period and into the Fifties and all the concern about why Johnny couldn't read. Then we went into the Sputnik era when I came on the scene in Washington. Suddenly, we couldn't count and we didn't know science, and that had to be the priority. Then, during the Sixties we went back again to whatever would seem progressive, where anything goes. Standards were made by yourself. Curriculum didn't matter. You could take basket weaving or whatever you wanted, and you defined for yourself what an education was. You had the control in your hands—you, the student. Now I guess we are back again to what I am told is the basics.
>
> What troubles me is the way we present all this to the citizens. No wonder they are bewildered. It's the new math and the old math. One is the wonderful way of the future and the other is suddenly rejected. And then comes another new form of teaching, or so we think about it at least. And I

think the coverage we have given tends to fall very much into this very easy quick fix. It's violence in schools. For years, George Gallup has told us that the primary concern of American parents is violence in the schools. Indeed, we do write about violence in the schools a great deal. We go through periods where we look at the newest things.

But what we don't do it seems to me—and this is the heart of my concern—what we don't really do well at all is look at the institutions of education and the attitudes that shape teachers and pupils.[7]

Johnson, of course, was reflecting on the responsibility of the press. It is a reflection that is badly overdue, for with few exceptions, American newspaper owners, publishers, and editors consider themselves the sole heir to the divine right of kings. The Pope, speaking *ex cathedra,* is no more pompous, remote, or less willing to accept facts than an American newspaper owner who has made up his or her mind concerning what is good for the community and the world.[8]

But that, essentially, is for another book, one about the failure of American journalism to exercise for the public good that privilege which the Constitution gives to it by name. Our concern here is what is wrong with the way educational managers take care of their end of the information pipe.

It is, as Johnson said, the "institutions of education and the attitudes that shape pupils and teachers" that are at the heart of things. The mote of educational blindness may very well be in the eye of the American press when it comes to proper reporting on public education. But until the educational hierarchy gets the beam out of its own eye, it can hardly see its way clear to practice its own profession.

How to Make Trouble for Yourself

The beam that is blinding so many educational managers and keeping them from understanding and implementing practical public relations comes in many sizes and manifests itself in many ways. Here are some examples from my own experience:

In one instance, a new personnel director for our school system was very much concerned over the teachers' union and kept demanding that the public information office do something to blunt the union's efforts. Of course, it is not up to a school information office to blunt the lawful, if inaccurate, attacks from a teachers' union. The best response here is to

---

[7] I am indebted to Chick Harrison, executive director of the EWA, for providing me with a copy of Johnson's remarks to the EWA meeting—and for not revoking my membership for having missed the speech.

[8] This is nothing but a reminder that this problem is going to get worse before it gets better.

make sure the system is itself doing everything it can do to *manage*, because proper management will, in itself, yield public support in any relationship with the union.

A few days later, I had to write to this personnel director as follows:

> I came in about 7:30 a.m. today and my phone was ringing. It was a substitute teacher named James _____ who alleged that he had been unfairly dismissed by your personnel department, and that no one in that department would tell him why his work was unsatisfactory.
>
> I don't know James _____, and everything he said may be distorted, but *if* he did not receive any reason for dismissal, then he is very much a public relations problem. He will be more than ready to believe anything the teachers' union says about us, and all the press releases or tv shows in the world about what a fine job we are doing won't change his mind.
>
> This is what I mean about public relations being the responsibility of all employees. . . .

Expectations of unenlightened or incompetent educational managers can also create problems in implementing a successful public relations program. In another instance, a group of psychologists in the school district for which I worked spent an entire day drafting a "press release," after first refusing the offers of the schools' information office to provide assistance. The release was delivered to the information office at 4 P.M. with a demand that it be printed verbatim in that afternoon's newspaper (which, of course, was already on the streets).

Here, then, are a few points to be remembered about any school public relations program by those who are employed by the district:

Points to Remember about Public Relations

1. The fact that a school is teaching children is no more unique nor newsworthy than the fact that an insurance agent is selling insurance. Doing something *genuinely* different and positive *is* news. Best of all, however, is doing the routine thing (teaching children every day) but coming up with positive, objective results that can be presented to the public in language the public understands. *That* is news.

2. It is not fair to anyone, including, but not limited to, children, parents, and teachers, to expect a public relations program to explain away crisis or to change failure of the schools into success in the eyes of onlookers. *To be credible, public relations must be honest, must be truthful.* It can advise. It can suggest. It can warn. But it cannot do the job for teachers, parents, pupils, or adminis-

trators that teachers, parents, pupils, and administrators must first be doing themselves.

3. Successful public relations is *everyone's* job. A media campaign can be destroyed by half a dozen insensitive administrators or rude secretaries. There is no way press relations can overcome that.

4. Successful public relations is tied directly to how parents perceive the schools. Public relations can capitalize on programs which are basically satisfactory to parents. Public relations cannot do very much with programs educators feel are outstanding but which parents do not like.

Over, and over, and over again the problem that keeps school managers from implementing a successful public relations program is the stress they wish to place on image instead of reality.

Robert Townsend, the business executive who rattled the cages of complacency in which business management has housed itself, says it well, and it can apply probably more to educational management than to business management:

> It seems to me that image is one of the most dangerous concepts in modern organizations. . . .A good image has to be earned by performance. . . . image is a by-product. Let's not chase image anymore. Let's go earn one by our own performance and by chasing the real goal of consumer satisfaction. . . .[9]

[9] As quoted by Donald M. Dible in *Up Your Own Organization*, which otherwise might have been called *Son of Up the Organization*. (*Up The Organization* being Townsend's book in which he first presented his management theories to a wide audience.)

CHAPTER 3

It's Reading and Math: Now and Forever

Ever since man first decided he had something to say, he's been trying to find how best to repeat himself. And that, essentially, is what this fuss over reading and mathematics is all about.

Given the current state of public education, it seems we are creating generations that must re-invent the wheel every twenty years, because the record of previous plans and inventions isn't getting passed on through the educational system to those who need to know how.

Reading and mathematics are the conventional ways for passing on truth. The former passes on truth which one human or one era saw; that it may not still be true today, or is no longer widely believed, does not change the fact that it is a true part of humanity's collective heritage and thus has influenced today's generation and will influence tomorrow's. Passing on this cultural heritage through reading presumes that someone somewhere still knows how to write, or at least to preserve and make available what others have written to those who can read.

While the reading/writing syndrome, whether represented by the stories prehistoric people sought to tell in the drawings on their stone walls or the latest hallucination of the syndicated columnist, deals with *perceived* truth, mathematics deals almost entirely with *actual* truth.

Both writing and math, of course, have much of their origin in symbols. The words and written language which are taken so much for granted today and which the schools seem so unable to teach to so many, had their origins far back in human development, although no one can say with certainty exactly where that point lies. Markings on bones from the second millennium B.C. in what is now China represent one early form of communication which developed into writing. Other evidence suggests that symbols with clay expressed an early form of writing in the Middle East 11,000 years ago.

Normally, we think of writing and reading as changing, and to the extent that new spellings and new words come into usage, and old ones are discontinued or disappear, that is correct. Primarily, however, the changes we believe we perceive in writing and reading come from the subjects described far more than from the techniques themselves.

Mathematics, the medium for expressing the objective as contrasted to the subjective with which language deals so often, is, a changing medium, not a static one. Fournier analysis, for example (named for the nineteenth century French mathematician, Jean Baptiste Fournier, who discovered it) deals with the principle of breaking complicated vibrations or waves into simple components that can be handled mathematically. It is still the subject of much investigation and few mathematicians would claim to fully understand it. Even calculus, the bane of many a high school student in a college prep program, is a relatively recent development (although anticipated by the Greeks, it was not perfected until the seventeenth century). And of course, there is the electronic computer, which grew out of an abstract mathematical design created less than fifty years ago. What Pythagoras and Euclid helped discover centuries ago is no longer the end of the line, or even the middle of it, in modern mathematics.

Given this analysis of the status of reading and math, brief as it is, are we to assume that the role of the schools in their teaching responsibility has somehow taken on a far greater difficulty than anyone imagined? Has some great leap forward in language taken place that is making it impossible for teachers to teach and children to learn in these areas today?

It would be a nice excuse and an easy out, but it just is not so. What children are so consistently lacking in reading and math today is not Fournier analysis or the ability to discuss at length the moral dilemmas in "Paradise Lost." No, it is simple literacy, simple competency and the lack thereof, which have turned the areas of reading and math into a public relations debacle so great that, as a curriculum issue, it must be examined with special emphasis.

A Look at National Assessments

The various national assessments of public education and pupil progress which show that reading and math are not being taught very well must be interpreted. Interpretation requires skill and knowledge, however, particularly in a public relations sense. Critics of the schools will look at any attempt to explain results as an attempt to dilute or minimize them. The school manager who chooses to speak about results whether of his own school district, or of state or national tests, must make plain that he is not trying to cover up, but to provide facts.

And what are the facts? First, this is no apologia for the schools' efforts in reading and math. Some are doing a good job, and are rightfully outraged by the national assessments which deal in norms and averages far below their level of achievement. But too many are not doing a very good job, and, more important, are not doing it for specific segments of the population.

The colleges and universities are prone to complain about the low level of student preparation they have to deal with in reading and math. In a sense this is true, although most colleges and universities would never be satisfied, no matter how high the quality of the entering class. In addition, they gloss over the fact that the teachers who trained the current crop of imbecilic college frosh were themselves trained in some cases by the very colleges and universities doing the complaining. Where this lack of preparation for college does exist, most institutions, except for the highly selective, simply require the students to take dumbell math or dumbell English to bring their knowledge up to a minimum before entering regular classes for college credit.

The specific segments of the public school population that are not getting adequate preparation in these key areas are, for the most part, those young people who will be entering the workforce, or who will be going to the least defensible colleges in the land, not those going on to the better institutions of higher learning. These students, it should be remembered, are those who, in another era, would have dropped out, frequently before even entering high school, and who would have become part of the unskilled labor pool where their academic deficiencies would have been neither bothersome to the employer nor a concern for correction.

Too often, those who do poorly, or who have been poorly prepared, are black, and this raises a spectre of testing and performance and discrimination and cultural bias and genetic abilities and environmental conditioning that scares hell out of school managers everywhere. It should. Because if we ever discover without question that genetic traits as well as the environment are causal factors in the failure to read and learn math, then we will have to abandon much if not all of what has been gospel concerning the teaching-learning process and the equal ability of the various races.

In the meantime, however, schools have to tread warily when looking at the statistics that show how poorly most blacks do in reading and math. The schools must try to improve that performance without getting blown up in the swirl of controversy as to why it exists among blacks and not among the Americans of Asian ancestry who were brought to North America under slave-like conditions little more than a century ago.

Any test or measurement is apt to be challenged as culturally biased, particularly by those who do poorly on it. This represents a significant problem in the teaching of reading and writing, but it should present no problem in the teaching of basic mathematics, which is immune to the charge of cultural bias. Five out-of-balance checkbooks times four unpaid bills divided by two unhappy adults works out to ten. Substitute rocks, snakes, or dinosaurs for any of the preceding and the result is still ten. If the cultural value is important to someone in this area, then simply adjust the problem to include elements that are culturally significant to children of different races.

Reading and Math: A Recent Requirement

Simply stated, skill in written language and basic math was not a requirement for cultural survival and progress among millions of citizens until relatively recently. The idea that all children learned reading and math seventy-five years ago is preposterous. For example, in 1901, only thirteen of every one hundred students who were in school at age seven would still be there at age sixteen. Rather obviously, students who were not there could not be tested; those who could not be tested could not do poorly; those who could not do poorly could not pull down the averages of the ones who were still in school, so schools came off looking pretty good.

Today, by comparison, three-quarters of all young people receive a high school diploma and six of ten go on to some type of post high school training. Yet, ironically, this very expansion of public education to serve larger and larger numbers of children may be its undoing. Hear now the words of Malcolm Muggeridge, a British educational critic of some note, who speaks from the pedestal of the born-again Christian:

> In my opinion, public education today is the greatest enemy that human enlightenment has ever had. Public education, supported by the media and by the scientific-humanistic consensus on which our society is based, represents the greatest menace to the free human spirit that has ever existed. Western civilization is not going to be destroyed by bombs; it is not going to be destroyed even by communists; it is going to be destroyed by its own educational system....
>
> (This is because public education) is based on all the great fallacies of our times. It's based on the idea of progress which is a completely absurd notion. It's based on the idea that through information and facts you can make

people rational and enlightened. It's based on the completely fallacious idea of equality, as distinguished from brotherhood. It's based on materialist values which, I think, must always destroy man.[1]

Muggeridge, I think, tends somewhat to the hysterical, but, like most hysterics, he is not without truth. It *is* the diluting of education that seems to disturb parents almost more than the bland allegation that public education cannot do anything right. All people may be equal in the eyes of God; they *should* be equal in the eyes of the law. But they *are not* equal, in learning or in anything else, and the schools should recognize it, since children already do. Yet there is probably no truth the schools have tried to kill with greater fervor than the truth of the inequality of children as far as interest in and capacity for learning are concerned. And since this capacity is traceable to the bedrock of reading and math, it is here that the foundation of the problem lies, and it is one of the schools' own creation.

The pandering platitudes which are repeated by public education in an attempt to make this truth of inequality go away change nothing at all. Within a week, a class of first graders can tell who among their number is bright and who is not; who is a leader, who a follower; who a speaker, who a ball player. Yet the educational establishment persists in its support of the heresy of equality—to the ultimate damage of all.

I have only to look at myself. As one who failed algebra three times in high school and once in college, it was nothing short of criminal to put me in a class with even average students of mathematics. If I was to make any progress at all, I needed the security and the encouragement of those as dumb as I (if indeed, a class of that many mathematical idiots could be found). This did not mean that I had to be relegated to the same status in all my classes, branded with Hawthorne's scarlet letter (in this case the "A" stood for algebra, rather than adultery) and cast into social isolation from the rest of the school.

Early Grade Emphasis

The solution to this problem is that the schools are simply going to have to do a better job of teaching these basic subjects during the early

[1] These comments are from an interview published in the *Washington Star* in February 1975. In another interview, this one in *The Washington Post*, Muggeridge lamented a "hideous experiment involving frogs, who were put in a pan of cold water, gradually heated to the boiling point. The frogs died, but so gradual was the increasing heat applied that it never occurred to them to get out."

That's us; those in public education management. And if we don't act to change the water or turn down the heat, we are going to wind up just as Malcolm Muggeridge's frogs—which is why we ought to appreciate it when the public applies the heat under curriculum and teaching rapidly. It give us a chance to hop.

grades. This can be done, I submit, without turning the primary school into a dungeon—a picture so many opponents of educational accountability always try to paint whenever objective academic goals are mentioned. Yet such does not have to be the case, and the critics know it. It is not necessary to have children immobilized in rows while a proctor with a whip prowls the aisles ready to strike out at the first inattentive movement.

Motivation, of course, is a factor, so why not award varsity letters for academic achievement, or conduct spelling bees or other academic competitions in which children can compete and excel just as they do on the athletic field? The comparison of academics with athletics is intentional. When it comes to learning, we too often figuratively put our children in bed and keep them there until they are eighteen. We do not allow them to exert themselves in any way.

But then, at eighteen, comes a different story. We tell them to enter the mile run and we expect them to win. But how can they run when they have never learned to stand, much less walk? How can they cope with the changes, the demands, yes, the unfairness, of vocational and personal and professional life when we have led them to believe such would never be a problem they would have to face? And when they discover that they have been misled, that life is not a game from which they can be excused, that skills and abilities are required, they are mad as hell at those of us in education, and I do not much blame them.

The problem is far more likely to be solved when the primary schools quit fragmenting the school day with desirable but nonessential programs and services; when teachers teach the academic subjects with genuine enthusiasm, excitement for learning, and reward for achievement. Until a competent program in reading and math is established, even if it takes up the bulk of the school day, then the formalized music, physical education, art, and field trip programs will just have to wait. To give in to demands for these programs before more important, more necessary, more basic ones are established is to exchange a short-term public relations solution for a long-term public relations problem.

In the later grades, a truly integrated curriculum would require some type of vocational education for the college bound; a continued emphasis on reading for pleasure for those in vocational courses. Through such a structure children at all levels cannot only learn the basics, but an appreciation for what goes into preparation for careers and vocations other than those they may have selected for themselves.

The emphasis on educating children—*all children*—according to their abilities (regardless of the origin, effect, or cause of that ability)—has public relations implications of the most serious nature. For where ability grouping has been continued in many public schools, its abandonment has been forced elsewhere by those concerned with sociological appearance rather than with the welfare of children. These are the folks who insist that ability grouping leads to the kind of in-house racial segregation that has otherwise been outlawed. That is not necessarily true (either that segregation results from ability grouping or that ability grouping is outlawed).

A Solution

The welfare of the children, all of them, requires that several points be made or repeated:

1. How is a child to make the most progress if forced into a class moving either too fast or too slow when, despite all the rhetoric about individualized instruction, class size can never realistically be reduced that much?
2. Ability grouping in academic subjects does not automatically exclude those of any sex, race, or class.
3. Ability grouping should *not* be permitted in physical education classes (except on physical ability bases), in study halls, at lunch periods, during assemblies, or in homerooms. This would provide for the necessary democratic contact among pupils which is a rightful part of learning.
4. If elementary schools will simply place the proper emphasis on reading, writing, and mathematics, particularly in schools that are black, or with heavy poverty-level enrollments, then much of the problem of ability grouping should be solved later.

It is my experience and belief that most of the problems of racial integration, and the huge public relations issues they involve, could be substantially lessened by following the four points just outlined.

However, this may require more courage than it is worth, for legal challenges lurk for the courageous school manager who would re-institute or establish ability grouping, particularly where black students are involved in any substantial number.

Things to Watch

There is some indication that this judicial attitude may be softening, as long as school management can show without question:

1. That ability grouping (or tracking as its opponents like to call it) is not arbitrary, but based on a combination of sound judgments and objective data.
2. That the assignments are not rigid and permanent. For example, a student who is assigned to a low ability math class need not (and quite possibly should not) be assigned to low ability English.

Proper evaluation may reveal that the child needs a mixture of low ability, average, and high ability classes, and the school must be prepared to recognize these needs and adjust assignments accordingly, even if it means doing so in the middle of a school term. (*Mills v. Board of Education of the District of Columbia*, 348 F. Supp. 866 (D. D.C. 1972) and *Pennsylvania Association for Retarded Children v. Commonwealth of Pennsylvania*, 334 F. Supp. 1257 (E.D. Pa. 1971) are two cases which, although they involve special education students, likely can, and should, be applied to the ability grouping of pupils when the schools fail to consider that variations in ability can occur from subject to subject in the same child at the same time.)

3. That there is no racial discrimination, or *intent*, in the application of the criteria for ability grouping. (A key case here is apt to be *Hobson v. Hansen*, 269 F. Supp. 401 (D.D.C. 1967), which outlawed ability grouping in the Washington, D.C. public schools and accelerated the flight of the remaining members of the middle class therefrom. The case should not necessarily be considered binding on those who support ability grouping, but should be studied carefully to determine what pitfalls must be avoided in its establishment.)

The Remediation Rip-off

Failure to establish such grouping has led to a rapidly growing problem of educational public relations: the secret scandal that is the rip-off of remediation. No business on earth could survive if it offered as many excuses for not doing the job it was paid for as the schools do; not even the American automotive industry could survive the number of recalls of its products that public education blithely demands that the public pay for in the name of remediation.

Remediation starts almost before the kids come to school. Federal money by the ton has poured into the schools under the near blasphemous guise of Head Start, Follow Through, and a dozen other programs that have bilked the public, bilked children, and encouraged teachers to take a why bother attitude—"Let the federal programs do it."

Remediation is more than a public relations scandal; it is a slanderous answer to the simple question: Why not do it correctly the first time? Parents, and teachers, who see their children having to make do, and frequently accomplish more, while the money and the programs and the people go to the remediated, those who could not or would not do the work in the time initially allotted, are bound to suffer depression and anger, and they are fully justified in their reactions.

But it is the child who is ultimately betrayed. It is he who has the right to the most anger when he finds that the remediation does not work. The child has been certified as having an education, only to find that society and employers laugh at him and tell the truth: the child has none.

The literature is replete with examples of functionally illiterate children having been graduated from schools, and not from programs in special education, either. The matter of the schools' civil liability for having turned out such children is not yet clearly established.

On the other hand, the much-heralded Baake case—the Supreme Court decision that denying a student admission to a California medical school while admitting another simply because the latter was of a minority (although less academically qualified than the former) was unconstitutional—may very well hold implications for the public schools. Wise school managers will see that they do not get caught in the controversy that may ensue. Although the court held that race could be a factor in college admissions, along with other conditions, the evidence available from the tragic record of some minority admissions to college suggests that both the colleges and the public schools have much to be ashamed about.

In 1974, a black student (we'll call her Melissa) from Washington, D.C.'s Roosevelt high school, graduated near the top of her class and was admitted to Georgetown University, a school with a sound reputation. The evidence suggests that the primary reason for her admisssion was her race, since the average scores for Georgetown freshmen that fall were 610 on the verbal test and 620 on the math. Melissa scored 410 on the verbal and 450 on the math.

Her class rank undoubtedly had led her to believe that she was a superior student, and by the record of the District's schools she probably was. (The District's average scores on the verbal were 330 and on math, 353. When one considers that only students who were considering college took the tests, and the fact that even a blank paper rates a 200 score, the District's record of preparation of its college-bound pupils in reading and math is almost unbelievable.)

Naturally, the child flunked out. Her mother blamed the District's schools, saying that even in junior high school her daughter "had no concept of multiplication." Why this mother did not take some steps to teach her daughter herself (although it was not her job to do so, some would say) or to insist that the schools do something, the mother did not explain.

Who was the loser here? The child, first; society, second. And who was punished? Again, the child and society. The schools got off free.

This case is not an isolated one. The practice of colleges and universities of taking students who are obviously incompetent either in their training or ability is nothing new. Athletic departments have been doing it for years, with the active cooperation of public schools always willing to try to take public credit when the athlete performed well. The scandal of inadequate preparation and acquiescence by the colleges is nothing new. It's just that more people than athletes are being hurt, and too many of them are the minorities for whom education, sound education, is the best hope of moving into financial security and self-satisfaction in North America.

The case of Jackson S., valedictorian of Washington, D.C.'s Western High School in 1976 is another example. Despite a near straight A average, Jackson was rejected by George Washington University after scoring 320 on his verbal and 280 on his math and comparably badly on other tests. The latter score put him in the lowest 2 percent of math test results in the entire nation.

In this case, the university at least rejected the young man out of hand, and the blame not only for not having taught him, but of having pretended to do so and of having made his record appear as it did, lies with the school alone. Grade inflation, as this practice is known, is a disastrous type of behavior on the part of public schools. Unfortunately, it is one short-term cover-up the schools are making for their failure to do what they were established to do. It is not necessary to stress what type of public relations problems are created by grade inflation once exposed.

The Washington, D.C. schools have come in for considerable criticism over the years, and deservedly so, but the problems we have been outlining can be found in most any urban school district in the nation and in some nonurban ones as well.

Of course, the immediate response to anyone who tries to use these examples is apt to be a defensive one from the schools, particularly where the school and the children are black. The old cry of cultural bias will be raised, or the defense will be offered that test scores had nothing to do with the ability to do academic work, a contention that simply does not hold up. What this type of excuse-making does to minority schools and students is confirm in the hardened hearts of whites, particularly those who are fleeing the inner cities (though most are gone now), that black schools simply cannot provide academic education that is worth anything.

The record does not always bear this out however. There is another side, one often overlooked. Take another Washington, D.C. high school, Dunbar, which today is as bad as any in the district. It wasn't always so.

For eighty-five years, between 1870 and 1955, Dunbar was an all-black public high school. But as far back as 1899, Dunbar students *came in first in city-wide tests given in both black and white schools,* according to Dr. Thomas Sowell, a black economist at the University of California at Los Angeles who has studied Dunbar extensively.

Sowell makes some other points which should not be lost on anyone, parent, educational manager, or the public in the attempt to understand basic education. Of particular note is his citation of a study of class records at Dunbar from 1938 to 1955, or a period covering the end of the Depression,

World War II, the Korean War, through the beginnings of the Eisenhower administration. Sowell contends:

> Although the local stereotype of Dunbar was that it was where the doctors' and lawyers' children went . . . , the percentage of Dunbar students whose parents' occupations could be identified as 'professional' never exceeded six per cent for any of the 18 years surveyed.[2]

Clearly not essential to the record of Dunbar students, he continues, "was racial integration, outstanding physical facilities, or generous financial support." What was essential, and was provided, he adds, "was a solid nucleus of parents, teachers and principals who knew just what kind of education they wanted and how to produce it." This production, Sowell notes, was "not done by teaching ethnocentric 'relevance' " yet was still accomplished in an all-black school with large numbers of children from low-income backgrounds.

Sowell's study has serious implications for other major areas of public relations concern, including those of parental relations, as discussed in Chapter 8, and that of the largest current public relations problem in some areas, busing (Chapter 9).

Probably the most controversial finding of the Dunbar experience, however, was that Dunbar showed what is still being proved: that "IQ tests are equally accurate predictors of black and white academic performance."[3]

A word of warning seems appropriate: to embrace a neo-segregationist attitude is not only a short-sighted public relations posture, it is unethical and unlawful. The problem is how to make the school serve all students; nothing less, nothing more.

It is particularly interesting that Sowell has a negative aside for the concept of "relevance" in education, a God-help-us-all sort of educational philosophy that has done much to damage student performance in reading and math and practically everything else of value.

Another economist, George Charles Roche III, writing in *Education in America* (The Foundation for Economic Education, 1969) describes a public education philosophy that is, sadly, still in vogue:

> Today, we are told that we have swept aside the dead hand of the past with its constricting and confining tradition and morality. We are told that the disciplines of former ages no longer bind us. We are told that, in view of these rapid transformations, all standards are relative to social considerations; man

---

[2] Dr. Thomas Sowell, quoted in *The Washington Post*, April 21, 1979.

[3] Sowell's remarks, ironically, have only recently begun to be echoed by such persons as Dr. James S. Coleman, the University of Chicago sociologist who is considered the father of the concept of busing as a means of integration. Coleman now contends that it is a mistake to believe that black children *automatically* learn better in integrated classrooms.

and society are whatever we choose to make of them. Thus, change itself, change for its own sake, becomes the dominant philosophy of the age. A variety of experiences (no matter what their quality) with constant growth (no matter in what direction) and constant activity (no matter how frenzied) are now to serve as a suitable educational goal. Here again, the decline of the intellect is most graphically demonstrated.[4]

The Need for Pride

Children will never learn their foundation material or anything else where pride in learning is not cultivated, and pride in learning will not exist in the absence of pride in teaching. Both are challenging, but the inculcation of both is the best way out of the public relations dilemma instruction in reading and math has become.

In a sense, of course, school is (and should be) a reflection of society. But not entirely and not always. To the extent that it is a reflection of society, and God knows it is reflection enough today, it becomes redundant, because a reflection is only an image, not a reality. And when a society has lost as much sense of purpose, substance, and something of value as our's has, there is no positive reason in school being a reflection of society.

Relevant? All right. A good word. But relevant to and for what? Is it relevant to load down a classroom of ghetto children with teachers and aides whose education, such as it is, merely reinforces the most negative values of that ghetto? This is the relevance of which too many of today's educators speak.

Pride? As Jesse Jackson, the black clergyman and columnist, puts it, the problem is students too proud to take off a hat in school—and too proud to work to put any knowledge under it.

Education must lead. It must reflect those values which are proven, which showed the way in the past and which will just as surely show the way and serve us in the future. The schools simply cannot teach everything all the time to everyone; they never could and never will. The only course of action therefore, is to establish priorities.

Educational managers must reform themselves, lead education back to a sense of substance, service, and stability as the answer to an age of ghetto pride, of pride in ignorance; of physicians seemingly obsessed with

---

[4] It is not just urban schools, black and white, that require this emphasis on a foundation of learning. Jesse Stuart, a backwoods Kentucky teacher, relates in *The Thread That Runs So True* how he took a handful of mountian children and in the midst of the deprivation of the Depression helped them become a prideful group that won academic honors year after year against the largest high schools in the state.

bringing down upon their heads the disaster of socialized medicine caused by their insatiable greed; of lawyers and judges who have no sense of justice; of legislators seemingly committed to an extension of the Parish beadle's statement in *Oliver Twist*: "If the law says that, the law is a ass, an idiot."

Yet, if reading and math are basic to all children, and if we must quit this silliness of remediation and see that all are taught a sound foundation, what about those children who are obviously blessed with the ability and the interest to take their talent, the foundation, and move forward, developing vigorously and rapidly, snowballing their learning into a challenge that wrings out the best that the best teacher has to offer and leaves him or her exhausted with trying to stay ahead? What, indeed, of them?

If there is a class of children that has been neglected in the public schools today, particularly if those schools are urban, and if the children are black, it is the children who are labeled "gifted." (The "talented" child is frequently included here, in such programs as schools bother to offer, but "giftedness" and "talent" are not the same thing, and do not always occur in the same child.)

According to the U.S. Office of Education's office of the gifted and talented, about one million school children in the nation are considered gifted. But, in 1978, only about 145,000 were estimated to be receiving any type of special attention in the public schools. As many as 20 percent of the gifted, according to studies conducted in Iowa and Pennsylvania, become dropouts.

The Tragic Neglect of the Gifted and Talented

What could be better public relations than to feature, encourage, and publicize programs for the gifted and talented in the public schools? How better to attract and retain the children—and the parents—of those who have the demonstrated ability to be leaders, to mobilize support for the schools, and to find the solutions to so many of the things which beset our society and our schools, either in this generation or in those to come? Yet many school systems consistently miss this public relations opportunity and the tragedy in so doing goes far beyond the affect on the individual children involved.

One of the obvious dangers in emphasizing gifted and talented programs is that some schools and some school systems will have far more of these children than others will. Schools will be labeled as "good" or "bad." This is already happening in more and more districts where school-by-school scores are released to the press. It is a tough comparison at times, but schools have no ethical right to hide this information. It is all the more reason that they should emphasize programs for their gifted children while they still have some with whom to work.

As an attempt to compensate for not having developed such programs, schools will sometimes pad their figures, or try to designate children as gifted, and force them into programs for which they are in no way qualified. The result, of course, is the discrediting of the program and the diminution of excellence for those few who may have been qualified in the first place.

For example, the Richmond, Virginia Public Schools officially proposed as an objective of its six-year plan for the period 1979–80 to 1984–85 the statement that, by June 1982, "The gifted and talented will represent the top 6 percent of the Richmond Public School population."

This, of course, is nonsense, and has the makings of yet another PR debacle. Giftedness does not occur in arbitrary percentages (any more than retardation does. If it did, it would be just as easy—and accurate—to say that by 1982, the bottom 6 percent of the population would automatically be retarded.) If, nationally, the average of gifted students is about 4 percent, it is obvious that an inner city school system such as Richmond, where test results show huge numbers of retarded and academically incompetent and reading and math scores are far below national norms, is not going to have 6 percent gifted—or 2 percent *higher* than the national average.

Another problem with giftedness, as an over-reaction to not having done an adequate job in teaching basic subjects for all children, is a variation of the idiocy of designating an arbitrary percentage of children as gifted when they may simply be just those who have the top 6 percent in scores. This is the kind of foolishness which led to the sad stories of Melissa and Jackson, outlined earlier in this chapter. In my experience, some principals have become so desperate to find some sign of excellence among their charges, that they would certify as gifted children whose scores place them in the low-normal range or below (IQ of 85–90).

In attempting to emphasize programs for the gifted and talented, however, educational managers may as well expect to be accused of elitism. The only answer is that if we are to serve all children, according to their needs, then all children includes the gifted as well as the handicapped.

Here, by comparison, is one more reason public education has lost touch with the priorities of its teaching role. In fiscal 1978, the federal government spent $6.5 million on the gifted, and *$600 million* on the 3.5 million children who are physically and mentally handicapped.

No one, of course, can afford to be an ogre and deny services to the mentally handicapped. (Indeed, it should not be overlooked that the physically handicapped and the academically gifted can be one and the same child.) But somewhere, someone is going to have to have the courage to say that public education is becoming a custodial institution for mental vegetables, and that this is not the role for the public schools. This is not education, and to get out of it, laws should be changed if necessary to put the schools back into the business for which they were established.

Nor is it elitist to suggest that federal laws which have brought about the so-called mainstreaming of retarded children have done much to force from the schools parents and children who are normal or above average in ability and intelligence. It is nearly impossible for even a superior teacher to do justice by twenty-five high school kids when all have the same general level of ability, interest, and background. It *is* impossible when the certifiably retarded, and chronically emotionally disturbed are forced into the same classroom.[5]

Let it be emphasized again, however: no one should try to deny custodial or educational care to handicapped children. But doing it at the expense of those who are not handicapped is no solution at all, although it may take more courage than most educational managers can muster to stop it.

Sell Your Success

Educational managers had best start remembering that the only thing we have to sell is success. In a sense, we have a captive audience, but it is one that is struggling to get free, and is choosing more conservative alternatives and traditional methods of education every day, despite the wailing by the public schools that play is better for children than work.

We do not mind children competing to play football, but God forbid intellectual competition and stimulation even in such enjoyable, productive things as spelling bees or math contests. But if such practices should be encouraged in the classroom, and should a healthy young sophomore standing six one, weighting 180, and with 9.5 speed choose to spend his afternoons with the math club instead of the football team, then a whole town is apt to go insane with anguish. What kind of teaching might a school be doing, anyway, where a youngster could be allowed to make such an asinine choice?

Inspired teaching, that's what, and inspired leadership. Time was, in many localities, where elementary principals prided themselves on the records the children from their schools made when they went on to junior high. And senior high principals and teachers could look at the junior high from which a child came and tell in a flash whether that child had had decent preparation in English, math, or anything else.

---

[5] There is, in truth, something badly wrong with American education when a full professor in a graduate school has only four or five students, all of whom are presumably mature and know how to work independently, and a primary teacher, in a situation where foundations are critical, is expected to teach thirty pupils of varying interests and abilities everything they need on which to build.

This is the kind of pride that schools should be encouraging today and advertising through planned public relations programs. It is the kind of teaching that needs to be encouraged: primary teachers who read with excitement and enthusiasm to children so that the children are set afire with a desire to do the same. Children need to work hard at some specific learning task, for only if they do will they be able to bask in the pleasure of having succeeded at something which challenged them. Many children have never succeeded at anything, and school management laments this. Management never stops to realize, however, that often the child has never succeeded because of having never been challenged; because nothing has been required. Only inspired leadership, inspired teaching can do this.[6]

Education *is* dangerous. The able student will challenge the teacher. That is as it should be. (Why else did Southern slaveholders oppose so violently those who would teach slaves to read? It threatened their own position. History proved them right.)

It is the building of pride, not in color, but in achievement that schools can accomplish if they will but understand that basic education is their lifeblood, their survival, and the way out of the wilderness of public discontent.

Many years ago I heard Dr. Walter R. Coppage, former president of the College of Charleston, make a speech—on what topic I do not now know—but I remembered and wrote down these words: "Anything of value is hard . . . taxes or demands. Looking at a picture or reading a poem are disciplines as demanding as prayer." It is a thought worth commending to those responsible for the curriculum in the public schools.

It is interesting to speculate, for example, how much of the 1978 tidal wave of taxpayer revolt that became the famous Proposition 13 in California originally began as eddies of protest over the schools' neglect of what parents wanted them to be teaching *first*. Now, in addition to taxpayer revolts, the public expects system-wide, objective testing programs to show exactly what children have learned. More and more states are developing such testing programs and the wise educator will remember:

KEY CONCERN FOR SCHOOL PR: *In the area of curriculum, quality education is no longer what the superintendents and principals and teachers and school boards think it is. It's also what mom and dad, and junior think it is. The educational manager forgets this at his peril.*

One of the more constant themes in public education which has helped it lose its way in the reading and math business, as well as in a lot

[6] The problem is not just that many children have not been taught what they need to know. As Eric Hofer, America's longshoreman-philosopher, puts it in his book, *Reflections on the Human Condition*, "An empty head is not really empty; it is stuffed with rubbish. Hence the difficulty of forcing anything into an empty head."

of others, is this matter of individualizing instruction. The theme, at first glance, is admirable. Indeed, good teachers have been paying attention to children as individuals all along, and will continue to do so, to the extent that it is reasonable, wise—and possible. Each child is special, we are told, and indeed each child is. But when we are also told that each child must be given the "freedom" to do his own thing, to grow at his own pace and rate like some magic flower that will bloom only if left alone, then it is time to remember that we are dealing with children, not hothouse plants.

The scientists tell us that no two snowflakes are exactly alike. Based on my experience with snowflakes, it seems reasonable. The anarchists of education tell us that no two children are exactly alike. Obviously.

But no matter how much one snowflake differs from all other snow-flakes, they have a common reaction when exposed to heat: they disappear. Keep the heat high enough long enough and the snowflake will be as extinct as the brontosaurus, a beautiful mega-myth in the wonderful world of the here and now.

There are other things snowflakes have in common. They tend to drift when the wind blows, they do not drift when it does not; they dissolve in water, or congeal if the temperature is just right. Children, like snowflakes, have a lot more in common than the anarchists of education want us to believe. They will endure in some instances, and vanish in others, and woe be unto the person who does not recognize this quality whether he or she is running a ski resort or, more important, charged with the responsibility of educating children.

KEY CONCERN FOR SCHOOL PR: *Failing to remember that children are as alike in some needs as they are different in others is a guaranteed way to destroy public support for your public schools.*

What are some of the many, many ways in which children are alike? They all need discipline, of the mind as well as the body, a discipline that requires that they make room for play in life, as well as work, but one which sees work as necessary for human survival and human progress. Discipline, in learning or in behavior, is not something a child is born with; it does not lie there, latent, waiting to bloom on its own. It is a conditioned reflex or a self-imposed one. The child who is taught to do his own thing as a substitute for disciplined learning is going to be unhappy and probably angry when a police officer says he can't walk against the light. And if the adult cannot read the sign that says not to walk, because he was not taught as a child, then the adult has reason to be angry.[7]

---

[7] Hofer again, this time in his *America*: "The more you know about a subject, the more reactionary you are going to be about it. It is only when you don't know nothing that you can be radical about it."

Yet, at the same time it almost seems funny to me to talk about the need for reading and math in the context of today. I've been saying it for five years. Now, at last, it's popular, *de rigeur*, to hold a cocktail at a party and bemoan the schools' steady decline in these two fundamental fields. Radical chic is the way the pop writer Tom Wolfe referred to it in another context. The danger here, of course, is that the current wave of interest in the schools' failure to teach these two most necessary of all academic "survival skills" will crest and disappear in a foam of dying fashion to be replaced by some new brand of educational chic. Perhaps the core curriculum. We haven't heard from it in a while.

The Eternal Adversaries

In fact, it's already happening. *The Washington Post, The New York Times, Saturday Review,* and a few other publications whose *imprimatur* certifies any issue, have already been testing the waters with snide articles suggesting that perhaps we have over-reacted in insisting that children be able to read, write, do basic math, and master other minimums of objective knowledge to the limit of their abilities.

It is wise to recogize that this swing, this change, can come. The reading-math dichotomy provides an excellent chance for the educational manager to prepare by looking at an issue without distorting it himself. The manager should begin by recognizing that others will distort any educational issue in the future, as they have in the past.

For example, Christopher Jencks, a Harvard sociologist and educational observer of some note, has already launched a counterattack of sorts on the current efforts to ensure that public schools cut down on their production of illiterates.

In a lengthy essay, "The *Wrong* Answer For Schools Is: Back to Basics," Jencks tries to justify the thesis contained in his title.[8] His quarrel is essentially a quarrel with tests. Some, he says, show children doing *better* than ever. But from a public relations standpoint, as the annual Gallup poll shows year after year, the public is convinced that children are doing worse and most test results confirm it. If this is not the case, then why isn't the public easily convinced by the evidence that Jencks *et al.* contend is so easily available?

As was pointed out in the preceding chapter, it is important from a public relations standpoint for schools to quickly and clearly identify those areas in which children are having objective success and to make public relations capital of them. Where those areas also coincide with the proven interests and concerns of parents—reading and math, for example—the

[8] *The Washington Post*, February 19, 1978.

school system that can stress success in these areas is going to at the very least be building an investment that can help it weather future storms.

To avoid another PR debacle, however, education won't over-react to Jencks and the clamoring converts he is sure to attract. If it does, it will be back at square one with an even more outraged public on its hands (presuming that is possible).

Although the debacle of reading and math is part of the substantive failure of public education in recent years, it does no good to institute a reign of terror by the conservatives and thus play into the hands of the closet anarchists of education who, like Jencks, are only now beginning to cautiously emerge once again from the thundering indictment of their educational philosophy.

A physician who discovers that a patient has been wrongfully and negligently dehydrated does that patient no service by drowning him. Sound conservative-progressive treatment is the answer for the patient, be that patient physically or educationally ill. Only in cases of life and death are rash, heroic measures required. Although many schools and systems may still need this approach to halt their declines in such areas as reading and math, the path of conservative progress must be returned to as soon as sensibly possible.

The Need for Self Reliance

If one of the major goals of public education is to make the individual self-reliant—or at least to give him or her that potential—then reading and math need no further justification. The self-reliance, self-development, do-your-own-thing kick is a favorite pillar of the anarchist school of educational philosophy. It is one that sane, balanced educators can safely adopt, however, by stressing that self-reliance in survival in the immediate future requires individuals who can ferret out and decode the written or mathematical word when the television and/or pocket computer is stolen, broken, or repossessed.

Now that schools are beginning the painful struggle to recapture their self-respect in the teaching of reading and math, they must make sure they never lose it again. The anarchists will use their old tricks of making schools feel guilty because objective teaching does not reach *all* children. The polio vaccine does not protect all children either. But that is no reason to leave all children unprotected.

The answer here is to insist that the anarchists demonstrate that their approach will produce greater success and self-reliance. Only with such unlikely proof in hand can the educational manager safely abandon his traditional responsibility for the teaching of reading and math. The record shows such proof is not going to be offered.

What we may be facing here, and reading and math represent a good place to begin, is a maturing of educational leadership that realizes it cannot justifiably be blamed, and need not feel guilty, if sound efforts to teach skills and knowledge of proven value do not take with all pupils.[9]

Objective teaching, no matter how much it should be implemented, is still subject to the fact that teaching is art as well as science. The late Columbia scholar, Gilbert Highet, said it eloquently and simply more than twenty-five years ago in a pair of small books: *The Art of Teaching* and *Man's Unconquerable Mind.*

In both books, Highet stressed the necessity for searching out among *all children* those who have the potential to achieve far beyond what we might otherwise expect. He cites examples from among the so-called over-achievers of history who came from just such backgrounds. But nowhere does Highet apologize for the fact that all children will not succeed or that some, despite the best, most reasonable efforts of teachers, will not succeed at all.

The changing nature of schools in our society has, of course, made the work of the educational manager more difficult in a sense. The well-intentioned policies of government, which force shools to keep indefinitely those who cannot or will not learn, have been self-defeating, and the result has been nothing short of turmoil for the teaching process.

Open School: An Appraisal

Much of this turmoil has come as the schools thrashed about, at-tempting to find a shortcut for doing what experience should have taught them requires effort and time in the learning process. To cite only one, the educator can look back on the fraud of the so-called open classroom con-cept. Originally started in Britain, this concept held that a child, no matter how small or ill-prepared would learn what he needed to know—reading and math among them—when he was ready.

The facts have proven otherwise. Perhaps the most damning indict-ment of this particular chapter of educational anarchy comes from the British themselves. The British study, released early in 1977, showed that formal teaching methods achieved superior results, not only in the basic areas such as reading and math, but also in the creative curriculum.

This is a point that some of the anarchists in education have been willing to concede, grudgingly, when backed to the wall. Their argument

---

[9] One reason they do not take, according to Scott D. Thomson, deputy execu-tive director of the National Association of Secondary School Principals (1977) is that schools have been *too responsive* to what they interpreted as a public mandate to keep as many children as possible in school for as long as possible regardless of the con-sequences.

has been, however, that this academic achievement was obtained at the expense of the child's emotional and social development, particularly in cases where the child was a bit shaky to begin with.

Not so, said the British study, which was done by a team from the University of Lancaster. Children with high levels of anxiety seem to do better all around in a structured, goal-oriented classroom, and there is no harm to the emotional and social development of otherwise normal children.

What makes the rout of the anarchists of the open classroom complete, however, is the fact that *all* the authors of the British study admit in their report (*Teaching Styles and Pupil Progress*, Open Books, London) that they began the study with a prejudice in *favor* of open education.[10]

The conclusions do not come from an isolated sample. The team studied third and fourth grades in 871 primary schools covering urban and rural areas, old schools and new schools alike.

The results say what parents have been trying to say all along.[11]

And The Answer Is . . .

But enough indictment of what has been wrong in the public eye with the teaching of reading and math. How can it be improved? First, some general observations:

Give the teacher time to teach. Reduce the field trips, and the class-room interruptions by the guidance people, and all the rest of the visiting consultants. (In 1978, Dr. John Davis, superintendent of schools in Fairfax County, Virginia, one of the wealthiest systems in the nation, found during an elementary school visit that the classroom teachers were having to make *appointments* to spend time with the children they were legally charged with teaching. A stop was put to this practice.)

Make certain the classroom teacher, particularly at the elementary level, realizes he or she, first and foremost, will be held responsible if his or her children do not make reasonable progress in reading and mathe-

---

[10] The fact that the British came to a self-critical look at what they themselves seem to have originated and advocated would have pleased President Thomas Jefferson immensely—and borne out his forebodings. In a private letter, Jefferson wrote thus about English education: "If he (the student) goes to England, he learns drinking, horse racing and boxing. These are the peculiarities of English education . . . He is led by the strongest of all human passions, into a spirit for female intrigue . . . or a passion for whores."

[11] Parents of this persuasion will also find much support in a fine book by Paul Copperman, *The Literary Hoax* (William Morrow and Co., 1978), which is an excellent analysis of the decline of learning in the schools. Copperman is a Phi Beta Kappa who graduated from the University of California in 1969 and who founded his own reading school one year later.

matics. Obvious as that may seem, the simple placing of priority on these subjects is one of the primary ways to better performance in reading and math.

It seems, at times, that public education has tried almost every trick short of the obvious one of hiring competent, compassionate teachers, giving them specific academic goals, and the time to achieve them, and holding them responsible for productive effort. The open classroom farce, the remedial rip-off, the federal boondoggles are by no means the end of the list.

Remember the teaching machines that were going to revolutionize the classroom? Certainly there is a place for audiovisual equipment (or "media," as it is now known), but how can a child use the technology intelligently when he or she has not mastered the language?

Or take the "new" math, which at last is falling into the disfavor it has so long deserved. Academically oriented students were able to master the theory of their subject. But an appallingly large number of them, to say nothing of the average or sub-average student, turned out not to be able to do multiplication or any other standard arithmetic, without which any citizen is at the mercy of the supermarket, the department store, and the income tax agent, to name just a few.

Some skills are acquired only through memorization (a wretched concept to many modern educators) and no skill improves or is even maintained unless it is practiced. Recognizing, then re-implementing, this simple fact of educational life would, in turn, make the lives of many educational managers so much easier.

Thus the case for basic education.[12] The statistics are there, and most of them are clear. As of 1978, the American public was paying $144 *billlion* each year for public education, a figure greater than that expended on national defense. Between 1968 and 1978, per pupil expenditures rose 132 percent, while the Consumer Price Index rose only 60 percent, yet pupil performance in the basic areas dropped. Take the college board scores, for example (and this, mind you, represents children who either have an interest in or, presumably, an aptitude for college). Between 1974 and 1975, the verbal score among public schools students in Atlanta was down 21 points to 334; in Boston, down 21 points to 396; in New York, down 13 points to 411; in Los Angeles, down 17 points to 406. Yet these are the same school systems in which the greatest proportional increase in public school expenses has taken place over the last ten years.

---

[12] Which the Council for Basic Education (725 Fifteenth St., NW, Washington, D.C. 20005) is always happy to elaborate upon, complete with case histories of graduates who cannot read and statistical data showing that traditional methods, particularly phonics, are the only ways to effectively teach reading.

And children aren't learning to read and do math? This isn't a public relations problem? The public doesn't have a *right* to be furious?[13]

[13] With regard to the reading aspect of the problem, it does not seem to me that there exists among teachers today a love of language, an awareness of its power, or an awe for what it can do. I fear that this is because teachers have not been exposed to language in either its written or spoken majesty during their lives or during their training, which is a problem we'll deal with next.

Many years ago, Gustave Flaubert wrote, "Human language is like a cracked kettle on which we beat out tunes for bears to dance to, when all the time we are longing to move the stars to pity."

Today's teachers sometimes serve the bears well enough; it is the stars they do not seem to know exist.

CHAPTER 4

Teacher Testing: Boon or Bugaboo?

The teacher shall be skilled in grammar and usage of the language; shall understand the principles of mathematics through algebra; have a mastery of geography, history and literature, including both English and American authors, and be otherwise academically qualified as required.
—a 1901 requirement of a
New York School Board

It have been a pleasure to writ you and I hopes to her from you shortly.
—a letter from a South Carolina teacher
of seven years' experience,
seeking a promotion, 1971

It is just another school board meeting, and the speaker who rises is one more parent with a complaint. The board members, the press, various administrative hangers-on, even some of the public, seem restless and ready to go home. But this time the complaint is not something that can be fixed by painting the classroom, carpeting the library, or adding a crossing guard. Money, for once, is not the answer. This time, the demand is for blood.

The parent is speaking for a delegation and in her fevered hands is the written evidence that one or more teachers has sent home messages containing atrocious grammar, indefensible errors in mathematics, or a blithe statement that the atom is the smallest bit of matter and the Earth is the center of the universe.

Board members look to the superintendent; the superintendent flinches, as he feels the bird alight on his shoulders, and another uproar has begun.

The public is aware and it's squawking. It's hard to blame them when they receive, as did visitors to the Manatee, Florida County Fair in 1976, a brochure from the Manatee Education Association containing at least one error in spelling or grammar in every paragraph and more than a dozen errors overall in punctuation and subject-verb agreement.

Or take the reaction in Lafayette, Louisiana, where in 1978, a teacher who had recently moved to Lafayette from Texas wrote an irate letter to the newspaper complaining about the low salary for substitute teachers. "What does the board expect to get for this kind of pay?" the letter asked. According to the newspaper, not much. The teacher's one paragraph letter, the newspaper noted, contained seven errors in grammar and spelling including two misspellings of the word *substitute.*

Meanwhile, in Richmond, Virginia, a four-page publication prepared by the superintendent of school's office during the 1978–79 school year contained twenty-four errors in spelling, grammar, and subject-verb agreement in four pages. The document was designed for mailing to the parents of all secondary students to build support for the superintendent's plan to create three additional administrative positions, each at a salary approaching $30,000 per year, while at the same time, to consolidate the city's senior high schools in the face of bitter teacher, student, and parent opposition.

Is the Case Hopeless?

Despite the fact that, as a California court held in 1972, Johnny's illiteracy in language, math, and science stems from his culture and his home, not just the school's failings, what excuse is there for the level of illiteracy among teachers and other staff which is breeding this public concern?

Is the case hopeless? Is teacher competency an impossible goal to obtain? And how, in retrospect, did we ever get in this mess anyway, where more and more parents and other people are challenging the credentials and the credibility of the classroom teacher?

There is no excuse, and school managers who thrash about trying to find one are just prolonging the agony. There is, however, an explanation or, perhaps, indictments which can be made. An examination of these may help explain the current situation, how to correct it, and what is to be done to prevent its recurrence.

The problem may be simple; the solution, somewhat less so.

How schools came to employ unqualified teachers begs the issue, in one sense, and tends to detract from the solution. However, there is blame enough to go round. Without trying to neglect anyone, let's look at some of causes.

Part of the blame can go to the teachers colleges of yesteryear (and some of those today as well) where anti-intellectualism was (and is) too often a knee-jerk reaction against the smug elitists of the liberal arts colleges. Yet the teachers colleges up until recently were themselves only responding to the explosive need for teachers; a warm body that looked intelligent, walked unaided, and did not drink in the classroom. (In 1957, for example, the movie theaters in Columbus, Georgia, were running advertisements before each feature which read, plaintively, "You CAN Teach if you WILL Teach." The ads may well have brought in some good teachers, but it was not much of a way to build quality control.)

Assembly-line production of anything seldom makes for the overall quality that the individual craftsman can provide. The mass production of teachers was no exception.

A Continuing Problem

Attacks on teacher education, however, are not new. The liberal arts people have been grumbling about it for decades. Even criticism from laymen is not all that recent. James D. Koerner traced the problems, which are now being faced yet again, twenty years ago in his definitive study *The Miseducation of American Teachers* (Houghton Mifflin Company, 1963). John Keats, in *The Sheepskin Psychosis* (J. B. Lippincott Company, 1963) also outlined much of the problem in the world which some schools of education inhabit, as did Paul Tractenberg in *Testing the Teacher* (Agathon, 1973).

Yet it was not the mass production, but the anti-intellectualism that lit the fuse of incompetence in the teachers colleges. A look at the requirements for a bachelor's degree in education in one of the Southeast's larger teachers colleges in the early 1960s will serve as an example. A teacher preparing for an elementary certificate was required to take 38 quarter hours in professional education, 38 quarter hours of elective, and 114 hours of general education courses.

Of the general education course, however, only 3 hours of the 114 were in grammar. Five hours were in "basic arithmetic" and 6 hours were in natural science. The latter consisted of 3 hours in something called "science at home" and 3 in "science in industry." There was, of course, no foreign language requirement, and there was no such thing as a competence test in any of the academic fields prior to receiving the teaching certificate (automatic with graduation).

It can be argued that those preparing for grammar school teaching careers sought out on their own from among their electives such non-required courses as biology, chemistry, physics, a foreign language, or other academic disciplines beyond the bare minimums. Yet human nature being what it is the number of college students who *elected* the more difficult and challenging courses was not high in the institution cited and it is doubtful if it would be higher today.

At the time covered by this survey elementary teaching certificates were good in many states through grade seven. This was also an era when admission to many teachers colleges carried with it extraordinary low standards. Admission to the institution cited here, a fully accredited four-year college, which is now a regional university complete with its own medical school, required of high school graduates only four units in English, one each in mathematics and science of an unspecified nature, and two in social science (also unspecified).

It was also generally conceded, even by some who were part of the educationist establishment, that the number of courses in educational theory and methods was disproportionately high in comparison to courses of academic content. This is a particularly sensitive subject, because the attacks on professional education courses continue to come from the liberal arts faction which sees education courses as having the same academic respectability as public school classes for TMRs (trainable mentally retarded). As with all accusations, there is, sadly, an element of truth in the charge, and this element has contributed to the low level of preparation and performance on the part of some teachers. However, it is unfair to label all education courses as being of this caliber. Some are not only rigorous and demanding, but could meet the academic credentials of any other offering in the institution. (As the product of many an education course, I can testify that, whereas the worst courses I ever took, both from the standpoint of teaching and content, were in education, so were two of the best and most challenging of my entire graduate or undergraduate career.)

So great has become the public's suspicion of the quality of education in many teachers colleges, that the name itself has almost disappeared. Most teachers colleges are now multi-purpose undergraduate institutions and if not, they label themselves as such. Many have begun a slowly increasing struggle toward academic respectability in an attempt to leave behind the wasteland of curriculum they offered during the 40s, 50s, and 60s.

The increasing academic respectability of some teacher training programs, together with a decline in the number of jobs for new teachers, offers hope that the disparities in training that many teachers now display are being corrected. This also provides a chance to correct the discrimination against liberal arts graduates who, though far better trained in the academic disciplines than most graduates of teacher training programs and frequently possessed of superior skills in teaching, were and are penalized by most states by being paid substantially less than teachers college graduates.

Another aspect of the training program which has caused this sad public relations problem of questionable competency of teachers is that so many superior teachers have to leave the profession altogether, or at least move on to the college and university level. This encourages the mediocre or the inferior to remain in the classroom until such time as they can win appointment to an administrative position. An example of this trend can be found by examining the backgrounds of those persons appointed to principalships, particularly at the secondary level, and particularly outside of the larger metropolitan school districts. Men were the overwhelming choice up until fairly recently (a blatant sexism that should have been corrected long ago) and almost all of the men had either a full-time or part-time background in athletic coaching or some aspect of vocational education.

This should not be interpreted as an indictment of the intelligence or the administrative ability of *all* administrators who have been coaches. I contend that the college preparation for coaches who were majors in physical education was lacking in the academic skills and abilities which the coach as *principal* is called on to administer.

The Legacy of Sexism

A side effect of the tendency to elect former coaches (males) to the principalship in disproportionate numbers has been to further discourage the competent teacher who wished to remain in the classroom with some hope of sympathetic, enlightened, and intelligent leadership. A high school chemistry teacher, for example, one who may have earned a master's degree in his subject field, can hardly be blamed for being discouraged if his competence and ability in the classroom is judged each year by a man who has never had a course in chemistry and who has never taught an academic subject in his entire life. As bitterly political as the pecking order for promotion among college and university teachers can become, at least those deans and other administrators who pass academic judgment on faculty have in almost all cases demonstrated that 1) they hold some academic degrees and 2) have had some successful experience as teachers of academic subjects.

The problem public education now faces with regard to teachers whose training was questionable is significant. That problem is exacerbated by the number of poorly trained teachers who have gone into educational administration and thus have gained broad influence as supervisors, principals, and even superintendents. The training offered in the advanced degrees of education, the M.Ed. and the Ed.D., for example, is superior in some institutions, but deplorable in too many others. It is a tragic indictment of educational management that some universities without campuses, resident faculty, or resident study requirement for so-called students are still licensed by certain states to grant doctoral degrees for work which amounts to little more than that required to obtain a "degree" for 50 dollars and the price of return postage. The one hopeful sign is that those institutions of highly questionable credentials are finding that other states are at least refusing to recognize the degrees they award and are refusing to certify, employ, promote, or otherwise reward those who hold them.

Institutions of this nature do not operate in a vacuum. The public is increasingly aware of the kinds of degrees teachers and educational managers hold and the quality of the institutions which awarded them. As more and more parents, particularly from the middle class, are themselves the holders of college degrees, they have first-hand information as to the quality, or its lack, of the teacher training programs which operate on the same campuses which they themselves attended. Some of these teacher training programs may have been a subject for humor while these parents were under-graduates; they become considerably less funny when these parents have to turn their children over to teachers who are products of such programs.

Attempts to reduce teacher training to a science that required little or no discipline, and where anybody's answer was as right as anyone else's in the names of democracy and openness, are still having a disastrous effect. The pseudo-science which resulted from the diminution of any requirement that teachers first know their subject (or, in the case of elementary teachers, a substantial amount about all subjects), cannot be corrected too speedily.

Teaching, successful teaching, requires the mental discipline first, of self, and then of those under one's authority. For that to be accomplished, a teacher must first know, and then have the commitment to be. William Lyon Phelps, himself a great teacher, put it this way in *Autobiography With Letters* (Oxford University Press, 1939):

> I do not know that I could make entirely clear to an outsider the pleasure I have in teaching. I had rather earn my living by teaching than in any other way. In my mind, teaching is not merely a lifework, a profession, an oc-cupation, a struggle; it is a passion. I love to teach as a painter loves to paint, as a musician loves to play, as a singer loves to sing, as a strong man rejoices to run a race. Teaching is an art—an art so great and so difficult to master that a man or a woman can spend a long life at it, without realizing much more than his limitations and mistakes and his distance from the ideal.

How many of the public relations problems involving teachers might be solved if schools simply insisted that the colleges turn out graduates who understood, or have at least been exposed to, what Phelps had to say, and were willing to rigorously apply it to themselves.

Still, defenders of faculty competence contend that whatever weak-nesses teachers may have in their academic preparation are small, easily overcome, and do not justify the awful fuss kicked up by the isolated incidents which come to light or the complaints of parents. Is there evidence, current evidence, which speaks to the current quality of teach-ers? Yes, and it tends to support the indictment, both for currently em-ployed teachers and for those planning to enter the profession.

One spectre which is causing as much concern as any to the teachers themselves is that of holding teachers responsible when pupils do poorly.

This is a short-sighted solution, because there are subjective factors in-volved. However, teachers who do not know what it is they are supposed to be teaching rather obviously cannot teach it, no matter what the quality of the children placed in their care. This was the reasoning behind a plan begun in 1977 by the State Board of Education in New Jersey. The plan, an attempt to bridge the ire of the legislature over what it felt was teacher incompetence, and the anger of the New Jersey Education Association at the requirement that teachers know their subjects and be able to demon-strate that knowledge, permits testing of employed teachers. Those tests can be used as one factor in evaluating a teacher whose students do poorly. Litigation may yet doom this plan, if it has not done so already, and school managers must expect any serious plan of objective evaluation to face such challenges.

The Dallas Debacle

In Dallas, Texas, in 1978, however, the objective evidence of poor teacher preparation was certainly concrete. Of 585 newly hired teachers who took a standardized test more than half failed—*even though they had to answer correctly only thirty-one of sixty questions in math and language.* [1] To make this a greater public relations debacle than the test results themselves showed, Dallas school district officials fought efforts by the Dallas *Times-Herald* to gain access to the test results—and lost. This is an excellent example of poor public relations—and poor judgment. The test results may have reflected unfavorably upon the institutions who certified and graduated the students, but the results also raised the question why the teachers were tested *after* being hired instead of before.

There is objective evidence to indicate that the poor test results run up by too many teachers are not unjustified. A study by Robert S. Zais, associate professor of education at Kent State University, reported in 1978, produced some interesting results—and some equally interesting inter-pretations. Zais tested 387 Kent State seniors who were in secondary edu-cation teacher training programs. The test used was the Diagnostic Reading Tests, Survey Section: Upper Level (Committee on Diagnostic Reading Tests, 1966). The results, according to Zais, showed that the reading per-formance of the seniors was well above the average for first-year college students and that one-third of his prospective secondary teachers might even read better than three-fourths of all first-year students.

Zais's positive interpretation does not seem warranted, if one remem-bers that the average reading level of first-year college students is not

---

[1] For a more detailed summary of the Dallas experience, see Richard Mitchell's account, "Testing the Teachers," *The Atlantic Monthly*, December 1978, p. 66.

generally considered to be very high. In addition, one would *expect* that the reading level of college seniors would be substantially higher than that of first-year students. To conclude otherwise would be to presume that college students do not improve their skills—and should not be expected to do so—as they progress through their college careers. This is both an unwise and an unjustified presumption, since the quantity of reading required in college generally is considerably more than that required in high school.

Of equal interest, however, is Zais's finding, and his explanation, that 15 percent of his sample read *less* well than three-fourths of the first-year students. Zais does not consider this to be alarming and cites as justification and rationalization prevailing estimates that 10 percent of American physicians and 25 percent of American lawyers are incompetent.

There is no intention here to defend the level of competence of American physicians or lawyers. The levels of incompetence cited for those professions are inexcusable and the accuracy of these levels is not questioned here. One cannot help but wonder, however, how low the level of competence might be among physicians and lawyers if those two groups did not have to take postgraduate licensing tests and examinations—conditions, it seems important to point out that many teachers are not required to meet. Or, put another way, how much would the competence factor of public school teachers improve if they were required to take a pre-service examination and post a reasonable passing score? (*Reasonable* here is projected as far greater than the 51 percent score which was passing in the Dallas tests previously mentioned.)

Zais's pointing to the incompetence factor among other professions is justified—as long as that pointing is done to attack the incompetence of physicians and lawyers and not to raise a smokescreen of defense, justification, or excuse for the incompetence among teachers. This type of argument is rather like saying that because your neighbor steals and gets away with it, you ought not to be punished if you're caught doing the same thing.

Further, the Zais study indicates serious concern about the competence of 15 percent of his prospective teachers (and serious concern is certainly warranted when one considers that Kent State is neither an institution of particularly outstanding academic quality nor by any means the worst institution now training teachers). If Zais's study is projected, then out of every 100 new teachers hired, 15 are language incompetents, based on his reported results. While this is nowhere near the miserable showing made by the new Dallas teachers in 1978, it is still far too great to be acceptable, even though there is a glut of applicants and few teaching jobs. Fifteen incompetent teachers out of every 100 times 10 years of employment times 100 students per year equals 100,000 children exposed to incompetence in the space of a single decade. Which school manager is willing to defend that to the public?[2]

[2] A summary of Zais's study is contained in *Phi Delta Kappan*, May 1978.

In-Breeding as a Problem

In-breeding in the educational establishment also appears to have caused part of the problem of incompetence in public education. Like the lawyers and the physicians, educators do not want the public to see their warts and blemishes. Despite all the professional codes to the contrary, it is far easier to cover up for the incompetence of a colleague than to take action. After all, on whom might the spotlight fall next? This is a very real concern for those educational managers who are finding their own training and performance undergoing objective evaluation.

The school boards themselves may also have a share of the blame for the current public unrest. Popular opinion to the contrary, most school board members do not dabble in the day-to-day administration of the schools all that much. Board members tend to be busy with their own vocations or professions. Thus, if the superintendent submits a list of teachers for employment, the board usually goes along without much question. Hindsight suggests this may have been a bad mistake.

The Layman's Share of Blame

And finally, parents, the public, and the press may all have a slice of the blame for the teacher competence issue so that everyone may feel properly guilty. For these are the folks who, at times, put pressure on the boards and the administrations to make schools "relevant"; to "open" education; to add "movement education," an "organic" curriculum, an organized physical ed program in every elementary school; to introduce the infamous "teaching machine" or a field trip for every whim. So what if this cut into time that might have been spent on math, or reading, or science, or history, or the mastery of electronics or secretarial science.

This pressure for innovation without excellence, for change for change's sake, runs through many of the public relations problems of public education. One of the organizations that has a continuing distress over this condition is the Council for Basic Education, a private, non-profit group organized in 1956 as an antithesis to "the view that the purpose of schooling was social development and life adjustment rather than intellectual training."

This concern, of course, has left the council somewhat at the mercy of those who support the idea that the greater the anarchy in education the better the schools. The latter group has been able to label the council, and many other supporters of traditional and proven concepts in education, as right-wing reactionaries. This labeling is fairly frequent in certain schools of education. No reasonable person wants public education to exclude any individual from educational opportunity. Certainly there is nothing entirely wrong with social or life adjustment, although one would do well to remember that historically those who have contributed the most to science, the arts, religion, and literature have frequently been those most out of step or least adjusted to their society. The council's position, therefore, might have drawn more support if it provided for intellectual training as the *first* priority of public education without attacking so exclusively the options of adjustment, particularly for those who will not be entering college to prepare for a profession.

Where the council is on stronger ground (and the council is certainly no fascist reactionary group, regardless of the narrowness of certain stands) is in its attack on the orgy of curricular innovation which has contributed so greatly to the problems of teacher training and an unhappy public. Among those innovations, each of which has been reflected by teachers colleges to the confusion of teachers and the detriment of students, are, according to the council:

The adoption of unproven innovations (new math, individualized instruction, open classroom); the proliferation of electives and so-called mini-courses, particularly at the high school level; teaching such subjects as health education and "career" education more properly the responsibility of something other than the public schools, and a decline in foreign language instruction.

While the council's objectives are probably too restrictive for the modern school, they are not unreasonable in that they help stress the morass of *expectations* the teacher faces. Teachers are often caught between fulfilling traditional expectations for which they have been poorly prepared and delving into the innovations that are pushed upon them, such as those about which the council complains. The wise educational manager will try to see that a situation is obtained in his jurisdiction which leads to teaching children what has been proven that they need, rather than what some individual or group suddenly concludes might be nice in the name of innovation, such as the ubiquitous "mini-course" with its equally "mini-learning."

As Eric Hofer, the longshoreman-philosopher of American letters puts it in his *Reflections on the Human Condition*, "Total innovation is the refuge of the untalented. It offers them a situation where their ineptness is acceptable and natural."

KEY CONCERN FOR SCHOOL PR: *Beware the teacher who prefers the sparkle of innovation to the solid shine of substance.*

Now that everyone has his share of the guilt and has cried an appropriate *mea culpa*, what's going to be done about the problem of teacher preparation and performance?

It must be approached from two levels: 1) what to do about incompetent teachers now on the staff and 2) what to do to prevent others from being hired.

Too many boards have been lulled into the belief that competent teachers were the only ones hired in the first place and that the periodic coursework most states require for continued certification ensured that the teachers stayed up to snuff. What they did not bother to concentrate on was that three courses in finger painting or the like would continue a certificate for most any teacher—and finger painting was not what the teacher was supposed to be teaching. This condition is being further aggravated in some states by the NCC (non-college credit) course which teachers can take in their own schools. Since there is no credit, there are no grades, no controls, no enforceable expectations. Yet this type of "advanced study" is being increasingly accepted as adequate for renewing a teaching certificate.

With current employees whose work is suspected of being substandard, the best approach is probably to consider minimum criteria of skills, to administer objective tests to determine if teachers have those skills and to provide, at board expense, remedial work for those who are deficient. (Example: A third grade teacher who cannot pass a test in multiplication, division, fractions, and decimals would have to show proficiency within a stated time.)[3]

The Union Issue

But whenever there is a move to correct deficiencies in tenured teachers, a fight with the union can be expected, particularly if remediation and testing are involved. In a forty-nine page report issued by the National Education Association in 1977 "indefensible" is the key word used to characterize tests for teachers, although it is difficult to understand how such a position can be ethically taken by an organization which claims a commitment to the welfare of children.[4]

Where the union is weak or non-existent, teacher testing can be implemented with less trouble. A strong union, seeking to buttress itself,

[3] M. Donald Thomas, superintendent of schools in Salt Lake City, described the best internal procedure for dealing with incompetent faculty that I have ever heard during a panel discussion involving M. Chester Nolte, professor emeritus at the University of Denver, and the author. The Salt Lake City procedure involves objective and subjective evaluation, keeps the incompetent teacher fully advised in writing of steps to be taken, assigns him or her to specific personnel for assistance, and, as of 1978, had resulted in forty teacher dismissals *without a single legal challenge.*

[4] The 1978 Representative Assembly of the National Education Association went a step further than just a report. In adopting resolution 78-52, the NEA said it "is convinced that no test now in existence is satisfactory for use" as even *one* criterion to determine teacher selection. It's hard to see how the adoption of such a resolution is consistent with the welfare of children.

is apt to see testing as another attempt to make teachers unfairly unaccountable for possessing knowledge they are already being paid to have. If possible, involve the union as educational management in Prince Georges, Maryland has done. This gives the union a share in the responsibility—and the blame—for finding the incompetent teacher and correcting his weakness. Public support at this point, however, is apt to favor school managers, and will be useful in any union relationships.

There is no public relations advantage, however, in trying to portray all teachers as mindless automatons opposed to any effort to improve teacher quality. Teachers today do waste a great deal of time, but much of this is because of fulsome programs thrust upon them. They *do* have reason to be concerned about pay that does not keep up with the cost of living and their attacks on non-productive administrators are not without merit.

Still, it may be tough. It's hard to do something about good Miss J's incompetence today when nothing was done with—or for—her in the five or ten years she's already been on the job. But the difficulty is simply one more indication of how badly overdue some constructive action is.

Part of the problem of having incompetent teachers of long standing stems from the in-breeding in public education, and part from less than adequate leadership. In too many school districts, for too many years, the annual evaluation of teachers has simply been a series of meaningless marks of a subjective nature made on a form that was filed unread in the personnel office while the teacher won automatic renewal for another term. No one was ever graded low enough to cause embarrassing problems. In fact, many districts have insulted their teachers in the same way that they have insulted their children on report cards—by abandoning any type of evaluation which indicates excellence or achievement. The result is that teachers are also being rated "S" after "S" (for satisfactory) regardless of whether their efforts and their achievements have been outstanding or just barely mediocre. Teachers, like pupils, should be entitled to some record of their excellence (and of something worse than an "N" for "needs to improve" as the only alternative to the ubiquitous "S").

Of course, a principal who seriously tried to weed out incompetent teachers was only asking for trouble. The incompetent would complain, perhaps to a political superintendent or a school board, and the principal who made the waves would find his own boat a-rock with analyses of his leadership and performance. Which, of course, is as it should be. But if one were to analyze the principal's performance, then what would keep this disease of evaluation from spreading to even higher reaches, into the bureaucracy of the central administration, for example. Danger here. Better to leave things be. Or so the reasoning has traditionally been.

Yet objective analysis of teacher performance is a must for good public relations, not just outside the school system, but inside as well. If a faculty has an incompetent teacher, other faculty members know it just about as rapidly as the pupils. But too often, when evaluation time rolls around, a principal either has ignored the incompetent or tried to quietly get him or her transferred to another school. At most, there has been some indirect counseling that he or she ought to seek another job.

Objective Evaluation: A Must

This won't work any longer, and is a downright dangerous practice as well. The principal who believes he has an incompetent teacher must find and follow *objective* procedures for counseling, using written records of shortcomings, and reports of progress, if any, if he is to effect a teacher's dismissal. Union contracts are too strong in some areas to do otherwise; the threat of lawsuit for failure to follow due process is adequate reason elsewhere. Even the most incompetent teacher is entitled to the protection of due process and attempts to circumvent this are not only unlawful, they are unfair.

A principal should have no fear of using an objective approach that may lead to the dismissal of an incompetent. He must, however, demonstrate that a recognized procedure that is fully understood by the teacher has been followed and that written statements have been given to the teacher periodically during the entire time she is under review.

Positive public relations will emerge from sound, non-biased attempts to weed out incompetence. Negative PR will be forthcoming if lawsuits result, particularly where such suits demonstrate sympathy for the teacher and where testimony reveals a level of incompetence at the administrative level equal to or greater than that among the teaching staff.

Court decisions, as will be shown, have strengthened the hand of the school board or other educational managers who may wish to use objective tests to get rid of the incompetent. These decisions, however, do not give school boards the right to rush carelessly into a program of teacher tests.

Keeping the incompetent out of the classroom to begin with is much easier. It requires no effort to mandate that each teacher applicant submit a 250-word essay, either biographical or expository, in his own handwriting as part of the application for employment.[5] Muddled thinking, obscure writing, and lack of simple grammar will show up quickly.

Prince Georges, Maryland has used such pre-employment testing in the form of spelling and grammar tests and found that this process quickly weeds out 20 percent of applicants. Similar tests can be devised for subject areas. This is particularly important in screening elementary school applicants for if there is one thing secondary teachers will do it is to blame the

[5] Torrington, Connecticut is just one of many small school districts in which the superintendent has assumed personal responsibility for the evaluation of essays by teacher applicants.

elementary teacher (frequently with good cause) for not having taught the foundation material and skills.

There is, of course, a difference in the skills and abilities which are required of elementary and secondary teachers. Elementary teachers are stuck with the same kids all day, while secondary teachers at least have a change of faces (and abilities). The elementary teacher is apt to complain because she is responsible for teaching in a variety of areas. What the elementary teacher will conveniently overlook, however, is that the level of knowledge required of her is no more than that any college graduate should be expected to have. Were the elementary teacher responsible for *in-depth* knowledge in history, mathematics, English, geography, and the various sciences, she might have a right to complain (although more than one child has been successfully taught in a one-room school by teachers who have mastered their subjects to just such a degree).

This adversary relationship between elementary and secondary teachers is further evidence for organizing a curriculum so that elementary teachers will know what objective skills they are expected to possess and teach so that their children will succeed when they reach high school. High school teachers, in turn, must be made to understand that their preparation does not begin and end with their subject field. A teacher who cannot command the written word is apt to do an unsatisfactory job even if his field of teaching is science or mathematics. An oral interview designed to determine how well a teacher candidate can think and answer unanticipated questions is a subjective test which can be included. In sum, pre-employment testing should concentrate on the academic skills in the subject areas for which the teacher is responsible and also upon the written and spoken command of the language. The only exception to the latter requirement might come for otherwise exceptionally well-qualified candidates who are teaching in some trade or industrial field.

Objections to Expect

A board which adopts this screening approach with new teachers, however, can expect squeals of righteous indignation from some teacher's colleges. "We have graduated these teachers," they will say. "Are you questioning our judgment?"

"No," you can reply in your best human relations manner, "just trying to vindicate it." Given the graduate glut now at hand, opposition from the colleges will not last long. Changing teacher training curricula to guarantee a consistent, well-prepared supply of teachers can hardlly be accomplished over night. In the last several years, as the demand for teachers has declined, there have been encouraging signs that the quality of the product is improving.

More devious, however, will be the accusations from some, including the well-meaning as well as the pompous, that attempting to ensure that teachers know the subjects they've been hired to teach is "de-humanizing." One of the favorite ploys of some teachers colleges, indeed of some superintendents, is that "humanistic" education is more important than knowledge, that innovation is more important than excellence. What has never been explained is why the teacher who knows his subject is automatically "dehumanizing" while the one who does not is somehow "more sensitive to the needs of children." That is no exaggeration. It has been stated in those very words.

Given that argument, of course, the public would all rush to a kindly, sympathetic old witch doctor for treatment of bacterial pneumonia rather than get a penicillin regimen in ten minutes from a qualified M.D., on the grounds that empathy is better for disease than knowledge and skill.

Put another way, what school board or community would tolerate an industrial arts teacher who did not know a wood file from a metal file? Or, for that matter, a football coach who did not know the difference between a fly pattern and a square out—and could not show his receivers how to perform correctly?

Too many school boards have neglected their responsibility to make sure their classroom teachers possessed skill and knowledge in their fields commensurate with that required of successful coach or shop teacher. After all, good PR from the football field can carry a school system only so far and for so long.

The increasing concern over the qualifications of teachers may not have resulted in sufficiently prompt action on the part of principals and other educational managers on the administrative team, but it has brought action of some type from many local and state boards of education. These boards, being more overtly political and, therefore, more aware of the potential consequences of an unhappy public, have moved in many directions and to varying degrees.

One report prepared by the Education Commission of the States in April 1978 cited action of some type to upgrade teacher qualifications in New York, Michigan, Idaho, New Jersey, Alabama, Louisiana, South Carolina, and Florida.

In Louisiana, where the steps to improve teacher competence were enacted into law, "considerable concern and numerous administrative problems (were caused) in the teacher preparation institutions . . . ," the study by the Education Commission of the States noted. An examination of that law (Act No. 757—1978) shows considerable awareness of the public relations aspects of the problem, not just as the act represents a response to concerns about teacher preparation but in how it affects the field of public education itself. In that sense, it is an excellent representation of the public relations implications, and the directions they may take in state legislatures unless the public education establishment itself moves to improve the quality of teaching.

The act requires, for example, six hours of reading methods for secondary teachers and nine for elementary teachers. This is clear evidence that the legislature has felt it necessary to use law to improve reading in Louisiana, because school management too often proved unable or unwilling to effect this improvement using its own authority. This is a dangerous condition for the public relations of public education, because a legislature that feels it can mandate in one curriculum area is unlikely to surrender that option willingly. The result is that the management of school affairs passes from the professional administrator and the local board more and more into the statewide political arena where it becomes more subject to patronage and political deals and is removed from effective local control. While state and even federal actions are necessary in some areas of public education, the management and public relations of public schools are best served when kept close to the patrons and children who are directly involved.

A second aspect of the Louisiana law stipulates that prior to admission to teacher education programs the prospective student must have three hours of counseling *"by persons other than teacher education faculty members."* While the effect of this provision may be to explain to the student the oversupply of graduates in teacher training and career options other than public education, it also is obviously a slap in the face of teacher education faculty for not realistically and adequately counseling their students. It is further evidence of a no-confidence vote in the teacher training institution.

The Louisiana law further provides that teacher training graduates shall be tested prior to graduation, that they must have field experience at the sophomore level (rather than in the senior year as is traditional), and must maintain higher grades than other students, specifically a 2.5 grade point average, in order to even be graduated.

The bothersome question that remains in the wake of the Louisiana legislature's action is not whether these steps were warranted. Those who attempt to argue this question (and a consortium of the teachers colleges, teacher organizations, and some public school managers is more than willing to do so) are missing the point, and exacerbating the issue. Clearly, there is no reason at all why the requirements stated in the Louisiana law should not be effective not just in Louisiana but all states. The requirements are specific, to the point, designed to upgrade the teaching force, and provide objective, high caliber instruction for children in the classroom. Anyone who argues against these objectives cannot be taken seriously. No. The bothersome question is not the validity of the results, it is this

KEY CONCERN FOR SCHOOL PR: *How did things get in such a mess that the legislature had to do what the teachers colleges, school boards, and local educational managers should have been doing for themselves?*

Perhaps the Louisiana development is a warning that education managers in some other states and localities can still heed: take action now, specific action, or the politicians, prodded by a public that perceives school management as unresponsive, unsympathetic, and unenlightened, will take action for you.

There is a danger here, however, for the localities and the educational managers who would help themselves, and it is a danger into which it is easy to stumble. Instead of taking dramatic, objective action, some managers will try to talk the issue to death or obscure it by taking what they perceive to be a minimum level of objective action in the hope that the public will be fooled into thinking something has really been done about the problem. This approach was taken in Florida, where the Committee on Teacher Education, which advises the state education commissioner, drew up a list of twenty-three generic teacher competencies. Those competencies, however, obscured the issue about which the public is concerned. Only six dealt even peripherally with the issue of teacher competence in academic fields and these were vague at best. The remaining seventeen skills included such down-to-earth objective statements as "Construct and sequence related short-range objectives for a given subject area." In other words, "plan."

It is this type of mumbo-jumbo which while reflecting a desirable end becomes instead an insidious attempt on the part of the entrenched and inarticulate portions of a defensive educational establishment to dilute, dissipate, or otherwise obscure what should be the first priority: *subject matter knowledge.*

As has been demonstrated before, all the peripheral skills of "relating" or "humanizing" are no substitute for knowing the material children need to learn and parents expect teachers to teach. The truly competent teacher is almost always a humanist and the way a teacher can best prove his interest in, and love for, children is by mastering his subject.

The Charge and Challenge of Racism

There is yet another issue that will confront school managers who try to weed out the incompetent and prevent their employment, and it is a painful issue undeed. Its name is racism.

For whatever reason, and the historical prejudices of racial segregation were surely a part, far more black teachers than white have consistently failed to show objective evidence that they have mastered the subjects they are supposed to be teaching. This becomes a particularly ticklish issue when one realizes that many black teachers of ten years or more experience most likely received part of their training in segregated public schools that may well have been as inferior as their colleges. Although that can be understood, it has never been excusable to impose an incompetent teacher on a classroom. Still, too many school systems across the country, whether prodded by conscience or the courts, have done it anyway. They have thus aggravated the problem by hiring minority teachers without requiring them to meet the reasonable and proper standards which all children—and minority children in particular—have a right to expect that their teachers have mastered.

The problem is not one that has just been discovered. Here is an example: In 1966, James C. Wallace, assistant professor of social studies at North Carolina State University, reported the 1961–1963 mean scores on the common examinations portion of the National Teachers Examination administered to seniors in North Carolina colleges who were planning to teach.

Although there was some degree of underclass integration in the state's traditionally white colleges at that time, institutions which had been historically white or black remained essentially segregated. The results of the tests showed that the mean for teacher training students at Duke University, a prestigious white private instition was 683. Second was the white University of North Carolina at Chapel Hill, at 633. The list continued through all 33 four-year colleges in the state until it hit Saint Augustine's, a private black college which had a mean of 424, or 259 points below Duke's.

Of even greater concern, however, was the finding that *every* black college in the state fell below every white college. The highest ranking of the eleven black colleges (Bennett, a small private institution) was 53 points below the lowest white college (Atlantic Christian, another small private institution).[6]

An Assist from the Courts

The problem of black teacher training and competence as a subset of the overall question of teacher competence reached the Supreme Court as an outgrowth of an uproar in South Carolina after only 3 percent of the seniors in the state's six predominantly black colleges passed the National Teachers Exam. The Court, acting in 1978, refused to overturn a lower court decision that the National Teacher Exam was not racially discriminatory as applied in South Carolina, even though it projects a demonstrably

---

[6] Although the Wallace study is now dated, it was one of the first to publicly pinpoint a problem that is still unsolved.

reduced percentage of black teachers (241 S.E. 2d 897), (15 FEP Cases 1196).

This action clears the way for the reasonable use of objective testing to improve the teacher pool for all teacher selections, even though it may have an adverse effect on the number of black teachers. At the same time, however, it may be a means to force black instituions into a more realistic level of preparation for their students and thus overcome a public relations problem that has reached historic proportions.

Educational managers must be prepared, of course, for continued controversy where objective testing is a requirement for teachers. Sadly, much of this clamor will come from the teaching establishment, the National Education Association, and its affiliates, who one would think would be in the forefront demanding that the levels of teacher competence be increased.

It is also necessary to remember that this issue is not restricted by race to the south, to all-black colleges, or to areas with a history of segregation.

Questioning the qualifications of teachers trained in black colleges —and of blacks trained under so-called open admission in white institutions—is as painful as it is necessary.

But, you say, isn't that just asking for a PR disaster? Not as much as trying to deny that the problem exists.

For much of the nation, particularly the white parts of it, the history of the black college and its role in the survival of the American black is not a matter of very high interest; a Sunday afternoon television type issue when there's no ball game to broadcast. Important as this heritage is, to the black community and to the nation, the time for change is long overdue. Preaching and teaching, so the saying went. This was all back colleges were good for. And for the most of that time, both the preaching and the teaching was to black groups. It is a sad commentary on American life that the qualifications of black teachers were never really an issue until after they began teaching white students. Shame is too soft a word.

It is too late for that. The public relations impact of teacher incompetence is too great for any school system to survive. It is a malignancy for which there is no cure short of surgery and a radical change in lifestyle.

What is happening in the academic world is much the same as what is happening in the athletic world. The black student who wants the best in training, or in athletic opportunity, is increasingly opting to attend a traditionally white school, knowing that he or she is going to get in on a quota system regardless of ability. That is as shameful as the racial discrimination which once kept the black out.

Three decades ago, Frank Howard, the old Clemson (S.C.) University football coach is alleged to have moaned as he watched Buddy Young perform on the football field for the University of Illinois: "If only I could have painted him white."

Racist? Sure. Gross? Perhaps. But true. Because Buddy Young was from South Carolina. Frank Howard knew how good a halfback he was. And he also knew he couldn't have gotten him, given the laws and practices of that era.

What all this means is that the private black colleges are struggling constantly just to survive. Formerly they took any black student because he or she sometimes had nowhere else to go. Now they take any black, period. The traditionally black state institutions in the south and border states have the same problem, even though they have the public purse in the form of tax monies to fall back on. The black student who can get into the University of North Carolina is not apt to opt for Fayetteville State, although his or her scores may not justify admission to either.

Fortunately, some black colleges and universities are beginning to recognize that their survival as meaningful institutions depends on establishing a reasonable level of quality—and requirements to go with it.

More than ten years ago, when the spirits, hopes, and fervors of the civil rights tides were still running high under the promise of the Johnson administration, Dr. Thomas H. Henderson, president of Virginia Union University, an institution both black and Baptist, warned that the equality brought by legislation was only half the fight; that the black student and the black college would have to find the *personal* resources to win the fight of equal performance. It was a courageous speech of a courageous man and it attracted less attention and less support than an afternoon movie on Super Bowl Sunday.

Dr. Henderson has long since gone to his grave, but he might well be pleased at a statement of standards endorsed in 1977 by the presidents of the forty-one member institutions of the United Negro College Fund.

Among the goals are these:

A proficiency exam is required for graduation for any student who has not maintained a "B" average in English.

A "C" average is necessary to pass first year English.

According to Charles E. Taylor president of Wilberforce University (Ohio) the nation's oldest private black college, "It is unfair to the students and to the institution to carry youngsters who for one reason or another are not prepared to function at the college level."[7]

This is the type of intellectual elitism—without racism—which, when applied to prospective teachers, will make the jobs of superintendents and school boards far, far easier when it comes to solving the problem of making sure teachers are qualified.

Dr. Henderson and the members of the United Negro College Fund are not totally alone, and never have been. But their voices have always

[7] In remarks prepared for delivery, May 1978, on behalf of Wilberforce and other midwestern colleges with black origins.

fallen most receptively on the ears of non-black Americans. In 1971, Bayard Rustin, then executive director of the A. Philip Randolph Institute and a leader in civil rights efforts before most blacks today were even born, had this to say:

> One of the new cults is 'black English.' Recently some 250 linguistics experts, teachers and students (most of them white) met to discuss 'Black English: Myth or Reality?' According to a *New York Times* report, the 'experts' seemed convinced that 'black English' is very much a reality. ('Black English,' according to these 'experts' is saying 'where Charlie?' instead of 'where is Charlie?')
>
> 'Experts,' the report noted, 'now say that black English has an identity independent of white dialects of English.' They also feel that it might be best to teach children in their native tongue rather than force them into the difficult situation of using English.
>
> There are already courses in "black English" being taught at a number of centers and colleges. Some are financed by foundation grants.
>
> No doubt the motives of some of these new "black linguistics experts" are sincere. They want to see black children learn, but do they want to prepare them for life outside the ghetto? Do they want to see them become first-class citizens? "Black English," after all, has nothing to do with blackness but derives from the conditions of lower-class life in the South (poor Southern whites also speak "black English"). Reinforcing this consequence of poverty will only perpetuate poverty since it will prevent black children from mastering the means of communication in an advanced technological society with a highly educated population.
>
> I am sure there are some black proponents of "black English" who feel that we must retain our racial distinctiveness and avoid the self-negating process of assimilation. But this is really a false issue. Immigrants who were much more foreign to American culture than Negroes realized when they arrived in America that in order to succeed they had to master certain skills, and they did so while retaining their ethnic distinctiveness.[8]

In New York City, for example, a clamor for a return to more stringent objective testing of teachers was accompanied by racial overtones. Louis E. Yavner, a member of the State Board of Regents from New York City, charged in 1978 that the city's public schools in some cases were staffed by barely literate teachers hired in a circumvention of what once was one of the more rigorous pre-employment testing programs in the nation. Ironically, New York City's testing program was once accused of keeping Irish Catholics and Jews out of the teaching force. Recently, however, even the watered down testing program has been attacked by blacks and Hispanics as discriminating against them.

---

[8] As quoted by Albert Shanker, president of the United Federation of Teachers, New York City, August 1, 1971.

That the issue does not have to be seen as racial, however, is shown by efforts by a black school administration in a 95 percent black system (Washington, D.C.) to establish objective pre-employment testing. The administration of Superintendent Vincent Reid of the Washington, D.C. schools sought to establish a testing foundation for excellence that would serve all children, regardless of their need. The backing of his board led to what many administrators had feared—increased accountability for them. Public reaction was highly supportive of Reid and his board. Yet this need for teacher competence, and the damage done to public confidence by failing to provide it, isn't anything new in Washington, though Reid and his board can't very well be blamed for that.

John Holland Treanor, who died in March 1978, at the age of seventy-five, was a teacher and principal in the Boston Public Schools for almost thirty years and an authority on English and teacher competence. His reports indicate how Washington failed in its duty to children.

In 1967, ten years before Washington began to move to correct its teacher inadequacies, Treanor had this to say of the Washington staff for which he was conducting classes: ". . . about 20 percent of your fourth, fifth and sixth grade English teachers are good. They're mostly the elderly teachers. Twenty-five percent should be thrown out the window. The rest usually have a poor cultural background that is reflected in their speech and vocabulary. And in their teaching."[9]

Boards and administrations will simply have to stand fast in the face of challenges to fair, equitable testing programs. The matter of "cultural bias" in tests will be waved like a flag; it is a hidden prejudice which must be guarded against. But it's almost impossible to have a "cultural bias" in long division, which applies in shopping at any supermarket, regardless of the race of the student who must one day do the shopping. And if "standard English" is considered culturally biased, the facts speak for themselves: While no one can, or should, try to destroy the cultural heritage or language of a sub-group, the fact remains that standard English is the language of access to most opportunity in this nation. If a black American and a white American were to be exiled to China, they could both sit around and talk of home—and they should. But if they want a piece of the action, social mobility, or whatever the good life is in China these days, then they'd better start hustling to learn Chinese. That's the issue.

As Dr. John R. Silber, the feisty president of Boston University put it: "We have paid a terrible price by consigning qualified minority members and women to jobs below their ability. We would have been spared this price by maintaining an honest and natural elitism."

Teachers *should* be more objectively competent in their disciplines than the average individual. And one way to determine if this is indeed the

[9] As quoted in his obituary, *The Washington Post,* March 22, 1978.

case is for school systems not to take subjective, second-hand reports, but to measure this competence themselves. Ah, well, you say. Very good and all that. You've stated the need. You've suggested ways to go about it. How about some evidence? Can we really succeed?

Yes, you can, now that the Supreme Court has effectively cleared the way. If you do not want to be charged with malpractice—like educators from Copiague, Long Island to San Francisco to Ft. Lauderdale, Florida in recent years—you had better get busy to establish that you have taken what the law calls "prudent actions" to prevent the exposure of children to incompetent teachers. This does not mean that you can apply testing, in whatever form, to everything a teacher does. Teaching is still an art as well as a science. What we are dealing with here is not passing judgment on the music teacher's taste, but measuring *objectively* whether the business teacher really knows enough shorthand to teach it.

Such skills as are tested must be: 1) those the board is formally committed to having taught; 2) those that are required to be mastered by *all* teachers in a similar state of employment (i.e., grammar for English teachers, equations for algebra teachers), while insuring that; 3) the testing is not used for purposes other than the legal and legitimate ones for which it was intended.

This last point is the pit into which so many schools fell with the National Teacher's Exam before the Supreme Court's decision. The U.S. Fourth Circuit Court of Appeals made this clear in a 1974 ruling (Watson v. County School Board of Nansemond County), in which it said that the test *as used in that instance* was clearly a matter of racial discrimination. Absolute care must be maintained, therefore, not just as a point of ethics, but as a point of law, to ensure that any testing designed to weed out, retrain, or prevent the employment of the incompetent does not become a screen behind which to hide racial prejudice.

Objective testing will benefit everyone, particularly the *minority* teacher who has lived with the suspicion or stigma that he would not have been hired except for his race. Given an adequate teacher testing program, an objective standard can be set that removes this question of privilege and patronage to a large degree.

The majority of Americans do not want their child's teacher chosen on the basis of anything other than superior knowledge and ability to teach. When other factors—race, patronage, whatever—become the factors for decision, a major public relations problem is created and public confidence in the schools, and the teachers, declines—as it should.

For this reason, it is particularly tragic that the National Education Association and its state affiliates, which should be leading the fight to increase teacher competence and accountability, choose so often, as they did in the South Carolina court case, to support privilege in employment based on race.

Leadership for Teacher Protection

Paternalistic as it may sound, superintendents and school boards have an ethical obligation to protect teachers from unfair accusations of incompetence. There are some children who, for reasons no one can divine, cannot or will not learn. Public education likes to compare itself with the professions of law and medicine. But lawyers and doctors seldom go to prison when they lose a client/patient to the undertaker or the state penitentiary. And both can usually find a way to avoid taking a case they believe is beyond help.

No such luck for teachers. Part of the greatness of public education in this nation, its promise and its pain, is that it has to take 'em all, give each child a chance, and a second, and a third.

This is why the public relations impact of failing to weed out or prohibit poor teachers is not just one which has disenchanted parents and pupils. School boards and administrations have paid too little attention to the impact that this neglect has had on the thousands of *good* teachers in American schools, those who do know their subjects and who have had to try to teach children who are constantly exposed to other teachers whose inferiority is patent.

Children bring a very special condition to schools. That condition is ignorance. It is the job of teachers to cure it. Educational managers need a sympathetic understanding of how it feels to be the teacher who is working to "cure" children of this condition, all the while knowing full well that some witch doctor is waiting in the next grade or class to undo all the efforts.

Teacher competence? Absolutely. Because the public, the pupils, and the good teachers have a right to demand it, and the school boards a legal —and moral—obligation to provide it.

Teacher competence is a concept whose time has not just come, it has been long overdue. Increasingly, the American public—and the American educator—has come to recognize that basic skills, survival skills, are not being mastered to the necessary degree by American pupils. The result has been the competence testing movement that has swept the country, establishing specific, objective, legitimate goals for pupils to have reached at various points in their journey through the schools.

It is wryly ironic, therefore, that the teacher competence movement has grown out of the minimum competence tests for children. But more than being ironic, it is just. For before we can fault the one who follows for having missed the path, we must first ensure that the one who leads can find it.[10]

[10] *Phi Delta Kappan,* the magazine of the professional education fraternity of that name, discusses the problem of poor training of administrators in its issues of November 1978 and February 1979. Particular emphasis is placed on the growing refusal of many states to recognize degrees by "universities" such as Nova which award degrees without many of the recognized academic requirements. When teachers see administrators getting pay supplements and promotions based on such degrees, resentment is understandable.

CHAPTER 5

The Language of Education: Problems and Solutions

The chief virtue that language can have is clearness, and nothing detracts from it so much as the use of unfamiliar words
—Hippocrates, 460–370? B.C.

Throughout this book, occasional bursts of sniper fire have been aimed at the hardened positions of language abuse which the educational establishment defends so fondly and at such expense to itself and to the public. In that sense, these comments have a definite relationship to teacher training and performance as a public relations problem.

The lack of literacy—specifically the inability of the employees of public education to put a fact or an idea into simple English, either spoken or written—is not limited to teachers. The problem is just as great the higher one goes in the educational tree.

To one who has labored in the field of public education in varying ways for more than twenty years, it seems obvious where public education first went wrong in its use of language. That, of course, is a risky statement and a popular one—risky to have to defend and popular because the public today is willing to accept uncritically anything critical about public education. And why shouldn't they? Most Americans are products of public education and have, or have had, children in it. In addition, they pay for it, a condition which automatically gives each of them a vested interest in their opinions.

After having watched public education and reported on it as a newspaperman and magazine journalist, having taught it at various levels, and having been an educational bureaucrat as well, my conclusion is that the place public education first went wrong with language is easily located. It can be described thus:

Public education is consistently guilty of violating what nationally syndicated columnist James J. Kilpatrick says is one of the cardinal rules of clear communication. Nothing is gained, Kilpatrick notes, by describing four bananas as "three bananas and one elongated yellow fruit." Four bananas, he contends with a simplicity which would seem to beg the obvious, is not only all right, it is better.

Yet how often has the public been steam-rollered with communications from a public educator which either try to find new names for a simple banana or else invent names for bananas that do not exist? "Career education, movement education, organic curriculum, open education, aural/oral concepts of learning, school leavers" are some of the milder examples, for the list seems endless. But who has ever heard or read a simple sentence definition, in plain English, of any of these terms?

Examples of Kilpatrick's "elongated yellow fruit" syndrome can be found in almost any written or oral communication from the managers of public education. It is very easy to slip into this jingle jangle jargon when everyone about you is speaking and writing it too and to nod sagely as if you understood in the subconscious hope that your fellow educators will extend the same charity to you when they next must face one of your communications. (One cannot help but wonder, however, if "organic curriculum" is related in any way to organic fertilizer. The evidence would seem to indicate that it is).

Kilpatrick's maxims were originally prepared with the idea of improving the writing of journalists, who are not entirely immune from obscurity of the written word. However, they have applicability to anyone who wants or needs to communicate, particularly in writing. A greater need than that of the American educational manager can hardly be found. Writes Kilpatrick:

1. Be clear. This is the first and greatest commandment. In a large sense, nothing else matters. For clarity embraceth all things; the clear thought to begin with; the right words for conveying that thought; the orderly arrangement of words.
2. Love words, and treat them with respect. For words are the edged tools of your trade; you must keep them honed. Do not infer when you mean to imply; do not write fewer than, when you mean less than. Do not use among, when you mean between. Observe that continually and continuously have different meanings. Beware the use of literally, virtually, fulsome, replica, many-faceted, and the lion's share. Learn the rules of that and which. When you fall into the pit of and which, climb out of your swampy sentence and begin anew.
3. As a general proposition, use familiar words. Be precise; but first be understood. Search for the solid nouns that bear the weight of thought.

Use active verbs that hit an object and do not glance off. When you find an especially gaudy word, possessed of a gorgeous rhinestone glitter, lock it firmly away. Such words are costume jewels. They are sham.

4. Edit your copy; then edit it again; then edit it once more. This is the hand-rubbing process. No rough sandpapering can replace it.

5. Strike the redundant word. Emergencies are inherently acute; crises are grave; consideration is serious. Beware the little qualifying words: rather, somewhat, pretty, very. As White says, "these are the leeches that suck the meaning out of language. Pluck them from your copy."

6. Have no fear of repetition. It is better to repeat a word than to send an orphaned antecedent in its place. Do not write horsehide, white pellet, or the old apple when you mean baseball. Members of City Council are not solons; they are members of City Council. If you must write banana four times, then write banana four times; nothing is gained by three bananas and one elongated yellow fruit.

7. If you cannot be obviously profound, try not to be profoundly obvious. Therefore, do not inform your reader that something remains to be seen. The thought will have occurred to him already.

8. Strike for a reasoned perspective. True crises come infrequently; few actions are outrageous; cities and economies are seldom paralyzed for long. A two-alarm fire is not a holocaust. Not much is imperative or urgent; still less is vital. To get at the size of a crowd, divide the cops' estimate by 3.1416.

9. Style depends in part upon the cadence of your prose. Therefore, listen to your copy with a fine-tuned ear. In the prose that truly pleases you will find that every sentence has an unobtrusive rhythm that propels it on its way. With a little re-arranging you can keep the rhythm going. But do not do this always; you may sound like Hiawatha.

10. Beware of long sentences; they spread roots that tend to trip the reader. The period key lies nicely on the bottom row of your machine, down toward the right-hand end. Use it often.[1]

Kilpatrick's little list is not unique, of course. There are many other examples and most of them have one thing in common: they make their point and quit; they make conciseness an art. One of the best, only seventy-one pages long in a volume that measures only five by seven inches, is *The Elements of Style* by William Strunk, Jr. (The Macmillan Company), which has gone through some two dozen printings since its original copyright in 1935. (My copy, incidentally, was rescued from a "media center" supervisor for an urban school system. It was one of the books she was planning to discard as without value because it had not been used in years.)

---

[1] Kilpatrick, with whom the author worked for several years, is not always the black-hearted reactionary that liberals paint him to be. He is essentially a libertarian, although the liberty he proposes for the business-industrial-military complex is frequently greater than that he would provide for you and me. But he is still the best user of vernacular English I know, and would be a model of style for all teachers and educational managers.

Some minor points have changed with usage, and this is recognized in an introduction to Strunk by E. B. White (to whom Kilpatrick refers in his list of rules). Language and its usage are not static. This truth is one of the more feeble rationalizations used by the educator who recognizes his illiteracy and does not want to bother to correct it. But the fact that language does change, is living and vibrant, does not give one license to ignore its basic principles, to mutilate and bastardize it, and to come up with an incomprehensible insult to the human eye and ear out of one's own ignorance.

Understanding Ourselves

It would seem, therefore, that the first problem about education is that things have deteriorated to the point that educators themselves do not know the meaning of the terms they use. For a long time parents and laymen have not understood what educators were saying. Now, the secret is out: educators do not understand what they write and say to each other either. It is not a consoling discovery.

In fact, one suspects a project worthy of at least a master's thesis, if not a dissertation, could be developed by designing a relatively easy formula which states that obscurity in educational verbiage (O) increases in direct ratio and proportion (R/P) to the degree at which the speaker (S) has no knowledge (X) of that of which he speaks or writes (Z).

There is a variation here, too. The worthlessness of a project tends to increase the degree of obscurity in the project's description. Sometimes this obscurity is intentional when a educator realizes that a pet project would be shot down in waves of laughter if he had the gall to describe it in simple English.

But even where something may have gone on that was worth knowing about, it's almost impossible, at times, to tell it, and this is one of the saddest results of the paralysis of the mother tongue that exists in education.

I once had the dubious privilege of working with teachers from two Philadelphia public schools. Here is the way they described their project:

> The students were then provided with the immeasurable opportunity of working with each professional and of acquiring significant information . . . ; hence, each student was the recipient of an imperial (!) experience relevant to classroom study.
>
> The students' immediate response to the program's educational sphere was paralleled only by the exhaustive manifestation of the inward work and worth of every professional, teacher, and parent responsible for the presentation. The expressive cadence of the entire program was strong assurance of dedicated involvement from all sides.

And what was this event? An "imperial" introduction to the Queen Mother? A description of an induction into a secret society? An experience of the Second Coming?

No. The teachers were reporting on a "career day" at a school.[2]

The obsession that most school people have against calling something by its real name is maddening, tragic, and, occasionally, funny. Here is another example:

In the summer of 1973, in Richmond, Virginia the cooperation of a metropolitan bus company was obtained to place advertisements on the interior and exterior of its buses as part of a program to get drop-outs back in school.

Yet without exception, the pupil personnel–psychologist–counselor clan in that school district agreed: the word "drop-out" must not appear on the posters. "Negative," they said. The word was used anyway, on grounds that you could not very well get a man's attention—at least that of most men, anyway—by yelling, "Hey, Jane" at him. Does a drop-out cease knowing that he's a drop-out just because some counselor takes to calling him a "school leaver," a term, it might be added, that can apply equally to the former student who either graduates or dies.

The bus ads brought several hundred drop-outs back. But by the time the counselors and psychologists got around to meeting with them most had already dropped out again.

This leads to the second basic problem: Because it doesn't understand what it's saying to itself, public education has become hopelessly confused as to its role.

Public education can advise, counsel, test, and motivate. Something called a Pupil Personnel Services Team can scrutinize; a media specialist has replaced a librarian; the assistant principal is now a curriculum specialist, something one would think would have been a fair description of a teacher, who is now known frequently as a resource teacher.

I am sad to report that a friend, reshuffled in a reorganization, came rushing up at a party and asked, in all seriousness, if I could tell him what his new job involved. He had memorized the title, you see; he just couldn't figure what all the words meant.

Examples of Language Problems

This redundancy and inexactitude of educational language is encountered everywhere, even on the side of the road. A state institution along U.S. 301 in Virginia advertises itself as the "Barrett Learning School."

---

[2] I will mercifully withhold the names of the teachers. The schools, however, were Philadelphia's Spring Garden Elementary and Samuel Daroff Elementary.

Learning School? Talk about redundancy! When all along what they meant, as the guy at the gas station explained, was "reform school."

Contrast this with a sign which appears in the Ikrsha Reformatory for juvenile delinquents in Moscow. The sign reads: "If it is difficult, we will help. If you don't know how, we will teach you. If you don't want to, we will make you."

Now, no one in his right mind is going to suggest that this motto is an example of public relations for American public schools to follow (although it might not be bad for our so-called Learning Schools), but one thing is certain: the aims, objectives, and goals are clear. The managers in charge of this school apparently know what they are about, be it good or bad, and it would be hard for any patron, parent or child, to say they did not understand what was being provided.

It would be funny if it were not pathetic. But because public education has so confused itself with a self-induced language of lunacy, it no longer knows what it is supposed to do. Like the Victorians who, out of a specious modesty, took to calling table legs "limbs," we succeed simply in making fools of ourselves with the language we create and use.

Is the child hungry? Feed him a "free" lunch, and a "free" breakfast, too, in many school systems. (In one system, for example, a high school student may be deliberately tardy for two hours or more. No matter. He is entitled to his "free" breakfast whenever he chooses to arrive.) But don't call it charity. And for God's sake, don't tell him he should work for his food. It's "free," isn't it?

Is the child unhappy? Adjust him with behavior mod, counseling, reassignment. Fix his teeth, take him on a summer vacation, get him free tickets to the circus. Every public school system of any size has countless people tied up doing all these sorts of things and more.

And, I emphasize, these are not always bad. They are generally good, laudable, commendable, *but they are not the primary business of the public schools.*

Most hospitals have provisions to help keep a child up with his lessons if he must be confined for a long time. Parents like this. Society benefits. It is commendable. But suppose your child had a compound fracture of his left femur and the hospital, instead of setting to work with dispatch to fix the break, first made sure that the child had a teacher to visit him, textbooks to use, an educational television channel to watch? And all the while the leg festered, swelled, and became more difficult to treat.

This is not what the public expects of hospitals, but this is the mess the public schools have got themselves into. *Because they don't know what they are talking about, they have lost all sense of purposeful priority and, thereby, both a sense of direction and much of their public support.* Each agency of society has *priority* responsibilities. That of hospitals is to mend broken bones. That of schools is to teach.

The First Priority

Teach a child to read, write, spell, add, and substract and find his home state on the map. Give him some understanding of his history, culture, and language and that of others. Expose him to the arts and music. Help him see the value of vocations and to practice one. Provide him time to study and to play in sensible physical activity. Do these things with loving discipline, joyful enthusiasm, all built on a foundation of sound knowledge and skill.

This is all the work any school system should want. All the other ministrations to the psyche of the child—be they genuinely required or imagined by some fuzzy-thinking educator seeking an empire to build—are the province of the home, the church, or some other social agency.

Yes, yes: it's much easier to have a system in which Johnny does—or does not do his own "thing" whenever he feels like it. It's much harder to teach Johnny his alphabet and language and how to use it effectively for the rest of his life, partly because of the lack of respect in today's schools for clear language and clear thinking.

But this is why public schools were established. This is what parents expect—rightfully—that the schools be about.

There is all the work the schools can handle right within the definition of a school. The school day is still only six hours long and an eight-year-old head or a ten-year-old or a fourteen-year-old head can still absorb only so much. It's time—past time—that those of us in public education, and those of us outside it too, insisted that the schools do the job for which they were established.

Make no mistake, this basic concern about language in and of the schools is survival itself—for all of us.

KEY CONCERN FOR SCHOOL PR: *If the program you or your staff are developing can't be explained in English, have it done over until it can. If your staff doesn't want to use English because of the way the public might react, junk the program. Anything you're afraid to explain in language the parent and the public can understand has a built-in booby trap and is bound to blow up in your face sooner or later.*

No one likes to be patronized. Yet this is exactly what most of the written communication—and a good bit of the spoken, too—does when aimed at the public by educators. Intelligent and educated parents will resent it, because they recognize that the same message could just as easily have been delivered in English. When it is not, they cannot be blamed for presuming that the educator either thinks the parents are too stupid to understand or is so ignorant he can't even recognize an insult when he originates it.

Less educated parents will feel much the same way. Although they cannot translate the jargon, they can and do wonder why a supposedly well-educated person will not address them in simple language they *can* understand.

The amount that has been written about the discontent of the middle class in paying for what it doesn't like, doesn't want, or can't understand must be measured in the billions of words. Few people in education have bothered to read them, apparently.

The middle class still pays for the school house in this country. How much longer it can—or will—do so is debatable. The middle class is not very enthusiastic about sending its children into classrooms where the culture, values, and language of the majority of students do not reflect middle-class values. And when middle-class parents cannot understand what educators are talking about either, that middle class frequently disappears, taking its children and its money with it.

This problem is a very real one; indeed, an urgent one for most urban school systems and, increasingly, for some suburban ones as well. Language that parents understand is the primary means of transmitting from one generation to another the values of a particular culture. And when any group of parents, and here we're talking about those who pay the bills, feels that the language of the schools is destructive to the cultural values of the middle-class family, something drastic is going to happen.

Signs of Encouragement

There are, however, some encouraging signs which indicate that something is being done about the problem of excess wordage and fulsome phrases coming from educational management. It should be remembered, however, that where the thinking is as muddled as the language, or where nothing of value exists to be described in the first place, then language and expression are not the problem; idiocy is.

A leading rescuer of educational managers who find themselves being choked by their own words is William Zinsser, author of *On Writing Well: An Informal Guide to Writing Nonfiction.* In an article for *The New York Times Magazine*,[3] Zinsser makes a point often overlooked by those seeking to correct language incompetence of managers, teachers, or children. Zinsser writes:

> One advantage that I bring is that I am not a grammarian. In fact, I can't make head or tail of the writing in most grammar books. I suspect I am not

[3] November 12, 1978

alone in this affliction, and if my advice is being sought it is because I am a practitioner, not a pedagogue.

Let caution obtain: this is no reason to suggest that language abuse is *caused* by an understanding of grammar and the possession of a good vocabulary. However, the suspicion here is that Zinsser is correct; the ability to speak and write clearly probably does not stem from the memorization of all the rules of grammar. It does consist of speaking and writing under guidance and review throughout one's life so that bad habits will be caught and killed. In other words, clear writing is not so much something that can be taught by rules; it is something that can be learned by effort, practice, and the use of common sense.

The Connecticut Experience

In an account of having tried to help a group of Connecticut educators out of the swamp of their own language, Zinsser offered this advice:

> Avoid fad words ("potentialize," "prioritize"). I don't want to give a school my input and get its feedback, though I'd be glad to exchange ideas and opinions, or even . . . some complaints.
> Don't use the special vocabulary of education as a crutch. Jargon is seldom necessary. There is almost no technical subject that can't be made accessible to the so-called average man. English is rich in precise words.

As another endeavor, and one that can certainly be commended, Zinsser took some of the ponderous presentations the Connecticut educators had previously sent out over their signatures and asked them to reduce each to English. This is how he described what followed:

> They scribbled on their yellow pads and scratched out what they had scribbled. They knit their brows. Some didn't write anything. Some tore up their paper and crumpled it . . . An awful silence hung over the room . . .

Zinsser might have elaborated upon several points implied in this scene. First, the agony he observed duplicates in many ways the agony that went into creating the original written monstrosity. It is easy to believe that all educational managers create their written and spoken horrors with ease. That is not always true. Many of them have to work at it.

A second point implied by Zinsser's description, and one we can only hope was not lost on his group, is that if they had to struggle so hard to turn their original work into English, imagine how the parents, teachers, and children who had to read it in the first place must have felt.

And finally, one wonders if the silence which fell over the room did not in itself testify to something—that the examples of hideous writing the educators were trying to resuscitate might best have been put quietly and permanently to rest. Both contraception and abortion have their places in controlling the malignancy of language abuse.

A Job for Private Enterprise?

The problems of inexact language have become so striking that they have received the ultimate American accolade. They have attracted private enterprise because a way has been found to make money out of them. Increasing numbers of private firms are offering to teach managers to speak and write clearly, and not just those in public education either. More and more private businesses, distressed that their public, their stockholders, and others cannot understand management's communications, have enrolled key personnel in courses on how to use the mother tongue simply, clearly, and correctly.

Tom Stapleton, owner of Stapleton Communications in Denver, represents one of the firms which specializes in this service. He offers the following example. The original statement read, "The proper functioning of this component is critically dependent upon its maintaining dimensional integrity." What was meant was, "The part won't work if it is bent."[4]

Such communication may not do much harm if it is between one incompetent and another. The danger in public education comes when such communication is visited upon the public that is paying for it. This type of fogginess then becomes a major public relations problem; a visible cancer rather than one that has merely been munching away in hiding.

Sloppy and obscure writing is not always the result of small brains and poor training. It can be an outgrowth of shrewdness and an animal caution of survival. This is particularly true when a subordinate must prepare a paper for his boss, when the subordinate does not know what the boss wants said. (Frequently the boss does not know either.) As a result, the subordinate writes so that anyone's interpretation can be supported. Stapleton makes three points in this area:

* Putting something in writing lends credibility to what they are saying, so people tend to be careful.

* People are afraid to take responsibility, so they try not to pin themselves down in writing.

[4] As reported by Gail Pitts, business writer, in *The Denver Post*, November 5, 1977.

* Some people use verbosity to convey how learned they are, a ploy that seldom succeeds.

All that is necessary to correct this problem, it seems, is to follow a series of rather simple steps:

First, educational managers should back off and perhaps not take either themselves or their communications quite as seriously as they do. A little sense of perspective may help.

Second, they may try what William Zinsser did: taking a close look at some of their communications with an eye to determining how the communications could be made simpler and clearer, or perhaps eliminated entirely.

Third, since communication is something all humans must attempt if they are to survive and prosper in an organized society, language should be given at least as much care, respect, and attention as the golf game, the family car, the mortgage payments or one's lover. A little scrutiny can lead to a more pleasurable and relaxed relationship with all.

For example, look at language as a tool and a friend. It can help you constantly if given respect and care; it can rip you up if neglected and betrayed. It can be an amusing companion. Many educational managers could improve themselves substantially if they just made a list of the terms they ran across, either in their own or others' writing and speeches, and tried to devise a simpler, clearer alternative. A beginning could be made by requiring a substitute for all words educators seem to think can be turned into verbs simply by adding "ize." For example: finalize, maximize, minimize, conceptualize, prioritize, structurize.

Another step would be to substitute in this manner:
Help for "assistance."
New instead of "innovative."
Soon instead of "in the near future."
Now instead of "at this point in time."
Slow learner for "unable to advance at an academic pace in keeping with others in his class."

These are just examples. As James Jackson Kilpatrick says, "Clarity embraceth all things." But redundancy, as in the patronizing and insulting habit of writing "ten (10); twenty (20); thirty (30)," is not clarity. This practice, which has become a favorite of educators, is an outgrowth of a communicative arrogance by which lawyers attempt to be erudite. This is one reason legal language is also under a fully justifiable assault. The school administrator who follows this practice will be making no contribution to clarity, but will manage to convey one of two impressions, either that he presumes the reader is an idiot or that he is belatedly trying to learn numbers at the reader's expense.

There are so many examples of the way errors in language make educational establishments and managers ridiculous in the eyes of the taxpayer that it is pointless to keep repeating them. But at least those in public education can take some consolation that they are not always alone.

At the University of Wisconsin in 1978 a member of the board of regents chastized two students leaders for their written complaint in which she found twenty-eight grammatical and typographical errors, which she circled. A newspaper reporter who reviewed the letter found that the regent had missed six other errors. And at the University of Arizona the same year, the Human Development Preschool announced its "sponcership" of a food program to be provided without "reguard" to race, color, or national origin at "sights" which were listed.

This does not mean, or course, that all college students or all employees of colleges write and talk this way. But the frequency with which these instances crop up in news reports, or in communications with the public makes for a very poor public relations effect. Just as a series of blunders by physicians, if they were made public, would lead to a demand for better medicine and less money-grubbing, the public exposure of educators' inabilities with language may yet benefit public education.

That a more healthy attitude is being taken toward this problem is shown by the National Council of Teachers of English, which each year singles out and widely publicizes a particularly atrocious bit of writing for its annual Doublespeak Award. Like the man whose fly is unzipped or the girl whose slip is hanging out, few people enjoy being laughed at under those circumstances. But it's a quick way to bring corrective action.[5]

[5] There is every reason to commend the National Council of Teachers of English for its work. Its 1976 award, for example, went to the State Department for announcing the appointment of a consumer affairs coordinator to "review existing mechanisms of consumer input, thruput and output" utilizing "linkages via the consumer communication channel." There was no explanation as to why the State Department needed a consumer affairs coordinator in the first place.

It is sad to report, however, that on the same page on which it cited the State Department for its verbosity, the October 1978 issue of the *English Journal* recognized five "promising researchers." A typical title of one such piece of promising research was "Toward a Systematic Description of Some Experiential Aspects of Children's Reading Comprehension."

CHAPTER 6

The Urban School Crisis

> *But, I thank God there are no free schools nor printing, and I hope we shall not have them a hundred years; for learning has brought disobedience and heresy and sects into the world and printing has divulged them . . .*
> —Lord Berkeley Colonial Governor of Virginia, circa 1650

> *What the hell good's school anyway?*
> —Richmond, Virginia high school senior, circa 1976

Lord Berkeley's hopes notwithstanding, the time is overdue to answer the question of the high school senior. Both parents and teachers are beginning to ask the same question, the public relations implications of which are little short of staggering.

To say that the small rural and town school systems of this country have no problems, including those of public relations, is nonsense. Of course they do. But the problems in these areas are apt to be with simple, objective, specific things: Do we put in the water fountain? Shall we add one more teacher? Shall we fire the principal (superintendent, janitor, etc.)?

Each of these issues is serious, of course, for the welfare of children is involved, but each is apt to be resolved with a directness not available to large urban and suburban systems. The solutions reached by the small systems may not be fair, or equitable, or in the best interest of anyone. But anyone who has ever lived, worked, studied, or taught in a small system can say that the public frequently gets its way by taking its relations directly to the educational managers who run things. And so although a senior in Piggot, Arkansas may feel the same way as a senior in Denver or Richmond, it is in the large school systems that the genuine crisis of public support continues to grow.

It is these bigger systems, where the sheer complexity, and needless growth of programs, personnel, policies, and platitudes has left everyone alienated. It's not just the students who are asking "What the hell good's school anyway?"

Those who want to get into intense, and wasteful, philosophical debate over this issue could start with Ivan Illich's primer for a classless state, *Deschooling Society,* and go on from there. The simple facts are that urban areas cannot afford, either in dollars or in lack of productivity, the public schools they now have, and the suburbs in many cases are busy digging themselves into the same pit, from which it is going to be one painful struggle to get out.

Illich, who is more interested in large scale social revolution than simple school reform, makes some valid observations. An elaboration of these is found in an essay, "After Deschooling, What?" which appeared in *Social Policy* for September-October 1971. Therein, Illich states, under the subheading superficial solutions,

> The curriculum is outdated, so we have courses on African culture, on North American imperialism, on Women's Liberation, on food and nutrition. Passive learning is old-fashioned, so we have increased student participation . . . School buildings are ugly, so we have new learning environments. There is concern for the development of human sensitivity, so group therapy methods are imported into the classroom.

So much for philosophy. The concern here is pragmatism, the simple fact that urban schools cannot survive in the wasteful, overblown, and non-productive manner which now marks their existence.

Attendance and Enrollment

To take just one small part of the mosaic: compulsory school attendance laws are engraved in the beliefs of most Americans almost as sharply as is indoor plumbing. But during the 1960s, when compulsory public school attendance laws were abolished in Virginia (to avoid coercive desegregation, admittedly), the percentage of public school dropouts went *down.* Now, compulsory attendance is one of the minor things against which Illich rails, but the Virginia experience has proved him correct. Putting the responsibility for student learning where it belongs, on the pupil and his parents as well as the school, may be a step toward simple sanity in the surgical salvation of urban public schools.

How long can this go on? How much is that besieged middle class of the last chapter going to pay for? Not much, as California's Proposition 13 has shown. And therein may just lie the answer, radical as it seems.

To state the proposition at its simplest, cities that are facing financial crises, or have every reason to expect they will, should get out of the business of public education as quickly and smoothly and to whatever degree they can. Like the British Empire of yesteryear, they should recognize that the jig is up, and begin implementing an orderly retreat from what has become a very costly and non-productive operation before bankruptcy finishes off everything and everyone.

Smokescreen maneuvers to increase or stabilize enrollment, such as establishing magnet schools, implementing new curricula, establishing "community ed," or any of the other vainglorious and fulsome phases and phrases, are not the answer. They have all been tried. None has worked.

The facts are these: in the majority of the older urban communities in North America enrollment in public schools is plummeting and costs are soaring at a far greater rate than can be attributed to inflation. Meanwhile, productivity, the turning out of students able and equipped to pursue either vocation or profession, is declining. Corporate studies, urban studies, even the studies by the professional education organizations and universities themselves all admit it and look for someone else to blame. The statistics are there. They have been quoted enough already. The solution to all this is not going to be found by providing more money for fewer pupils, the ravages of inflation on school budgets notwithstanding. The money sources are vanishing, and reality needs to recognize that fact.

A Future for Urban Education

This does not mean, however, that urban public education—and, increasingly, urban, rural, and small town education as well—be closed down tomorrow and children and staff put out on the pavement forthwith. But it seems particularly necessary that a caliber of courage be found in urban school leadership which will say to its state legislature—education being essentially a state function—that local governments are going to provide only those educational services required by law, not by fiat or mandate. In the interim, localities will work to get the law changed so that they do not have to provide some of the more outrageous and extravagant programs the state frequently can order.

Further, the locality should spend only the money the state and/or federal government provides on an optional basis that is essentially free of long-range commitments from local funds or services and, in addition, will cut out locally originated programs of questionable value.

The short-term results of such a policy may seem at first to be traumatic. Such a policy will mean an end to so-called matching grants. But more and more localities have nothing left with which to match, and it's time they admitted it to themselves and to their public. Most controversial, perhaps, will be the necessary reappraisal of expenditures for stadia and interscholastic athletics. The same amount of money, spread properly, can provide more opportunity for student participation in intramurals and a broadened program of a more realistic approach to football expenditures is taken. That broader-based level of student participation should bring about the public support necessary to offset the cries of the football partisans who are used to spending most of the budget.

But most important, the city councils and school boards of these cities will say freely and candidly to all: If you have school-age children, and do not plan private or parochial education for them, please do not settle in our city. Go to the suburbs where wealth sometimes still runs riot and public education, although somewhat tarnished, is still subject to occasional worship and the possibility of success. Some suburbs, however, are getting uneasy over the prospects of growth, particularly those areas that still have rural and agricultural interests. These interests know that expatriates from the city expect costly services—such as new schools—and do not mind raising real estate taxes on large landowners to pay for them. Meanwhile, as the urban exodus goes on, those who run the cities can set about making sure the streets are safe, business is developed, and housing is improved.

In no sense is this a proposal for the abandonment of the city. Not in the slightest. But with a commitment to a phased withdrawal from the costly, nonproductive burden of urban public education as it is today, the city will be in better shape as a place to work, to live, to grow, to play.

All urban public schools cannot—and should not—be eliminated. But they can be reduced through a phased withdrawal by 75 to 80 percent at a concomitant level of savings. The process of abandonment by natural forces is already underway. Parents who can afford it have voted with their feet and moved out already. The answer, then, is to *quit trying to stop the process and help it along.*

Look at urban schools now: building utilization is frequently 50 percent or less. Yet a school 50 percent full still has to have a principal, and an assistant, and a librarian, and a nurse, and a cafeteria with staff, and a handful of guidance counselors, and a psychologist, ...

Oh, yes, one more thing. If the obstacles to this phased and sensible withdrawal from the lunacy which urban public education has become is attacked by your neighboring suburbs, then city councils have one sure-fire step which can succeed: Give the charter of incorporation as a city back to the state. Go out of business as a city entirely. Let the area that is now the city revert to its original political control, the surrounding counties.

And when the counties realize the burdens of welfare, law enforcement, fire protection, sanitation, etc. they would have to assume if the city surrendered its charter, they will be delighted to help you get out of the public education business—if you just won't give your troubles back to them.

It's worth a try, because the time is ripe, overripe, and the foundation has been laid. A survey released in 1978 by the U.S. Department of Housing and Urban Development stated it clearly.[1] While rural and suburban residents see the city as a viable place of culture, recreation, and service, most also see cities as "wracked by crime . . . centers for racial conflict" and most of all, a tough place to raise children because of poor schools.

Hope in Seattle

And in Seattle, some public officials are beginning to say that the gradual decline and disappearance of the public schools is not really so bad. An iconoclastic study done by the city's Office of Policy Planning gives official credence to the unthinkable—considering that public education, what it should be, rather than what it is, is probably the closest thing to a national belief and religion this country has ever had.

The Seattle study has the advantage of stating things simply: that there is little the city can do to attract more families with children and, *most significantly,* that the city can jolly well get along without them, seeking instead to attract young singles, the childless, and the more mature.

"This policy," the study says, "accepts the loss of the white middle class upper-income families" and says no "special efforts" should be made to attract them as long as the other adults who do find the city attractive reflect the positive values of the middle class.

The Seattle situation is in many ways classic, although its financial position and racial and cultural postures are nowhere near as bad as those of many other cities. Seattle has lost people—from 550,000 to fewer than 500,000 in less than a decade. The number of households keeps rising, however, which seems to indicate more and more single-person residences. During this same period, white population dropped 16 percent, minority population rose 62 percent and the schools, which had 100,000 enrolled in 1962, are now below 60,000 and are projected to go as low as 40,000 or fewer in less than ten years. The revival of Boeing's aircraft business has brought some revitalization to the area—but not to the schools, even though the unemployment rate dropped to 5.5 percent and housing occupancy rose to 98 percent. In this sense, the improved economy

[1] "A Study of 11 Metropolitan Areas," Kathryn P. Nelson, U.S. Department of Housing and Urban Development, May 1978.

of the latter part of the 1970s shows that not even prosperity can rescue urban school districts when the middle class has lost faith in them.[2]

Will Seattle enact a sort of "benign neglect" toward all public education and allow it to seek its own level? At this writing, no one can tell. Those with a personal profit in schools obviously hope not. Others, such as former Mayor Wes Uhlman, apparently remain unconvinced that letting the schools go their own way is wise.

But why not? How, indeed, can a strangled public purse keep propping up schools parents won't support in that most crucial of ways—by sending their children? The answer is simple: it can't.

Such a recommendation as a solution to urban ills, particularly those of the schools is neither radical nor restricted to Seattle. In 1967, a team which included sociologists, psychologists, a professor of education, and one advanced graduate student from the Universities of Richmond, Tennessee, and North Carolina approached a similar problem with regard to Richmond, the capital city of Virginia.[3] The drain of the middle class, particularly whites, was already underway from the quarter million population inside the city limits to the suburbs.

Unless annexation were effective, this report said—and this is increasingly difficult for more and more cities in the nation due to legislatures dominated by coalitions from rural areas and the suburbs—the "city of Richmond (should) give up its charter entirely, creating (thereby) two metropolitan county governments." The recommendation, which has yet to be acted upon, did not beg the obvious: that the problems of the cities would thus automatically become those of the counties.

And in 1978, a group of urban scholars told a Congressional committee that the drastic loss of population which is remaking the face of the American city—and that of its schools—is by no means bad. Typical comments came from David L. Birch of the Massachusetts Institute of Technology and Charles L. Leven of Washington University in St. Louis. Birch, speaking to the House Select Committee on Population, suggested that the American city may be a better place to live and work if its population falls to half what it is today.[4] Leven told the committee that instead of trying to reverse history, cities might simply be helped to "grow old gracefully." Their remarks, while not advocating steps quite so direct as those implied in Seattle, recognize that the cost of stemming the migration from the city is prohibitive.

---

[2] It is a sign of the times, perhaps, that Seattle consistently ranks in the top three choices among surveys to determine the most livable city in America. Further study of the Seattle phenomenon is surely warranted, because a city that can control school costs and still attract new residents is bound to be doing something right.

[3] Conclusions were reported in the so-called "Sartain Report" named for Dr. James Sartain, the University of Richmond sociology professor who headed the study.

[4] Minutes of the House Select Committe on Population, 1978.

A housing expert, Anthony Down, a senior fellow at the Brookings Institution, went so far as to say that "a total city revival aimed at restoring all large cities to their past peak populations is undesirable, as well as impractical."

So far, however, no educational manager of any leading school system in the nation has apparently had the courage to suggest a similar approach as a solution for the schools, and the result is another:

KEY CONCERN FOR SCHOOL PR: *If education managers do not recognize the inevitable, they can't complain when solutions are forced on the schools by other governmental, political, and parental groups.*

The economics of this is not lost on landlords, either, which is one more reason urban public education managers had better get their act together and start providing schools which produce if they want to stay in business. A single family house that houses a batch of children can frequently be refurbished into a charming series of apartments for lease to young singles and young marrieds. The idea that single family housing must become a slum is not true.

Add to this the fact that only four states have laws (which are quite probably unconstitutional) which prohibit landlords from refusing to rent to families with children, and you have further evidence of a trend.

A Limit to Public Support

Urban school managers in urban areas are fond of proclaiming the light at the end of the tunnel, that victory is just one more bond issue, or millage increase, or budget boost away; that if the public will just ante up one more time, victory is assured and the steady loss of population, enrollment, and the middle class will end. If this sounds suspiciously like the kind of talk the national administration was handing out during the worsening years of the Vietnam war, it should: it is compounded from the same kind of self-serving malarkey.

As emotional as the idea is that a benign neglect should be the fate of urban public education—at least until it quits lacerating its own body with fulsome programs of great expense—the facts support the contention that public education in many urban areas is *in extremis.*

John F. Long, chief of the U.S. Census Bureau's population projections branch, conducted a special study of the nation's 153 cities with populations exceeding 100,000. He could not find any trend that indicated movement of population back to the central cities. In addition, his study showed that, generally, the bigger the city the greater its population decline in the period of 1970–75. Of six cities with more than one million population (New York, Chicago, Los Angeles, Philadelphia, Detroit, and Houston) only Houston grew faster than the national rate of 4.8 percent during that five year period, and Houston's growth was traceable to annexation of suburbs.[5]

Of twenty cities between 500,000 and one million in population, only four—Phoenix, Jacksonville, San Antonio, and San Diego—grew faster than the nation as a whole. This does not suggest that any of these cities grew because of an increase in either school-age children or parents of child-bearing age. Since each is a so-called sunbelt city, increases in population undoubtedly reflect an immigration of the elderly and the retired, groups which are not likely to vote support for increasing school budgets no matter how worthy the expenditures may be.

It should also be remembered that the elderly who cannot afford to move to retirement communities are apt to remain in the central cities, partly because if they cannot afford to move out of state, they are reluctant to seek expensive suburban life in the same climate where they have lived all along. In addition, the elderly who might be able to afford a move to the suburbs tend to prefer the convenience of medical care and grocery stores in the urban area, even at the expense of street crime.

Another study which tends to support the declining fate of urban public education was conducted by the Department of Housing and Urban Development (HUD) in 1978. It concentrated on eleven metropolitan areas and found that, as of 1975, the number of people returning to the city was "small in magnitude and did not represent much of a departure from past tendencies toward decentralization."[6]

It is probably not just coincidence, either, that urban areas have felt a particular impact from court-ordered busing, and that the reaction of the white middle class in urban areas outside the south has been precisely that which has taken place in the south—a speedy departure to areas where stability in school assignment and the danger of being innundated in an alien culture are less.

Where some in-migration of young adults who are white and middle class has occurred, the impetus appears to have been in so-called home-steading or in the reclamation of older homes the cost of which has been somewhat less than that of suburban housing. Where this has occurred, however, a study by the National Urban Coalition indicated, the effect has been spotty, sometimes concentrated only in a few blocks. There also are indications that the white middle class which has been participating in this in-migration consists disproprotionally either of childless couples or of

[5] As quoted in the *Washington Post*, September 4, 1978.
[6] "A Study of 11 Metropolitan Areas," *op. cit.*

those who have planned or received guarantees that their children will be educated in non-public schools.

In addition, such urban homesteading has proved attractive to homosexuals who have found urban areas more tolerant of their lifestyles than suburbs. Such a trend was reported by Jon Wright, a San Francisco sales manager for a real estate firm, as being responsible for many of the middle-class migrants who have been returning to the Victorian homes in the blighted and crime-ridden areas of Haight-Ashbury and Hayes Valley.[7]

There are other exceptions to the national pattern of urban decline and always will be, but this does not mean there is an imminent reversal of the trend. The affluent will frequently remain in the cities with the poor long after large segments of the middle class are gone. This is probably because their money provides them the insulation from the negatives they perceive in urban life (crime, public schools) in return for a convenient proximity to their financial and cultural interests.

A Simple Matter of a Loss of Faith

In 1975, Stanley Marcus, chairman of the huge Dallas store, Neiman-Marcus, addressed a group of business executives in Omaha.

> There is a massive loss of faith in the business community by the American people—and perhaps a loss of faith on the part of businessmen as well.
>
> Let's not kid ourselves into believing that the negative attitude . . . is merely part of an 'anti-Establishment' mood throughout the nation. It is a lot more specific then that—and a lot more justified than that."[8]

Marcus, of course, was talking about American business. He could just as easily have been talking about American public education, and American cities.

Americans don't want to lose faith in their schools—urban schools or any other—but a loss of faith has been forced upon them and educational managers are largely to blame. Part of the problem here in the urban area is that public education is no longer the heterogeneous thing it once was.

---

[7] As reported by *The New York Times*, August 6, 1978.

[8] Lay leadership such as that demonstrated by Marcus is absolutely essential if the public schools are going to regain their balance. Too often, leading spokesmen for the business community see the schools as nothing more than a drain on their profits. But waste and corruption are not restricted to the public sector, and the business community must clean its own house, not just point fingers. Marcus's understanding of this does not appear to be shared by the rest of the business world.

Although the middle class is frequently accused of being elitist, seeking only its own kind, history proves this charge false. The middle class has never wanted to abandon public education. Throughout North America, in small town and small city, the doctor's son went to school with the barber's alongside the daughters of the garbage man and the farmer and the real estate agent. That was the glory of American public education. Most children, and their parents, rejoiced at the success of a child whose parents came from lesser backgrounds—just plain poor.

But what does the middle class have now in the urban public schools—being swamped in an alien culture, alien to the nation, alien in goals, achievements and, too often, abilities. It is not the sort of thing many middle-class parents will permit. Equal educational opportunity cannot be achieved solely for the underprivileged. Urban schools which spend millions on special education and nickels on the gifted bring about their own downfall. As Stanley Marcus said, "it's a lot more justified than that."

The peril of what urban public education has become is spreading through to many suburban school systems. It is not here the place or intention to single out the ills of the affluent suburbs—and God knows they have a plenty, including a sort of mindless mirror image that makes them believe every one else is as they are—or should be.

But suburban educational managers who forget, as many of them are doing, that the patience and the pocketbooks of their constituents are not endless may wind up going the same way as the cities—by the time the cities have gone through the process which Seattle predicts and have begun to rescue themselves.

Can this be? Oh, yes. For what Seattle has projected, the diminution, a sort of zero-zero base budgeting, does not mean the end of urban public education or even that it will never grow nor thrive again. Not at all.

For if, by necessity, urban public schools have to go back to the concept of having one reasonably qualified public school teacher per elementary class, teaching a reasonable number of children in the same room each day (a room with four stable walls); all kids in the same desk each day (a desk assigned by the teacher if necessary); learning reading, writing, spelling, and speaking ("yes, ma'm; no, ma'm; please; and thank you") instead of "communication arts" from a team of "resource people," why, what may happen?

Remediation may become a thing of the past. A child may learn the first time around. Then the secret of what can be accomplished with sound, sensible goals and objectives in education may just get out. If that happens, suburban parents, who by now will be undergoing the same malignancy in their schools which brought radical surgery to the cities, these parents will set up such a clamor that either the suburbs will reform, or parents and children will move back to the city and thereby restore it to the rightful place in education it should have now.

Then, of course, given the helpful ministrations of the education professor, the social worker and the absence of a wrathful God, the whole mess
can get started again and urban schools can head right back to the stew in
which they are now simmering.[9]

[9] For a further study of how Seattle residents are reacting to declining enrollments and school closings, see the Ford Fellows in Educational Journalism Report,
"Declining Elementary and Secondary School Enrollments: Problems and Approaches of Selected Cities", by Monte Trammer, pp. 33–37, March 1979. Trammer,
education writer for the *Baltimore Sun,* also discusses the problem as it has been
encountered in a suburb (Arlington, Virginia) and on a statewide basis (Minnesota).

Politics and You (The Ultimate PR)

There once existed a strange little man who ran a school system. He was strange because he insisted that politics was beneath the dignity of a school administrator and that such a dirty world would never be allowed to rub off on his schools. The strangest thing of all was how this little man ever got the job in the first place, with an attitude such as this. And when he lost the job, he was the first to scream "politics" as the cause. He was right.

In the euphoric world where so many educational managers would like to—and try to—live the dirty intrusions of back-scratching, knee-jerking, and boot-licking simply would not be permitted to exist. Schools would run on some unseen flow of financial, political, and parental support like a steady breath of wind; children would gambol in grassy playgrounds and march happily off to class; teachers would all be fully qualified, never demand pay raises, never question an administrator's judgment, and never quit; buildings would be self-maintaining; there would be joy, joy in the wonderful world of learning.

Lots of luck! You'll need it because of this

KEY CONCERN FOR SCHOOL PR: *Everything the schools do or don't do has the potential to become a political issue. Just because something was not an issue this year doesn't mean it won't be one next year, particularly if there's an election. Politicians have long memories concerning your mistakes—if by remembering and recalling them they can get some votes.*

To say that schools can exist separately from the political process is as ridiculous as saying that a citizen who never votes is not affected by government. The difference between the two is that the one who never votes abdicates any right he might have for influencing his own future, while the other, by participating, obtains some positive sway over things.

At the risk of over-simplification, let it be said that public education cannot exist in a vacuum. Furthermore, it never has.

Good Management Equals Good Politics

Still, public education, if it is to do its job of transmitting truth and preparing for the future unknown, cannot be prey to the whim of every peristaltic political trend. Public education must be protected, where possible, from too much violent interruption in the same way that an unborn child is guarded to a degree by the amniotic fluid. Without this precaution, public education in many of its stages will die, and with it will go the key ingredient which makes Western democracy work that 51 percent of the time necessary to keep us out of both the intellectual dark ages and the quagmire of dictatorship.

The irony, and this is one public relations failure of public education and the political process, is that most of the unstable concepts and practices which have come ultimately to damage public education, have not always been forced on the schools. Rather, education managers have found a herd of little demons; clutched them to their breasts with money sought out from legislatures, congress, and city councils; raised, nurtured, and supported them; and now are being eaten alive. We have introduced, too often, the pox into our own houses, and now we cannot understand why we are fatally infected.

On the very day I am writing this, I have been in touch with an old friend high in the management of an urban school system. This system is laying off teachers, closing schools, poor-mouthing with the best, and poorly educating with the rest. The problem is simple. My friend has just been advised that his department has come up with $600,000 which it does not know how to spend before the fiscal year runs out in thirty days.

To his credit, my friend is astute enough to know that failing to spend the money would be politically devastating to the same degree that returning it with candor to the city council would be political suicide.

But how did his system get the money in the first place? Why they lobbied for it, they padded their budget in every way possible, they called in all due bills from board members, PTA officers, members of the city council. It is a sad procedure, but it is the way the game is played, and the primary rule of the game of political education economics is that It Is Better to Have Than to Need, for He Who Hath Can Always Dispose, But He Who Hath Not Cannot Always Get.

In a sense, it was always thus. The history of public education in the United States, from its beginnings in New England, its flourishings in the midwest and far west, to its relatively late arrival in the south, has been adequately told elsewhere.

Good Education Equals Good Business

Public education, despite its early initial obstacles (primarily from the church, which considered this part of its sacred turf, and sometimes still does), was pretty well guaranteed in some form once it became clear that the community with the school house attracted people and people brought business. Americans have always had a grudging respect for literacy (which persists to this day in a few areas), and thus the establishment of the one-room school at the crossroads slowly became a matter of community pride. Not, mind you, that local governing boards were not tight with the dollar right from the first. Impecunious as they were, however, the wrath of local political authorities was never greater than when the school consolidation fever began to spread across the more sparsely populated rural regions, once it became possible because of automobiles and improved roads. Many were the politicians who remembered that the community that lost the railroad was the community that died. Keep the school house!

This attitude, in part, is probably what is behind the reluctance of even the most hard-pressed business community to back off from unnecessary support of today's public schools, as the situation in Seattle demonstrates. Once it can be assured, however, that a limited public school system will not keep young couples, the retired, and the unmarried away from the urban areas and their still powerful, though crippled, marketplaces, the chambers of commerce and similar organizations which dominate most city councils will realize that they can reduce public school support in keeping with enrollment declines, not hurt their own pocketbooks, and actually help the public's. For it is all too obvious that in many urban areas, public education has succeeded only in keeping within the city those with the greatest educational, social, and health needs and the least social, educational, and financial productivity. No one knows this better than the urban businessman.

Supporters of the cyclical theory of history will no doubt draw an immediate comparison between the fights over the closing of one-room schools in rural areas forty and fifty years ago in the name of consolidation, cost effectiveness and better education and the demands being made currently by urban neighborhoods who do not want to lose their schools even though the schools are falling down and less than half full.

Educationally, of course, consolidation of rural schools made sense in many ways. (Unfortunately, consolidation has since been carried to ridiculously nonproductive extremes in some urban areas on the faulty thesis that if a 1,000 pupil school was working well, a 3,000 pupil school should work three times as well. Not so.)

Politically, the consolidation movement, although bitterly resisted, did make a start toward a more equitable distribution of funds. For if a state with one hundred county and city school systems still had a disparity in the distribution of state funds, it was nowhere near the disparity which existed when every crossroads and pig path jealously guarded its own one-room school. (This establishment of reasonable school districts is not as far advanced as some may think. New Jersey, for example, maintains high school districts and elementary districts which frequently have no coincidence with township or other political subdivision boundaries. In some states, junior college and/or community college districts are also imposed and each district has a governing board of some type.)

The Myth of Money Problems

The fund distribution problem, however, is not as crucial today as the proponents of that myth believe. For example, almost all urban school systems get far more money per child enrolled than suburban systems do, but show far less in the way of pupil achievement. The problems of community attitudes, environment, and social deprivation, of course, have an effect, but the yowls of school districts which say they are not getting enough money come frequently from those which are already getting the most. Funding inequity thus emerges, in today's light at least, not so much as a true deprivation, but as a complaint by the schools against not getting all they want.

The fight over funding for schools always has political overtones, or undertones, perhaps, if the fight does not break into the press or otherwise attract much public attention. The problem is that school managers frequently have to develop three political strategies, with three public relations approaches, depending upon whether they are dealing with local, state, or federal authorities in their pursuit of funds.

One survey which shows the pattern revealed that in 1968, 52.7 percent of school revenues in the United States came from local sources, 39.3 percent from the state, and 8 percent from the federal government. By 1978, the federal share had remained essentially static at 8.3 percent, the state share had risen to 44.1 percent, and the local share had fallen to 47.6 percent. Given the magnitude of spending for education in the United States, these changes represent billions of dollars on the local and state levels.[1]

Thus, if the trend outlined in this particular survey holds, local school managers must concentrate their public relations effort either on convincing local politicians to reverse the declining level of their financial support or else work on the state legislatures and state departments of education to make certain their particular localities get a fair hunk of the coin. Given the declining ability of localities to support increased tax levies for public education or anything else, the wise move may be to try to talk hold-the-line politics and public relations before the city council, while pushing hard politically for increased expenditures at the state level.

The politicians, however, can have as much of the blame as anyone else for the confrontations that have recently occurred in the politico-economic rebellions and battles surrounding the schools.

In 1970, I listened with wonder as Senator George S. McGovern, the South Dakota Democrat who would go on to become his party's presidential nominee, talked with a group of educators in New York at a seminar sponsored by the Center for Urban Education.[2] McGovern was speaking the language of the times, and heads were nodding in agreement. Among his proposals: to move social services for the community into the schools; to open gymnasiums, libraries, and classrooms to the public at night; to use college campuses as places to send ghetto children in the summer.

Now, none of these programs was entirely without merit, but nowhere did the Senator indicate who would pay the tab or what would be done if, once the programs got started, a taxpayer rebellion set in. The prevailing feeling seemed to be that there was money a-plenty from someone; that that was the least of the worries. In 1970, that may have been true, because the Senator's speech, and the reception it got, was being duplicated in dozens of similar conferences across the nation. Yet this is the kind of euphoria, a political euphoria, that helped breed the taxpayer revolts not

---

[1] "Survey of School Support," *Education Commission of the States,* Denver, 1978.

[2] The seminar's topic, "How To Restore Parent Confidence in Public Education," was certainly appropriate, which is more than could be said for Senator McGovern's recommended solution.

only in California but in Cleveland and Columbus, Ohio and in so many other cities and communities where citizens have simply said NO to bond issues and other levies.

The wise superintendent, when faced with the type of local taxpayer political rebellion which has emerged, is going to have to find supporters who can convince the mayors and city council members that they are going to have to twist federal and state arms to slow the waste of tax dollars.

If this political tactic sounds like it will merely compound the political and economic chaos the schools are facing on the local level, remember that state and federal spending have contributed more to taxpayer unhappiness than have local or school waste. It's just that the local schools and pols are easier to get at when the public is angry and looking for something to take it out on.

But the big reason local leaders in education and politics should stand together in calling for a reduction in state and federal spending is that this level of spending reduction will give the local taxpayer the most meaningful, long-term relief. That relief, if granted, will make the taxpayer more willing to again support *reasonable* expenditures for local schools and government where he can at least see some effects of his tax money. Further, unless educational managers and local politicians seek a reduction in state and federal spending, even if it means tighter local budgets in the short run, the ultimate result will be to run the risk of greater and greater state and federal control over public education.

Given a local taxpayer rebellion, state and federal agencies, being further removed and less accessible and having greater fiscal resources, will be tempted to toss fiscal life preservers to local schools and governments. In most cases, the localities will be wise to reject them if at all possible.

The hustle and jive with which educational managers have enjoyed juggling politics to shake out the bucks had better end. The bucks are not there to be shaken anymore, at least locally. "We're movers and shakers, shakers and movers," an Oregon superintendent once told me. "That's the way to get the bucks. Just keep things moving, keep'em confused." It may have worked then, in the mid-70s, but I doubt it. It certainly won't work now.

What the critics of the taxpayer revolt against the politicians have overlooked, however, is that taxpayers do not just want to get out of paying taxes; they want to get out of paying for what seems wasteful or outside the province of government as they perceive it.

In the wake of the now legendary Proposition 13 referendum in California in 1978, a poll by the *Los Angeles Times* revealed that those who supported this radical reduction in property taxes and government services had no regrets for their actions.[3] At the same time, however, these same supporters of Proposition 13 made it clear in their poll replies that they wanted no reduction in police or fire services or in *essential* educational services. What the public considers educationally essential—and what the educators have come to think they have to have—are very different, and the political implications of this gap for education are overwhelming.

Living with Politics

Political control over public education in this country is, to a large degree, something the individual education manager has to learn to live with rather than expect to change. Since education in the United States is essentially a state function, in that it is generally mandated by state constitutions and/or ultimately controlled by state law and regulation, the local superintendent of schools is simply out of luck unless his tenure is long enough to allow him to act in concert with other superintendents of similar mind to bring sufficient pressure on the legislature.

What his local school board (or boards, depending upon the state) may think about this is another matter entirely, for local boards are themselves a hodgepodge of altruism, political fiefdoms, and raging disinterest. The latter condition exists most frequently when a local board is *fiscally dependent*, in other words has no fund raising authority of its own and cannot set levies, tax rates, or property assessments, or call millage elections. The fiscally dependent board is thus less likely to be a target of the voter's ire since it has to go hat in hand to the state or local governing body for the bulk of its funds. School board members are not automatically endowed with either brains or common sense, however, in fiscal-political matters or in anything else, and what they say, through either idiocy or intent, can get the educational manager snarled in a public relations fiasco almost faster than the manager could have done so himself.

Selection of Board Members

The three primary means of selecting school board members in this country, although not all states have all three systems, are: (1) direct election by the people of the district; (2) appointment by the government body (county or city council), either at the pleasure of the individual council members or for staggered terms; and (3) appointment by a court or some special body whose sole duty is the selection of the school boards.

[3] *Los Angeles Times*, July 9, 1978.

Dealing with each body requires a special type of public relations, and each has concomitant problems that an educational manager has to understand if he is to succeed in growing old in the job.

Direct election is probably the true democratic way. It certainly keeps the schools in political contact with the community, and enables the community to make its will felt immediately and dramatically, particularly where all board members come up for election at the same time and when the terms are short, less than four years in length.

The disadvantages here stem primarily from the fact that partisan politics can gain a stranglehold on any attempt by the schools to operate with intellectual freedom and professional objectivity. In some districts, the firing of a single teacher, to say nothing of the superintendent, becomes the major issue of a board election while more telling needs are ignored. The pay for school board membership alone is seldom enough to make a decent candidate want the job, although the graft can sometimes be nice.

The other major disadvantage of this type of election, given short terms, is that long-range planning and achievement are impossible. This is not all bad, given the penchant many school managers have for saying they cannot deal with a problem because of a "long-range study" being conducted by their "research" people or "advisory" committee. However, on the other hand, it makes little sense to start on a needed building program in a community, then have the thing jerked to a halt at the end of two years because the entire board is thrown out by angry voters.

Conversely, a special electoral board or a county judge appointing school board members removes the board too far from the reasonable and proper wishes of the public, particularly where the appointing judge is the beneficiary of appointment by a state assembly or governor who can grant long terms on the bench.

Probably the best of the systems, and the one a prospective superintendent would do well to try to find if his state has it, is one in which school board members are appointed by elected local governing bodies. It is necessary, however, for those appointments to be on a staggered term basis (no more than two appointments per year, for example, from among a seven-member school board or one from a three- to five-member board) so that the public will can be heard and heeded, but the partisan politics of the professional council member cannot intrude too far into school matters.

This latter condition is probably almost mandatory for any kind of continuity in local education given the attitude which developed in the mid-1970s and which has shown no sign of abatement. That, of course, is the matter of Proposition 13 and its offspring.

The educational manager needs to understand that, grim as this public relations problem is for the schools, it is not only the schools that maddened voters are after, as the post-election survey of voters showed in

California. It is, however, still true that the fulsome practices of educators have brought much of the public resentment toward government, and the manager who disregards this legitimate concern will be not long at the public trough.

Remember the Chain of Command

The educational manager should also understand clearly the public relations perils of failure to follow an appropriate chain of command in dealing with the political community. The temptation to go outside this chain, led on by the euphoric feeling that "all my friends in the PTA et al. will keep the political hacks off my back," is always strong. This seldom works.

The manager who does not defend the board's right to set *policy* is on shaky ground when he tries to defend his own right to set procedures and establish rules. The superintendent also must make sure that his staff understands this. Neither superintendent nor staff should contact elected governing officials without the knowledge, consent, and probably the active participation of the board.

Most of the public relations and political problems that beset educational managers today have at their root one word: money. This does not mean that the public is pressuring its local politicians to gut the schools' budgets simply because they think the schools' economic waste, if eliminated, will cure all problems. Rather, it is the *accessibility* of local political affairs in general and schools in particular that makes them so vulnerable to citizens outrage over rising taxes and government waste.

The education manager's position requires exceptional balance and political judgment in this public relations area, because although he should be rightly concerned that overt politics be kept out of the classroom, day to day school affairs, and management where possible, he must realize that it is the bureaucratic insularity and aloof "we know what's best for you and your kids" that has contributed significantly to the taxpayer revolt against the schools. Such an attitude and its implications will be discussed further in the next chapter.

The Continuing Growth of Small

What should be obvious to more and more educational managers by now is that political capital and public relations hay can be made by recognizing a trend which many in American government have been slow to pick up on. That is the value which is being assigned to Small. For in just a few years, the space of a single decade of the 70s, waving the flag in support of the United States Biggest, Most Expensive, Longest, Loudest, Most Expansive, has become anethema to the public. Fortunately. For given the historic American obsession with growth as the equivalent of both God and Good, we seemed well on the way to the automatic deification of cancer.

The catalyst of the oil crisis and embargo of the early 70s is frequently cited as the point of origin for reversing the United State's think big mentality and increasing its obsession with Small as Good. Not so. The trend was underway long before the Arab world realized that the American gonad was fueled by oil and squeezing it was the quickest way to get the American attention. Look at the evidence:

The transistor shrank the size of the electronic hardware long before the oil crisis shrank the size of the car. The size of the American woman as a measure of beauty has been declining for years. Models who are on the verge of starvation and whose bust size is measured in millimeters are the vogue, the envy and the objective of men and women alike. Television screens shrink, the paperback book market continues to grow; the long-long-playing stereo record has long since replaced the older, bulky albums.

But perhaps the most significant factor that affects the public and the schools is the miniaturization of the middle-class American family. As this family has declined in size, producing fewer and fewer school age children per unit, the size of the welfare family has not declined accordingly. And since it is the middle-class family that pays the freight for the schools, an increased hardening has taken place in its willingness to pay for what it is using less and less and those who don't pay are using more and more. Yet the vote of the welfare mother counts just as much as that of the department store manager, a point not lost on politicians of the urban area, where there are more of the former than the latter.

This is one more factor in the decline of public school enrollment particularly among upper middle-class families. Let us hold down public school taxes on the one hand, they say, since we are not getting much for our money even when we send our kids to public schools, and spend the cash instead on a private school that reflects our values.

The Issue of Tuition Grants

The national drive for tuition grants as an option to public education is one result of this attitude. Smaller schools *and* smaller bills. That's what the middle class wants. But a superintendent who must deal with a constituency which is of a racial/welfare minority (even though it may be a numerical majority and has yet to elect local government office holders) must be aware that any mention of tuition grants is apt to be seen as elitist.

Among the proponents of the tuition grant, however, is University of Chicago sociologist James Coleman. Coleman, author of a 1966 report that was widely used by the government and others in support of busing for desegregation, believes that a tuition grant program gives black children and other minorities the same options from public education as it does white middle-class children, since private schools can no longer legally discriminate on the basis of race. It is a good authority for a superintendent to be able to cite when dealing with racial/welfare minorities who are becoming politically active.

"Parents and children have a better sense of what's a good school context for them," Coleman is on the record as having told a Black Student-Fund program at Georgetown Day School in Washington, D.C. "I trust the parents and children more than the professional (educators)."[4]

The political implications of the tuition movement are substantial, as are the adversary educational priorities of the various classes, and no education manager can afford to ignore them. This is apt to be particularly traumatic, and politically perilous for the schools, when a system is in racial transition and the power structure is not.

Failing to Look Ahead

Take for example the Arlington County (Virginia) Public Schools. Arlington County is probably the original suburb of Washington, D.C. and during its greatest period of growth (the ten years immediately following World War II) was home to substantial numbers of influential generals, admirals, top level government bureaucrats, and politicians. It was certainly one of the wealthier localities in the nation. It enjoyed strong support for its schools and, indeed, had one of the better public school systems in the nation.

By the mid-1970s however, all this was gone. The county was losing population both in the schools and out. Pockets of poverty (at least by the standards of Washington, D.C.) had appeared. Racial minorities now made up 20 percent of the school population.

Instead of anticipating these events, of adjusting to the positive dictates of Small and profiting by the experience of other localities which had been through them; instead of tightening belts *before* the politicians saw the votes to be gained by tightening them for the schools, Arlington diddled and dwardled, while trying to think up and add more and more programs for fewer and fewer students. Visitors were struck with a sense of *déjà vu,* listening to the Arlington educational community adopt the word games which had long since betrayed other school systems: "alternative" education; "non-directive authority;" "individualized" learning. The county school administration had even taken to calling itself an "urban" school district, and woe be unto the employee who forgot to do so. Instead of

---

[4] As reported by the *Washington Post,* May 1, 1978.

sticking with proven practices in education, Arlington thrashed about looking for a panacea, and the anti-education politicians moved in for the kill.
It was a sad demise for what had been—and could have continued to be—a
great public school system.

These and other economic trends make it certain that the school
manager will have to constantly deal with issues of high public impact:
layoffs of teachers and other staff and the closing of schools and other
buildings. Each is apt to upset the teacher union and the parents, and both
groups are almost certain to excercise whatever clout they have to bring
pressure on the school administration, elected officials, and school boards.

The politics of the successful education manager of the future require,
simply, that she or he have the guts of a burglar, the self-discipline of a
pirate, the nerves of an astronaut, and the sixth sense of a wild animal, for
the public is a treacherous creature. The educational manager must have all
these abilities—and two more: a commitment to preserving the traditional
values of public education, its humanism and its heritage, and the wild
desire of the surgeon to cut out every shred of the unnecessary.

In 1973, the late E. F. Schumacher published a book that drew
immediate widespread support in Europe, and, several years later, attracted much the same kind of reaction in the United States. That book was
Small is Beautiful (Blond & Briggs Ltd., London; Harper & Row, New
York). Although concerned primarily with economics, it pointed out quite
reasonably the necessity for using resources wisely and the fact that economic advancement and decline has an inevitable peristaltic effect on all in
the Western world. Having stated the case for Small as frequently more
functional than automatic Big, and also more humane and less wasteful,
Schumacher went on to point out (p. 91):

> The true problems of living—in politics, economics, education, mar-
> riage, etc.,—are always problems of overcoming or reconciling opposites.
> They are divergent problems and have no solution in the ordinary sense of the
> word. They demand of man not merely the employment of his reasoning
> powers but the commitment of his whole personality. Naturally, spurious
> solutions, by way of a clever formula, are always being put forward; but they
> never work for long, because they invariably neglect one of the two opposites
> and thus lose the very quality of human life. In economics, the solution
> offered may provide for freedom but not for planning, or vice versa. . . . In
> politics, it might provide for leadership without democracy or, again, for
> democracy without leadership.[5]

[5] It should not be surprising that such a book would be written by a native of
a small nation (Great Britain). Western Europeans—like the Japanese and their miniaturization of the electronics and automobile industry—seem to grasp the need for
Small more readily than residents of larger nations who tend to think space and
resources are limitless.

The educational manager must understand that his public relations role with the animal Politic is like that of Sisyphus with his rock: he is condemned to roll it forever and the job is never done. There are those who contend that politics is a body contact sport. No way. Dancing is a body contact sport. Politics is war. It draws blood and breaks bones (to say nothing of careers) and it never ends. The secret educational managers must master is how to engage in it without fatal damage to the public whose support, for their schools and themselves, they must have.

Is this always possible? No, of course not. Some persons who exercise regularly, watch their diets, never drink, never smoke, and breathe only smog-free air (if that can be found) still get cancer of the respiratory tract or premature heart disease, and no one can say precisely why. Therefore, an educational manager who makes all the right moves in his public relations is never guaranteed that things will work out. The best one can hope for is a playing of the odds, knowing when (and how) to cut one's political losses, and resigning oneself to the fact that no one wins it all.

How to Make Bad Worse: A Case Study

A case study in a bungled political relationship can be found in the following set of events which illustrate the inter-relationship of so much in the school public relations picture. These events also show what any poker player knows: everyone gets dealt a bad hand that cannot be won. Only the smart players know how to cut their losses. Those in this contest did not.

The issue became public when an English teacher wrote a long letter to a large daily paper. The teacher contended that she had resigned from one of the city's more infamous schools because of repeated harassment, threats of rape and murder, drug addiction among pupils, and a do-nothing attitude on the part of the authorities.

The editorial page editor sent a copy of the letter, which was specific and detailed, to the superintendent, told him that the paper planned to publish the letter and invited the superintendent to make any response or comment he wished for coincident publication.

This superintendent, attacked by the same type of paranoia which seems endemic in his breed, decided to stonewall it. When the teacher's letter was published, together with an editor's note that the superintendent had received, and refused, an opportunity to comment upon, deny, or explain the charges, political opponents were quick to gather around the wounded body to snatch a bit of flesh. One councilman, in particular, appeared before the school board to demand a response on behalf of the teacher, the public, and anyone else who might be favorably impressed with his action. Naturally, a long and detailed uproar ensued in which much political hay was set by for use at the polls. The schools finally were forced to trot out a watered down disciplinary program which pleased neither the attackers, who thought it not enough, nor the defenders, who thought it capitulation to the attackers.[6]

The loss of public confidence might have been diminished; diminished, mind you, not prevented, not at this stage. (Of course, the whole thing might have been prevented had administrative leadership been alert to the conditions the teacher was to cite and put a stop to them during her tenure. That not having happened, however, the superintendent was faced with what the poker player knows—that when the cards are already dealt you're not just in a win/lose situation, but one in which the loss has already occurred and the issue is simply how to minimize it. It is a situation businesspeople and military officers also understand, but one which seems to slip by superintendents and school board members.)

This case had been lost, of course, and the superintendent should have known it when he first saw an advance copy of the letter. He could have cut those losses, however, by drafting a low-keyed response which might have gone something like this:

> We regret very much that Miss _____ does not feel she had a successful and happy year at _____ school and has found it necessary to resign. I am always disturbed when a teacher leaves with bad feelings because it shows that neither she nor her students probably achieved what they had wished.
>
> Since this is the first notice we have had of Miss _____'s complaint, and since the school in question is now out for the summer, we cannot, of course, take action on history. However, it is better to know of these concerns in this manner than not to know of them at all. You can be sure I will see that the matters mentioned are reviewed with the principal and, if they can still be verified, steps will be taken to make whatever improvement may prove to be necessary.

Had this been done, the platform which the councilman used to attack the schools for stonewalling would have been cut down before he had a chance to climb upon it. Certainly, damage was done by the letter (particularly since many parts of it rang true, as other teachers testified). But a low-keyed, concerned answer would have cut the public relations loss and, because that answer was not delivered in the proper form and at the proper time, a bungling administration found itself forced to take premature actions that angered its few remaining friends and did nothing to assuage its enemies.

This is certainly a point too many school managers will not recognize in their political relations: some politicians historically built a power base upon support for public education, thus turning the Parent-Teacher Asso-

[6] The Richmond (Virginia) Public Schools, 1978.

ciation, teacher groups, and other educators into a vast constituency which helped get them elected.

But the tides have now turned. An equally large constituency can now be built by politicians who recognize the stunning vote total which can be gained from among those many groups and individuals who feel alienated from, and betrayed by, the public schools. No superintendent who wants her or his own career to last very long, or advance very far, can fail to recognize this nor fail to take whatever internal or public actions are necessary to neutralize it.

Crises Management and Survival

In summary, therefore, the political survival of public education in North America is apt to be seriously challenged in the years ahead. Public education will survive, however; we have not yet done so much wrong that the public wants to destroy it entirely. The educational manager who must face these problems while working from a declining base of public support does not need to start new fights (unless, of course, they are ones he is sure can be won and that they will distract from other battles he is sure to lose). The educational manager does need to plant the idea that the waste and incompetence in the public schools does not exist in a vacuum with a recalcitrant public.

No. The huge amount of waste in money, talent, resources, and intelligence of which so many, many school systems and organizations have been guilty grows out of historic American attitudes, a first cousin to the American preoccupation with the idea that Big is good. Waste and incompetence are not indigenous to government in general or public education in particular. It is the American business community that has fostered a lifestyle in which we are not supposed to be too concerned that products do not work. Just throw them away and buy new ones. The American automobile industry is probably the classic example of this type of thinking, and its specious productivity and waste could hardly be duplicated by any government alive.

Further, in any analysis of the use of public funds to prop up the empires of educational bureaucrats the loudest voice often comes from American business, which complains about the waste of the taxpayer dollar for non-productive special interests. Yet these are the same businesses and industries that want tax money to pay for subsidies to tobacco growers while health services are wrestling with waves of tobacco-related disease. These are the same critics whose businesses are subsidized by the tax dollar, either in favorable postal rates, such as newspapers receive; outright grants to the transportation industry; or control of tariffs to protect the free-enterprise United States from the free enterprise of the rest of the world.

Public education managers who understand the political process whereby American business wants to feed at the trough filled by the taxpayer, but does not want government to do anything at all—even something right and necessary, must take care in pointing out this syndrome. What is fair for one should be fair for all, however, and the American educators who receive their salary from tax sources are, themselves, as much taxpayers and voters as any member of the National Association of Manufacturers, the Chamber of Commerce, or the AFL-CIO.

Some means must be found therefore, to put the political problem of economics for the schools into proper perspective. This is why responsible educational managers must clean up their act, and get control of their own operations. They should recognize, for example, this

---

KEY CONCERN FOR SCHOOL PR: *Federal aid of any kind should be accepted only under dire circumstances, as a post-surgery patient would accept morphine. As soon as the condition is under control, the use of the aid (drug) should be stopped. Otherwise, the penalty is addiction and loss of control.*

School managers who have the courage to take such a stand, and make it work, will then be in a better position to gently remind their business critics that the schools are trying to get out of taking irresponsible government handouts at taxpayer expense and wouldn't that be a good thing for business to do as well? In sum, if there is to be a cutback in government expenditure, and the public certainly seems to want it, then let us take the rich off welfare too.

All of these efforts, of course, will require political ability of the highest order. Special interests abound. Educational managers will need a sense of humor when they find themselves (and their budgets) subjected to the political pressure from the right-wing of the American Medical Association, proposing reduced waste of tax dollars at the same time the AMA is fighting valiantly to keep down the number of doctors so that present practitioners may each have a larger share of the public's purse. Politics is not practiced only by those who hold public office and greed is not limited to those who draw their salaries and their operating budgets directly from the tax dollar.

It is a period of stormy political pressures and relationships into which an ethical educational manager must now steer. And there is no sign of calm in sight. It is this type of relationship, in other forms and circumstances, which has concerned Eric Hofer, American's longshoreman-philospher, and toward which he constantly points his literary finger. In *America*, he says:

> Jefferson said that in a totalitarian country the government was afraid of the people while in a free country the people were afraid of the government. Now, what do you have when in the same country, the people are afraid of the government, the government is afraid of the people and the people are afraid of each other? . . . what the hell kind of country do you have then?[7]

What kind of country, indeed. It is a sobering question, which cries for a leadership that can provide a sane and sober answer.

[7] One answer to Hofer's question is the reason the closing chapter of this book is called "The Positive Value of No."

CHAPTER 8

The Public and Its Wishes

Of offering more, than what I can deliver,
I have a bad habit it is true
But I have to offer more than what I can
deliver,
to be able to deliver what I do.
—from *The Dog Soldiers*, by Robert Stone[1]

Whatever skills are required for living successfully with the body politic as described in the preceding chapter are needed just as badly for enjoying successful public relations with the family and the good old, anonymous silent majority; a group no longer either silent or anonymous.

For all their unpredictability, politics and politicians are reliable in one way: go with the winner. Do not rock a winning boat or trip a front-running horse. If you have power (money, clout, a tap on the opposition's phone) then we will find a way to let you help us. Ergo: GET ELECTED.

The non-political public could care less. Politics, insane though it is, at least responds to laws and rules all the players understand (although they will change the rules whenever it's to their advantage to do so). The public is not interested in the rules, does not care if they exist, and is frequently perfectly willing to tear down an entire school system (or superintendent) to get its way in whatever issue has angered it, no matter how trivial or transient that issue may be.

How then can educators have any kind of successful public relations with parents, *et al.*? It's impossible; at least it's impossible all of the time. The best bet is to figure out what is apt to get the educational manager in the worst trouble the fastest with John Q. Public and his relatives and then try to avoid or minimize those things before they get out of hand.

[1] Houghton Mifflin Company, New York, 1973, p. 273.

KEY CONCERN FOR SCHOOL PR: *It's what is—or is not— happening to the kid that makes or breaks relations with mom, dad, and the rest of the family.*

Sound obvious? Well, it should be. Yet why is it that so many school managers seem to disregard this fundamental procedure and then cannot understand why they are in hot water? These things do not occur in isolation. If Johnny's dad expects Johnny to have homework in algebra, and Johnny doesn't, because Johnny's teacher doesn't "believe" in homework, and if Johnny fails the class, or doesn't get the foundation he needs for calculus or trig, then other families probably are experiencing the same thing. That means the educational manager responsible has the makings of a major public relations problem on his hands, one that, treated with enough benign neglect, can quickly grow into a political malignancy.

Let the Public Be Proud

Basically, this is because Americans *want* to be proud of their schools. When they feel the schools' failure is not the fault of the public or the student, they get upset. I don't blame them. It would be one thing if an upset parent charged off to the school, got a positive reception, and had things set straight. Too often, however, the reception is a runaround from the secretary, the guidance counselor, and the vice principal and *then* is when things really start to deteriorate.

The parent complains over the backyard fence, encouraging the nearest neighbor to tell *his* horror story of how he feels the school has let down his kid. And when grandmas and grandads get involved with this problem, watch out. It's one thing for the schools to neglect to teach, discipline, or otherwise attend to somebody's kid; when they do it to someone's *grandchild*, it's bad, bad. Moral: mad as parents can get, grandparents, who have lots more leisure time in which to call the mayor and write letters to the editor, can get even madder.

Bringing Trouble on Yourself

Is the current falling out between public and the schools strictly a product of the present? Is it caused only by poor teaching, violence, busing, social conditions, economics, television, or phases of the moon? Or do its roots go back further than the here and now and the immediate yesterday?

A case can be made once again that educators have brought it all on themselves, though not necessarily as recently as either they or the public imagine. The history of public relations blunders by the schools is not quite as short as we might think. An examination of one such instance can provide some perspective.

Historically, there are four great professions, four learned areas: law, medicine, the church, and the academy. However, the quality of the practitioners in each area has varied widely from generation to generation and sometimes from year to year (scholars of the middle ages, for example, knew far more about astronomy than, by comparison, the physicians of that era or, for the matter, of the eighteenth century, knew of the functions of the human body).

Still, in the formative days of public education in the United States, the lawyer, the physician, the pastor, and the teacher covered most of the market on formal knowledge. What they said pretty much went in American society, and although many in these classes felt the stir of *noblesse oblige,* many others could have cared less what happened to the education of masses of Americans as long as their own families and classes were taken care of.

By the early twentieth century, however, the advantages of an educated citizenry were becoming more and more obvious and more and more necessary. Part of the reason, ironically, was a grudging recognition by national leaders that a literate soldier was a better one than an illiterate; he could understand and carry out orders better—other things being equal—and more readily learn to operate the rudimentary technical devices that began to emerge during the United States' rise to true international prominence with the Spanish-American War of 1898.

The concurrent growth of the business, industrial, and professional classes—helped along admittedly by public education—led more and more Americans to believe that the American dream could become a reality, and that education, public education, made it possible. The sons of immigrants became small businessmen; their children became engineers, accountants, and journalists. A new herd of specialties, each with a debt to education, had joined the four historic professions, and each, in turn, expected to have a say in, and, more important, to be listened to by, government and society.

Education continued along these lines until the impetus of World War II touched off a new wave of concern for more and more education of more and more students. Although the dropping out of the non-college bound students, or those not obviously scheduled for a career in marketing, commerce, or a recognized trade had long been considered not only sensible, but desirable, the emphasis following World War II changed. Keep 'em all in school regardless of ability, interest, effort, or anything else became the cry. And crying the loudest were the school people themselves, motivated partly by the altruism of Education for Everyman and partly by a shrewd recognition for building bigger empires with more students.

Yet here came trouble. For a literate public is less likely to accept without question the actions and decisions of the traditional professionals than an illiterate one. No more did those who were not lawyers, clerics, physicians, or teachers approach the representatives of these classes with hat in hand and shuffling step, begging for an oracular word or grain of wisdom for themselves or their children.

If a little learning is a dangerous thing—and a little learning is usually far better than none—the American public became increasingly convinced that a little education made it an authority on the subject. Part of this stemmed from the mushrooming demand for teachers which required the invention and expansion of the teacher's college, an institution almost as efficient in turning out scholars and teachers as army KP is in turning out chefs (a PR disaster which will be discussed in a later chapter). Parents who had earned a college degree themselves—and many who had not —became aware that they just might know almost as much, just as much, or quite possibly more, about public education as those who were teaching and running it. The lawyer, the physician, even the clergy of the less hysterical faiths, had to obtain at least two *legitimate* academic degrees requiring study and effort to practice. The public school teacher, though degree-holding, was still apt to be a fresh-faced girl with no idea how to speak or read a foreign language (such courses were banned from most teachers colleges except for the few students who planned to teach them), and little knowledge of literature or history, math or science, but lots and lots of "methods" and half-baked educational psychology.

As a result of all this, parents in the post-war era began a slow but steady push for accesss to the evidence (such as books, lesson plans, test scores, IQ results, and subjective evaluations) of specifically what the schools were doing to and for their kids. Part of this momentum came from a growing suspicion that the kids were not being educated to the parents' satisfaction and part from the fact that an increasingly well-educated laity was convinced it now stood on equal footing with that traditionally deified class: the teacher. No longer was the word of the experts alone enough to satisfy.

What happened, of course, was perfectly predictable.

The shamans of the clergy, law, and medicine would have behaved the same way, and still do, when they can get away with it. In the more learned denominations, only the clergyman may handle the communion, administer rites, and pass binding moral judgments, and the faithful are never allowed to forget this. Although a good legal secretary can provide a couple with all the paperwork and advice for an uncontested divorce just see what happens if she or he tries. The thugs of the state bar association will be on her or him quicker than June ticks on a North Carolina hound. As for the physicians? Well, have you ever tried to get a refill on a pre-scription that you have taken for ten years without getting the magic O.K. (and paying the appropriate fee), to cite only one of many examples?

Whose Kids are They?

Sure, educators reacted the same way when parents started asking too many questions; when they wanted to see too many records; when they wanted equal partnership in the education of their children.

You're "unqualified" to interpret the data, some parents were told. This is "professional" information others heard. The lawyers, physicians, and clergy would have been proud. And through it all, not lost on the parents in the slightest, ran the unjustified elitism: *we* know what's best for *your* kid, so you just *go away.*

Today, of course, that's all so much stuff. But it took the Buckley Amendment (1974) which put federal law on the side of the parents to legally guarantee them what common decency and ethics had dictated that they should have had all along: access to the school's records concerning their kids.[2]

Sure the educators wanted to protect what they saw as their turf, their clout, their privilege. But the public wasn't fooled.

The public understood then, as it understands now, this

KEY CONCERN FOR SCHOOL PR: *If you're ashamed to put into English, written or spoken, whatever it is you're doing to a kid—or have done—and to show it freely to a parent, you probably didn't—or don't—have any business doing it in the first place.*

That it took until 1974 to get the Buckley Amendment passed and to guarantee parents' rights is an indictment of public education practitioners from the standpoint of public relations, and more important, from the standpoint of ethics and common decency.

In fact, long before Buckley, courts throughout the land were rolling up an impressive array of decisions to the effect that parents did indeed have a right to access to the records showing what the schools had done and were doing to their kids.

In 1961, for example, a parent in Nassau County, New York sought to inspect school records concerning his son. His request was denied at the local level, so he appealed to the New York Commissioner of Education, whose decisions, as do those of so many administrators in government today, have the force and effect of law.

Once again, the parent was denied. In an historic proceeding before the Superior Court of Nassau County (*Van Allen v. McCleary*, 211 N.Y.S. (2d) 501 (1961)), the parent won the right to access to school records concerning his son. This was achieved despite *amicus curiae* briefs filed in defense of school secrecy by two organizations one would have hoped

---

[2] Named for the then-Senator James Buckley of New York.

would have been on the side of the kids: the New York State Psychological Association Inc. and the New York Teachers Association.

The court, in its ruling, quoted at some length from the essay "On Liberty" by the English philosopher, John Stuart Mill, and concluded with a ringing indictment of the arrogance of educators. The parent's rights, the court wrote, "stem not from his status as a taxpayer seeking to review the records of a public corporation, but from his relationship with the school authorities as a parent who, under compulsory education, has delegated to them educational authority over his child."[3]

There were other legal precedents which would have made the Buckley Amendment unnecessary had the schools taken it upon themselves to simply do what was right. In *Harfst v. Hoegen* (163 S.W. (2d) 609, 349 Mo. 808, 141 ALR 1136 (1942)), a case decided almost twenty years before the New York case, a Missouri court ruled that where the will of the school board and the will of the parent conflict, the school board must find statutory authority for its exercise of power. Few, if any, school boards adopted rules prohibiting parents' access to their children's records. Then, almost without exception, prohibiting access was an arbitrary action of educational managers.

The amazing thing, at least in the appraisal of the issue I have undertaken, is that Buckley was so long in coming, given the obstinacy of school systems where parent rights and pupil records were concerned. The point here, as any student of law knows, is that the rulings of courts form a body of "case law" which, in similar cases, has an applicability across state lines and which can be just as binding as statutory law, or law enacted by legislative bodies.

Two other cases establish the precedent that the child is not a creature of the state and that reasonable access cannot be denied. Neither case involved the public schools, but, under the principles of case law, both bore upon it in matters of parent access to pupil records. The first, a landmark case, *Pierce v. Society of Sisters* (268 U.S. 510, 45 SCt 571, 69 L.Ed 1070 (1925)), established the freedom of parochial schools to operate in the nation. In so doing, however, the Supreme Court made a simple statement of graphic importance to all: "The child is not the mere creature of the state." One can only wonder what the implications for parental access to the school and its records—and concomitant support for public education— might have been had this simple sentence become more widely accepted by the public schools.

The second non-public school case which could have had positive affect for parents was, strangely enough, *Eagan v. Board of Water Supply* (205 N.Y. 147, 98 NE 467 (1912)), a case decided seventy years ago. In that case, a contractor who did not receive a contract won the right to inspect

[3] *Van Allen v. McCleary supra.*

the board's records to determine who had received the contract and under what specifications.

This decision established what might be called the interested party doctrine under which the nature of circumstances surrounding a request to review records should be considered. Are parents an "interested party" in a child's education? Obviously. Therefore, they are legally entitled to inspect their children's records.

There is a certain irony in the continual grumbling which comes from school officials even in the wake of Buckley. This grumbling comes because, yes, it is some trouble to have to haul out student records and explain them to parents and, worse, it is embarrassing at times to have to explain what's in the records. That it can be more than just an embarrassment has been established, in part, by cases in which parents have sued, successfully, on the grounds that information contained in school records was libelous.

This is indeed another

KEY CONCERN FOR SCHOOL PR: *Every pupil record should be made so that the person making it could defend its accuracy or its professionalism in a court of law.*

This does not mean—and need not be interpreted except by the careless or the cowardly—that derogatory information cannot be contained in a child's record. It *does* mean that that information must be accurate, pertinent, and professional. In *Iverson v. Frandsen* (327 F (2d) 898 (1956)), for example, parents sought unsuccessfully to challenge an opinion about their child entered in a school record by a psychologist. But, the court ruled, the opinion was *within the range of the psychologist's professional competence and thus was not libelous.*

Liability and Character Assassination

It is not, therefore, just what is said in a school record, but who says it.

There is still room to shudder, however, over the possible effects of a young music teacher's tossing into the cumulative records subjective, pseudo-psychological analyses of his students.

That this sort of thing happened, and may still, should not be seriously questioned. That it stemmed from the ignorance or stupidity of teachers alone is not always the question. In a graduate class I was visiting at Virginia Commonwealth University fewer than ten years ago, a professor recommended—and distributed—a checklist which he said should be compiled on all pupils. The checklist, in part, suggested the compilation of information on pupils with regard to family status, such as drinking habits, the status of the marriage, the presence of live-in adults in the home who were not members of the family, and the family's economic condition.

Now, it is conceivable that some of this information might have to be compiled by a peripheral arm of the schools in cases of documented child abuse or other such serious condition. But to suggest that it be compiled on all children—as was the case here—represents a flagrantly unethical violation of the rights of personal and family privacy and makes those parents who find out about it wonder, quite logically, if the schools and those who run them have taken complete leave of their senses.

Even more serious, at least from the schools' standpoint, is that the manner in which it is suggested that this information be compiled leaves open the probability that most, if not all, of the data recorded will be hearsay. That, of course, is not admissible in a court of law to prove defense. It can very well be admitted, particularly when written into a record, as evidence of libel and slander. The question then becomes not just one of unethical conduct on the part of the schools, but one which opens them, individually and perhaps collectively, to suit with a strong likelihood that they will lose. Of course, such a suit, if well-publicized, would do far reaching public relations damage not only to the schools and individuals involved but to schools and educators wherever they might be.

This, then, is a brief historical look at how the obstructionism of the educator class not only denied parents what they were legally and ethically entitled to, but contributed directly to a suspicion by the parents that the schools had something to hide. A legitimate partnership which could have been a source for substantial and continuing public relations support for the schools was not just neutralized, it was turned into a nest of disenchantment with the schools.

There simply is no legitimate reason, and can never be, for concealing from parents, or from failing to explain in clear, concise language (if the educator is capable of it) what a child's record says. How can educators possibly blame parents for being furious when parents with two and three college degrees are told by implication or direction that they are not intelligent enough to understand what the school has to say about their child?

It is only fair to note, however, that the loss of confidence in the schools by parents who had been denied access had a substantial ripple effect, spreading to others who might not have had the same experience directly. The fuss over school records was primarily a middle-class phenomenon in that it was the rising middle class that first developed the confidence to challenge the educational establishment directly.

Increasingly, however, the poverty classes have come to understand that all those little numbers and scribbles educators make about their children and carefully file away can have a direct bearing on their children's future and these parents, too, want to see what's going on.

Explanations of the results of a test—means, averages, stanines, and percentiles—can indeed be over the head of many parents. This does not mean that they are not entitled to the information on their children *and entitled to it in language they can understand.* There are very few things in professional languages, and education's is no exception, that cannot be reduced to simple English (see Chapter 5). A school official who takes the trouble to make these explanations to poverty-level parents, or those of inferior education, and who does so without being condescending, may be building a considerable reservoir of public relations goodwill.

It should be noted, however, that despite parents' legal and ethical right to school records concerning their children, they have no right whatsoever to a fishing expedition involving the children of others. Nor is the school under any obligation to hand out without explanation the contents of a child's file to the parent. There is room—and reason—for interpretation. Matters often do need to be explained. How this is done frequently determines whether a positive or negative public relations impact will result.

How to Guarantee a Reaction

Enough though about student records as a public relations problem. Do parents really want to know everything that's going on in the schools, every day and in every way? Do they really want to be involved in all this decision making? Is participatory democracy in education what parents are waiting for with glazed eyes and sweating palms?

Not really. The parental posture over student records was more a reaction than an action. *This is almost always the case in the school's relations with its publics.* School in our society is a continuing thing; it is not new. Therefore, the public's postures are almost always reactive ones to stands, postures, or perceived failures of the schools themselves.

Part of this, of course, comes from the history of arbitrary authoritarianism employed by many schools in their relations with the public (as the instance of student records shows very clearly). For if there has ever been a fiefdom, a duchy, a baron of the manor in American government, it has been the principal and the school. Today, principals seem to last no longer in their jobs than superintendents do. Many are ambitious; many are removed. But there are still a few around, in rural areas and large cities, whose sole vocational objective was a principalship and, once achieved, they held on to it. (Amazingly, there was once a gentleman in Richmond,

Virginia who was principal of the same school for 67 *years.* He began at age eighteen and died in office at eighty-five.)

Whenever a lasting tenure was established, many principals began to think of the school as "my" school in the same way that an English baron spoke of "his" lands and "his" peasants. You cannot blame the principal. The faces changed, but he stayed on. And when a parent came in to register some mild concern, question, or complaint, it gave the principal an omnipotent and omniscient feeling to be able to remind the visitor that in some cases he had disciplined not only him but his father before him and his grandfather before that.

These principals, in particular, have been the ones who have had to bear the heaviest crosses, not only in letting parents see records, but in extending due process in disciplinary matters to pupils who formerly would have been suspended or expelled by a wave of the hand or the principal's royal edict. In this sense, principals and police have begun to sound almost alike: the cops' bleatings over the protections extended to suspects by the *Miranda* and *Escobedo* decisions could just as easily have come from the school house as the precinct house.

As a result of the judicial or legislative changes which extended individual rights into the schools, some educational managers (though admittedly, few principals) panicked and made their next public relations mistake: they gave up too much.

But Parents Don't Want to Run the Schools

It is the contention here that parents don't want to run the schools. They want reasonable access, answers to questions, protection for their children, cautious expenditures, and, where possible, winning athletic teams.

They do not want to assume the school's role for curricular decisions, for the teaching of algebra, the selection of textbooks, the running of the cafeteria, or the like. Yet the number of school managers who *think* that parents are sitting around all day with nothing better to do than jump to perform all these duties is legion.

Parents don't want these jobs. The fact that they *do* expect the school to be doing them is something else entirely. Most parents feel that in providing the kids, the cannon fodder on which the educational process works, and in paying the freight, they've discharged their responsibility. Now, they want the schools to discharge theirs.

Put it this way: most parents don't know how to take out an appendix. They'll be the first to admit it. Yet if a member of their family comes down with a localizing pain in the right lower quadrant, rebound tenderness, nausea, lack of bowel sounds, constipation, and the like, it doesn't take a genius to figure out that the individual needs to see a doctor fairly soon, and probably go into the hospital as well.

But once the patient is in the physician's hands, few parents want to be called into a meeting where everyone sits down in a circle and with equal votes decides what should be done—one vote for the physician, one for the nurse, one for the janitor passing by, one for mom, one for dad, one for the uncomfortable patient. Hell, no. What the parents have a right to expect is that the physician and/or surgeon will advise them of the diagnosis, tell them what is going to be done, get their permission, and get on with it. The parents are paying for a certain expertise. They want to see it exercised. They have a right to demand it. They have neither the time, desire, nor inclination to sit in on surgery, offering advice, and taking votes on which way the scalpel should be held or what kind of stitch should be used.

Yet this is just the kind of parental public relations mess that many educational managers have managed to create. And they can't seem to understand why the public is outraged. For years, educators have been talking about how they were "professional." The public bought this. Now, the public wants them to act the part.

Providing a reasonable accounting of what has been done (an appendix in a bottle and a child returning to health would be a satisfactory result, to use the medical analogy again) will satisfy the parent. Thus, this

---

KEY CONCERN FOR SCHOOL PR: *It is not comforting to the public when it becomes obvious that the schools do not know which way to go or why and must ask parents to help make* routine *decisions.*

It's simple: parents are not authorities in teaching academic subjects. But they have the right to expect that the schools will be. And this leads to the next pothole of public relations into which today's school manages to step: how do we tell mom and dad how Junior is doing in his "learning experience?"

Report Cards Can Make Trouble—For You

There once was a time—and fortunately, it seems to be returning—when the school used a report card parents could understand. I doubt seriously that there is a public school student or adult who does not understand what the A–F grading system means. Of course this system was not perfect. It is not perfect today. It never will be perfect. But in too many school systems, educators, under the guise of refining the system, developed report cards that managed to say even less than A–F and in far, far more words. Like a fussbudget who does not want a lukewarm cup of tea, they have boiled and boiled and boiled the water of its making in order to get it just so until at last there isn't even any steam left and the pot that the water came in is scorched and ruined too.

One such modernized report card, for use with grades kindergarten through five consists of about 120 simple sentences grouped by academic or study areas. Each sentence is reasonably clear as far as it goes (although the report card contains six errors in spelling and grammar, but that's another PR problem). All the sentences, however, are in positive language and the teacher is expected to simply circle the numbers by the sentences in the category he or she desires. For example, in grade two, a teacher could check a perfectly simple sentence saying, "Understands what s/he reads."

Very well. Very good in fact. But what is the child reading? Is he reading on grade level? And is his understanding the understanding of the average student, the above average student, or the superior student? (Read C, B, or A.)

Or, for grade five, a teacher may check a sentence saying, "Uses spelling skills in writing." By grade five, most parents should hope as much. But how well is the child using them? As well as he should be?

The alternative to all this inexactitude is two-fold. Both folds have public relations implications. On the one hand, the parent should come to school regularly to discuss with his child's teacher face-to-face how well the child is doing. Ideal as that may be, however, it just is not practical for many parents, particularly when the child goes into secondary school and has half a dozen teachers. The other alternative, which has been tried and found wanting (primarily because it unreasonably taxes the teacher) is for each teacher to send home each six weeks a personal narrative for the parent in which he or she describes in detail how well the child is doing in his various areas of academic endeavor. This would be a reasonable substitute for the A–F grading system if, of course, the teacher knew what to say and how to say it. But it is unfair to expect a teacher to do this in the detail which would be required—at least most teachers seem to think so—and this method of parental reporting seems to be largely in decline.

As an alternative to a lengthy narrative report, however, many school systems, particularly in the elementary grades, have tried to compromise and have created a mutant.

The mutant frequently uses the worst examples of obscure pedagogical language ("expresses felt needs;" "utilizes the aural-oral concepts of learning") and manages thereby to patronize parents. The tendency to use this language seems, in my experience, to be particularly prevalent where the poor and the black are involved. Most poverty-level parents have very limited reading skills. Whereas the A–F grading system means something to them, this business of "aural-oral concepts" does not mean a thing and they know it. And when they find out that all the teacher meant was that their kid had learned to listen and to talk, they do not forget that they have been patronized, and who it was who did it.

One other aspect of the report card business has helped cause a public relations problem for the school. Some schools, for reasons no one seems yet to be able to explain (that they are ashamed of the whole thing might be the reason), are using letter grades to report pupil progress, but, as in the instance before me, restricting them to two letters: S (for satisfactory) and N (for needs to improve).

Granted, these letters do tell the parent something, but they do not go far enough. What's the matter with the rest of the alphabet? All this S–N business does is desolate the student who is trying to do better than average, "S," or C-grade, knowing that his report card will never show it. The kid who makes 100 on a test after hours of study and struggle, who turns in a paper carefully researched, which has taught him something through his own labors, winds up rewarded with the same neutered "S" as his fellow student who loafed through, doing only what was barely necessary to get a respectable grade.

Conversely, the child who gets the ubiquitous "N" has not been told all that much either. Since there is no provision for a "U" (for unsatisfactory), a letter that once was adequately expressed by "F," the child and the parent have no way of knowing whether the N stands for one point below passing (whatever that might be; there's no way of telling), or whether it means the kid got a dead flat zero and is all the way down to the bottom of the academic pile.

In sum, the matter of pupil reporting is pretty much a public relations shambles in many school districts. There seems to be no provision in the "innovative" reporting systems for regularly and consistently recognizing excellence or above average performance, nor is there any way to report specifically and directly that a child has failed; yes, failed—I know the word isn't supposed to be used in schools any more—to make the required progress.

This continuing breakdown in reporting to the home comes at a time when school officials keep talking about the very types of communication that they have either destroyed or have not really had. The "newspeak" language of educators in this regard is designed, so many say, to build bridges. The language bridges that they build, however, may simply speed their own collapse, as the report card issue has shown.[4]

In due time, of course, another fashion in communication concepts will appear. (The use of "linkages" as the word of educational fashion is enjoying a surge in popularity just now. The new superintendent employed

---

[4] An analysis of report cards to see if they are understood and accepted by parents is one of the first steps a new educational manager should take. Silence does not mean acquiescence; it may be all the warning you get.

by the Boston School Committee in 1978 used it repeatedly in his first press interview in which he talked of his priorities. It sounded rather like he was going to make sausages.)

The schools' apparent failure in the matter of pupil reporting should not be taken as a call for abandonment of efforts in this area. Parental communication is critical to the public relations success of the school. In that sense, if the in-term "linkages" implies proper communication and support for public education, it's probably justified. Obviously, there are plenty of other ways in which the schools can and should be communicating with parents.

The PTA: Strength and Weakness

The most obvious is the Parent-Teacher Association. And if the schools have been torn by confusion about their roles and responsibilities, PTA has suffered just as much. As originally established in 1897, the National Congress of Parents and Teachers was known as the National Congress of Mothers, but later amended its membership rules as well as changing its name. Its membership grew slowly during the first three decades of the century, reaching 1,500,000 by 1930. It then increased with considerable rapidity until its membership had reached approximately 10 million in 41,000 local branches by 1970.

PTA's goals, of course, included most everything that could be considered to affect a child's welfare and did not restrict itself simply to in-school education. During most of its career, PTA has been an essentially low-profile group and has received much criticism for being simply a cowed rubber-stamp organization for the principal's whims and wishes.

Although this accusation has certainly been true in many areas, in others PTA has been a vibrant force of parents which has sought to lobby for collective school improvements and to benefit individual schools. The question how far to involve itself in school issues of controversy has been something of a setback to PTA in recent years.[5] During the early 1970s, many PTAs broke away from the parent organization, because of controversies over the busing of pupils for racial purposes, and set up autonomous local units which kept all dues and funds raised for strictly local purposes. So divisive did the issue of busing become to PTA that major lobbying attempts were successfully made at national conventions to defeat candidates who were thought to be pro-busing, or whose records had shown them to support it in their local school districts.

---

[5] As a PTA president, I once had to remove a tape recorder stuck under a guest speaker's nose by an anti-sex education trespasser, and throw it out the door (the recorder, not the trespasser) in order that the meeting might continue.

By the mid-1970s, the national PTA had suffered such fund losses that it had had to curtail some of its major publications. Its membership had dropped by more than a million, although this was certainly influenced by the decline in school enrollment and the direct involvement of fewer parents in the educational process. At the same time, however, the national PTA began a substantial attack on television shows it considered deleterious to youth because of so-called violence or explicit sex. This, in turn, brought the national organization under attack from groups who perceived PTA's stand to be little less than censorship which would deprive adults and older youth of the television shows to which they did not object.

Despite these controversies and obvious setbacks, PTA, or any similar organization, still represents a potentially viable outlet for public relations involving the schools. An educational manager who handles the development and cultivation of such an organization with both candor and professionalism can improve substantially his future prospects of success and establish a foundation that may help him over the problems even the best of managers is sure to encounter.

One of the unwritten practices of many principals, however, has been not to encourage any such parent organization unless he was sure it could be controlled. Such organizations do at times get out of hand. "Booster" clubs which raise money for athletics and bands can become so possessive through their efforts that they feel they and they alone should determine schedules and performances. In addition, few things are worse than establishing a parents' or citizens' group to provide "input" or to serve as an advisory committee and then ignoring its recommendations or trying to deliberately kill it with senseless meetings and endless paperwork.

These instances, however, are exceptions. Most parents and citizens, even those who wish to be active in such organizations as PTA and "booster" clubs expect school managers and teachers to do what they were hired to do: to manage and to teach. If parents had felt they had the time and the competence to do these things themselves, they would not have authorized the hiring of the managers and the teachers in the first place. School employees should not forget that simple lesson.

The Aims of Education: Sex or Not?

Understanding the public relations dilemma that has beset school management in its workings with parents also involves goals and objectives of the curriculum. School managers should be very cautious in introducing subjects that are difficult to justify when public support for public schools is as questionable as it is today. This is no time for confrontation politics with the people who pay the bills. It's hard to think of anything the schools do which cannot become a public relations issue, but let's just choose two: sex and morals (we'll leave race until the next chapter).

Many critics of so-called "sex education" programs in the schools seem to feel that this is some type of communist plot devised by those who want to undermine and destroy American morality, government, and the balance of trade. It seldom does any good to point out that calls for sex education in the schools go back well into the early part of the twentieth century and that these calls have come most frequently from groups of impeccable middle-class credentials such as the PTA (which first called for sex education in 1898).

The superintendent or school board which is being masochistic, however, and feels that a sex education program is necessary had best watch its step and measure what might be gained against what might be lost. I know. It was once my duty to defend a sex education program (a good one, I might add). It soon became an eighteen-hour-a-day job with one or more speeches every night. You learn to quote the Bible effectively, since this is one of the favorite tools of the attackers. You learn to keep, or develop, a sense of humor, since your attackers are always singularly without one.

There is, of course, a serious need for sex education among American youth (and their parents, too, if the ones I encountered were any example). But the proper question is not whether sex education is needed, the question is whether it belongs as a prominent, separate part of the public school curriculum. If an educational manager concludes that it does so belong, then he has a serious problem of implementation ahead. In my judgment, and in my experience, a separate program has little value that will outweigh the time it takes from other things, and the disasters that hang from it like leeches.

Parents in our society do not mind their kids knowing more algebra than mom and dad; they do mind them knowing more about sex. A parent who can take one look at an algebraic equation and blithely tell junior to take its solution up with a teacher is not likely to respond the same way if junior asks whether erotic dreams are normal. (Sometimes I think we were better off when, in a simpler world, the Baltimore catechism of the Roman Catholic Church could teach, as it did near the turn of the century: "Q. What does the Christian young man do when he has an erotic dream? A. Say two Hail Marys and change position.")

School managers are thus ill-advised, in my experience and judgment, to start off on a new sex education program, not because the instruction is not badly needed in our sexually ignorant and neurotic society, but because the fuss is not worth the frequently limited achievement.

Second, sex education (more properly—and safely—called "human growth and development" from a PR standpoint) should not be a separate course; there is not even enough room in the curriculum or the day now for those courses the public is convinced we should be teaching.

Conversely, however, there is no way to teach high school biology without teaching human reproduction, and no school should apologize for doing just that, as long as it does not spend a month on that aspect of biology alone.

Neither should a health class teacher be afraid to mention rudiments of hygiene which are sex-connected, although this was far safer in the days when classes segregated by sex were more possible.

The critical need for sex education, however, is at the upper elementary level. Any elementary school principal can tell horror stories of having to calm a terrorized little girl who has begun to menstruate before anyone had ever warned her about it. *Compulsory* sex education, particularly at this level, is an almost certain public relations disaster, as school system after school system keeps finding out, as if it were rediscovering the wheel.

Where sexual instruction would occur *normally* in the curriculum, a well-run school can go ahead with it, and, if handled correctly, encounter no serious problem. A parent who objects can—and should—be told that he can sign a written exemption for his child and that that child will be excused from class and not penalized for the one or two days during which sexual matters might be referred to. However, it is *equally important* when dealing with such parents that they understand that they do not have the right to deny other children the same instruction, any more than they could if the sex education program was being held separately after school and taught by physicians and clergy.

Of course, the confidential relationship between counselors, teachers, nurses, and children provides a means for transmitting appropriate information in response to appropriate questions.

The big public relations danger of a formal sex education program is not so much that teachers today will turn out to be perverts or will transmit inappropriate information (though, God knows, they should be chosen with exceptional care). The problem is that such a program, started as a separate school-wide or system-wide course, may bring the kooks slobbering out of the trees and touch off a witch hunt that cannot be stopped, and which will include textbooks, library books, and the personal lives of the faculty.

If you do have a program, however, there should be no hesitancy whatsoever in making materials and lesson plans available for public inspection. In fact, this applies to any curriculm, not just a controversial one. In defending such a program, on one occasion, I would show any and all films that we used to any group who requested it. Most got bored and walked out before it was over. I would normally introduce one film (about eggs and fertilization) by warning that the producer was so infamous that his films were banned in many foreign countries. I did not mention until later that those countries were in the communist block. The film was produced by Walt Disney.[6]

---

[6] "The Story of Menstruation."

Book Burners, the Clergy, and the Radical Right

The danger of sex education, or other highly controversial curriculum, to existing school programs is, of course, the matter of censorship. Right wing groups, for some reason, continue to believe that the
Bible has been banned from the public schools and, while they themselves
are among the most dangerous book burners and banners, the fact that the
Bible has not been banned (and never should be) never seems to register
on them.[7]

(Before another anti-sex education group in a school library one night,
I was faced with the Bible-ban accusation. Having heard it before, I was
able to turn to the shelf (which I had previously checked) and ask my
interrogator whether he preferred the Revised Standard, King James,
Douay, or some other version.)

The use of clergymen in schools is dangerous for much the same
reason—competition among them for the captive audience and a "divine
right" concept of their own personal idea about morals and truth.

The hearts of the book burners are not always allied with the
right wing. A shameful number of schools in this nation have removed
Little Black Sambo from their optional reading shelves because of the
arrogance of black pressure. Even worse, Mark Twain's classics, *Tom
Sawyer* and *Huckleberry Finn,* have so often been bowdlerized because
of the term "nigger" that their consistent theme of human rights is
obviated.

Thus it is by no means just sex that can cause a public relations
problem. Race is close behind. "Dixie," for example, a stirring fight song
for use at athletic events and written, ironically, by a Yankee, has been
banned from many Southern and border state schools while the red, black,
and green symbol of black racism is flaunted. The school manager who
cannot tell the difference among overt racism, which cannot be permitted,
constitutionally protected self-expression, and harmless student enthusiasm is really asking for PR trouble.

Race as a source of curricular trouble, and thus a PR confrontation
with parents, may be newer and more popular, but the older issues of
morals and politics remain with us.

The Daughters of the American Revolution, for example, as recently
as twenty years ago, made a study of all available public school texts and

---

[7] In defending the sex education program, it was frequently necessary to deal
with self-styled clergymen trying to build a flock. Most of these preachers, however,
get so carried away with the sound of their own shouting that all but the lunatic fringe
soon deserts them. One such preacher who found himself unable to wreck our program, announced to the media that "God has called me to Florida." It probably wasn't
good PR, but when a radio newsman asked if I had any comment on the good rever-
end's decision, I felt compelled to reply that if God had indeed called him to Florida,
it was because He felt we had suffered enough.

branded hundreds as "unacceptable" for use because they did not reflect what the DAR felt was an appropriate attitude of morals and Americanism.[8] In most cases, this meant that the texts stuck to the facts, or insisted on giving both sides of an issue.

School systems that have made serious attempts at studies in comparative government such as communism *and* capitalism have run into trouble and probably always will (particularly where some good could be said of the former and some bad of the latter).

What many educational managers may forget is that parents have a *right* to challenge materials which may be made available to their children, particularly where the use of the materials is required by some authority. As difficult and ridiculous as it was to have to keep showing completely harmless sex education films to reams of parents, or to have to pull out book after book after book for the DAR or someone else to examine, this is part of the price school managers had best learn to pay. As the sales manager used to tell the young salesman who was tired of being chased by dogs as he made his rounds, "It goes with the territory."

Any parent—any citizen—has a right to object to any material, but as stated earlier, he does not have the right to ban or deny that material for use by other children. Here, indeed, is a

KEY CONCERN FOR SCHOOL PR: *If you, as an educational manager, have built a climate of performance and confidence regarding yourself and your school, you are far more likely to weather the charges of the crackpots and the kooks.*

The National Council of Teachers of English (NCTE) is particularly sensitive to attacks by those who would snatch books and materials from the hands of children, and they have done something about it that can help school managers who think ahead. It has devised a simple, non-defensive form to be filled out by those who complain about books or other materials. The form asks for specific objections, which seems a not unreasonable request. It also gives the complaining parent a chance to indicate that he would accept the withdrawal of the material from his child only. This gives both school and parent a way out, for there are very few courses, particularly in the areas of history or literature, which cannot use a variety of materials from the same author or from different authors to make the point that is desired.

[8] This "study" was conducted by the DAR's National Defense Committee in 1959 and cropped up frequently throughout the 1960s to plague unsuspecting and innocent schools. The current climate in the United States is just right, I fear, to revive such efforts.

The element of morals, which anti-sex education spokesmen contend is always missing from schools, is probably going to rise to greater fashion as a public school PR problem as the "born again" movement of evangelical Christians assumes the "right" to dictate its values to everyone else.

But let me not be misunderstood: schools have an obligation to teach morals. They are not obligated to teach religion (although they must teach about it if they are to do a decent job of teaching world history). A system-wide emphasis on honesty, respect for property and rights of others, ethics, humane behavior, common courtesy, and common decency will never be out of place in the school program. Trying to deny this entirely will bring a public relations problem from parents almost as quickly as a one-sided advocation of abortion, contraception, or sex outside of marriage.

Concerns with what the schools are—or are not—teaching, as well as concerns over race and violence, which are the subjects of the next two chapters, may very well be playing a part in the serious PR problem of declining public school enrollment. Not all parents who are enrolling their children in private schools want them to receive religious indoctrination, or are all who are doing so segregationists of class or color. Some simply want from the public schools what they feel—legitimately—that they ought to be getting and, not finding it, are willing to pay the price to look elsewhere.[9]

The public school management reaction against those who leave for private or parochial education is nothing if it is not evidence that the public school people do not understand the problem. It is a symptom of a massive public relations failure.

Find Out Why They're Leaving

Instead of attempting to determine rationally why the public is leaving the public schools, public school managers turn defensive and suggest that such departures are treasonable and the public schools can survive quite nicely without those who have left. Well, they can't, and it's about time school management began to understand this, or they will wind up with schools populated only by those who can't escape to some other alternative.

Of course, not all of the reasons that parents have for leaving the public schools are ones which school management can control, either through realistic public relations or through anything else. The busing

[9] Private school enrollment held up remarkably well during the inflationary period of the 1970s. Between 1970 and 1975 private school enrollment went from 8.1 million to 8.2 million, a greater percentage increase than the rise of 52.2 million to 52.8 million recorded in public school enrollment during the same period. (*Statistical Abstract of the United States*, 1976, U.S. Department of Commerce, Bureau of the Census, p. 117).

controversy alone is a prime example, as we shall discuss in the next chapter. But at least the public school people need to know why parents pull their children out of the institutions they must continue to support with their taxes and then pay an added tuition to send them to private or parochial schools which are in many ways apparently inferior to that which the public sector provides in the way of physical facilities.

The basic concern, of course, is with perceived threat to a lifestyle parents value. This is the kind of thing that gives rise to so many schools of the Jesus Church Basement variety in areas where that particular Christian heresy, fundamentalism, is popular. Often, this involves race. It can involve culture and textbooks, as the explosive situation in the Kanawha County, West Virginia schools showed.[10]

Parents are jumpy over what they perceive to be the moral devaluation of the public schools. And although the morals of the parents may, in some cases, be no better than the morality they fear is being subjectively endorsed by the schools, they want their children to be better than they are.

Most people, if they stop to think of it, realize that for the first time in history we have a true freedom for sexual promiscuity without serious risk of *physical* damage. Neither church nor society seems to have the power to enforce chastity, or the appearance thereof, that they once had. Young adults, including teachers, live together out of wedlock, without apparent negative effect on their employment. There is no excuse for an unwanted pregnancy, and only a little more for the contraction of venereal disease (although gonorrhea is now almost as prevalent as the common cold). In short, science and social change have made a true moral choice possible in the matter of sexual conduct and lifestyle, and parents are jumpy about what if anything, the schools are doing, to see that their children go the right way.

In addition, when parents see school officials who are arrested and convicted for various crimes, but who are not only retained but subsequently promoted, they do not gain much confidence in the moral stability of the schools. (I once knew a principal of a high school whose social life revolved around after hours clubs frequented by gamblers and pimps. He never could understand why he had trouble disciplining children or teachers, for he seemed to think that his out of school lifestyle was not known by those with whom he worked.)

---

[10] In Kanawha County, West Virginia, a dispute led by fundamentalist religionists over textbooks in 1974 escalated to gunfire and dynamiting and practically destroyed the entire system. During the same period, textbooks were burned in Drake, North Dakota and Junction City, Kansas and an uproar broke out in Bennington, Vermont over which magazines should be in the school library. ("It Starts in the Classroom," a publication of the National School Public Relations Association, December 1974).

When you combine this fear for values, perceived values, with the evidence that children are not receiving the caliber of basic education which parents value, you have established some major reasons for the desertion rate from the public schools that don't have anything to do with race *per se.*

It is not fascism which parents seek, I don't believe. They do not want to surrender human or Constitutional rights simply in return for order or for stability or the mere protection of their children from that which may be new or challenging. But what they do seem to want is substance of learning, be it tangible or intangible, and some semblance of progress.

Why Parochial Schools Are Surviving

Probably nowhere is this expression of public attitudes more prevalent than in the parochial school system run by the Roman Catholic church. In a sense, the fluctuations in enrollment in this system reflect parental satisfaction or discontent with the public schools. This is true because it is only the Roman Catholic Church that operates anything that can be considered to vaguely resemble a national system of non-public schools, even though each is controlled primarily by its own diocese or parish. One can also consider that the liberalization of the Roman Church, its increasing willingness to accept non-Catholic students (and their money) without open proselytizing, as factors which make the parochial schools not only an acceptable alternative to many public school patrons, but establish those parochial schools as a viable competitor for the available children.

A remarkable example of this trend can be found in a place one might least expect it, and that very fact has substantial implications for public schools: the ultimate "inner city," Washington, D.C.

Our Lady of Perpetual Help Elementary school is housed in a sixty-sixty-eight-year-old building in the district's Anacostia section, a ghetto neighborhood of welfare housing. Yet in 1978, the 517 students—all but 3 of them black and 42 percent of them Protestant, were establishing marks such as these:

- A daily absentee rate of 3 percent, as compared with 8 percent in Washington's public elementary schools and 18 percent in the public junior highs.
- All but 15 percent of the children lived in the District and most of the remainder came from Prince George's County, the District's most heavily black suburb.
- Test scores were within six months of the national average, while

children in the neighboring public schools averaged two years *or more* below national norms by the eighth grade.[11]

But perhaps the most significant point for the public schools is that more than half the children at the school came from homes so poor that they qualified for federal financial assistance. This is a critical concern for the District's schools, because the poverty classes have been the one continuing captive audience that the public schools could rely on to provide children for the public classrooms. Yet what if this trend were to spread, not only in the district, but in the other cities which are heavily black and heavily poor? The implications are substantial, and give credence to the trends in Seattle and elsewhere which show that unless the urban schools begin to concentrate on basic, traditional offerings and performances, they might as well go out of business.

Such an emphasis seems to be precisely what attracted so many poverty-level children to Our Lady of Perpetual Help, despite the fact that the per pupil expenditure, a traditional (if erroneous) measure of the quality of an educational system *was only $500 per pupil in 1978 as compared with more than $2,000 per pupil in the district's public elementary schools,* including the one directly across the street.

Uniforms are required at Our Lady of Perpetual Help for all children; homework is assigned each day and requires about two hours a night, depending on grade level. Respect for faculty is required; fighting, theft, and abuse of the rights of others are not tolerated and are dealt with swiftly and directly, in some cases with corporal punishment.

Is this the ideal education for all children? Of course not. But the important thing is that this represents a symptom that public education must recognize: at a time when traditional Catholic opposition to public school education for Catholics is weakening; at a time when more and more money is being made available to public schools, particularly those in the urban ghetto, *Protestant* parents, *black* parents, *poverty-level* parents are willing to turn their backs on the largesse which public education offers and make the painful personal and financial sacrifice necessary to give their children *the kind of education which they deem valuable.*

Parents Are Your Bellwethers

Parents are pretty good bellwethers. It's time public school managers who want their public to survive started listening to them; not in the sense

[11] According to Sister Loretto, the principal, and Father Leonard De Fiore, superintendent of schools for the archdiocese of Washington. (The *Washington Post,* December 25, 1977).

that they should react to this noisy pressure group or that rowdy self-appointed advisory committee, but to the parents who have been passing judgment on the public schools with their feet, or with their articulate silence, or by withholding their funds, or, more important, their children. The evidence is building, and school public relations policy must consider it, and act accordingly, no matter how painful the process is to those who are entrenched in the nether regions of educational management.

Take several additional examples, which come from different points on the educational compass, but all of which zero in on the center: public confidence and public school achievement and accomplishment.

- An exhaustive review of research on class size as an effective force for learning conducted in 1978 by the Educational Research Service showed that smaller classes by no means guarantee that pupils are going to learn more or better—even though this has become an article of faith in the demands by school boards and superintendents for increasing budgets. (The experience in the Washington parochial school just cited, where class size was frequently from five to fifteen pupils higher than that in the public school directly across the street seems to bear out the research survey findings.)
- As far back as 1969, the first national evaluation of the federally funded Head Start program for so-called disadvantaged children, a study conducted by the Westinghouse Learning Corporation and Ohio University concluded that the program had negligible positive effect on learning among pupils enrolled in it.
- More recently (1978), the non-profit Rand Corporation concluded that the multi-billion dollar program of educational assistance that grew out of the Elementary and Secondary Education Act of 1965 has failed because of the simplistic assumption that more money, more technology, and more employees would improve pupil learning.
- As early as 1974, the National Committee for citizens in Education concluded that public education was "out of control" and responsive simply to one pressure group or fad after another.

These studies, these implications, point out the kind of conclusion many parents who've never heard of the studies themselves are already reaching. As the singer Bob Dylan used to say, in another context, it doesn't take a weatherman to tell which way the wind is blowing.

Schools which can find time, frequently with the mammoth amounts of money made available from the various federal programs, to take large numbers of children fishing, but not to teach them to read; to take them camping, but not teach them to write; or, in a personal instance, to put them on buses and airplanes and spend each summer hauling them across the state staying in motels and at beaches and mountain resorts, are not doing anyone a favor.[12] The people who have to pay for it, which is everyone, seem to resent it. Even the parents of children who are the supposed beneficiaries of this sort of entertainment in lieu of education seem increasingly to recognize that the best way out of poverty in this society is still to get the education that will lead to college, business, or a marketable technical skill.

Resisting Pressure—from Right and Left

The conservative tide that is running in America today has, of course, profound implications for public education. Any educational manager who is not aware of that fact deserves the worst that can happen to him.

Because of this tide, therefore, educational managers would do well to anticipate the breathing of renewed strength into certain pressure groups and demands from the more simple-minded and reactionary parts of the American right.

No intent is here manifest to indicate that the conservative position has no place in the public school curriculum (as will be demonstrated in just a page or two). The point here is the same for left: No simple-minded, doctrinaire political position can be allowed to dominate curriculum. Short-sighted accommodation of such demands simply breeds worse public relations problems in the long run, to say nothing of what is done to a balanced, effective education for children.

An example of the type of organized curriculum pressure from the right which may be expected to enjoy a revival given the current climate of public opinion is the witch hunt conducted in the late 1950s and early 1960s by The Daughters of the American Revolution against almost 200 black-listed public school textbooks, many of which were quite simply beyond reproach.

But it isn't just a case of getting things out of the curriculum.

For years, millions of Americans were brought up to believe that a glass of milk at every meal was mandatory for good health, and the American Dairy Council did—and does—everything possible to get schools to encourage that belief. Such a belief is relative, however. In the urban slums of another generation, regular glasses of pasteurized milk represented a quick, cheap way for millions of immigrant children to get protein, fats, and vitamins which their diets would otherwise not have provided. Sadly, that

---

[12] This project, known as COW (for Classroom on Wheels), is paid for by Title I of the Elementary and Secondary Education Act. I am sure it is enjoyed by those who get to participate at taxpayer expense, but for those taxpayers who are not eligible and who could never afford a similar vacation out of their own pockets, this type of school-related activity is inexcusable.

is probably true for many children in today's urban ghettos where parents are unable or unwilling to insist on proper diets.

But for the majority of middle-class American children with diverse but balanced diets, three glasses or more of milk each day simply are not necessary. Indeed, many pediatricians and other health professionals suggest a *reduced* intake of milk and other dairy products, if the diet is otherwise healthy, because of evidence that regular ingestion of such products has a causal relationship to some types of heart disease which are prevalent in later life in our society.

But has the American Dairy Council gone along with this medical recommendation? Of course not; no more than the tobacco industry will concede that smoking causes cancer. The tobacco companies, however, do not have a history of providing free books, pamphlets, films, and guest speakers to unwary schools under the guise of health education. The American Dairy council does.

Thus the unaware educational manager may be setting himself up for crisis and confrontation either with parents who are better informed of the latest implications of dairy products and health, or, if he over-reacts to these changes, with a powerful dairy lobby that will accuse him of being anti-business.

The campaign to make the children of today's parents into captives awaiting indoctrination by special interests from all levels and all directions represents an investment of considerable amounts of money and time on the part of those who want to implant their message in the little hearts and minds. The best in advertising technology frequently is behind such presentations, and "public relations" in the Madison Avenue sense becomes a very real practice in the campaign to capture the classroom for purposes of indoctrination.

Today's Education, the Journal of the National Education Association, gives one small indication of how pervasive this campaign is. In a single issue, out of seventy-four "free" or minimal cost services teachers could request, twelve involved propaganda from various manufacturers or businesses under the guise of "educational materials."[13] The gamut of those offering this service was wide, but with a concentration among the so-called producers of "junk food" whose market is frequently dependent upon the shool age child. McDonald's, for example, offered a Nutrition Action Pack; Coca-Cola provided free films about its manufacture; Tom's Foods offered its "nutrition brochure and snack nutrition posters;" Burger King promised an "exciting new board game." Others with so-called educational offers included Procter & Gamble, the American Gas Association, General Mills, the Commercial Union Assurance Companies, and the American Textile Manufacturer's Institute.

[13] *Today's Education,* September-October, 1978, p. 124–125.

The problem is not that these, and other reputable profit-making businesses want to infiltrate the schools, although the ethics of it are certainly questionable. Some of the information offered might have a use, if critically and carefully examined. However, this whole business is part of a

---

KEY CONCERN FOR SCHOOL PR: *You can never know enough about your curriculum. Never forget that no matter how established the subject, there is probably more than one side—and children need to know it.*

Part of the public relations problem that ensues over curriculum is because some parents and some groups, either deliberately or through ignorance, see the role of the schools as one of indoctrination rather than education. The AFL-CIO would like nothing better then to have the history of labor in this country taught from their point of view, replete with heroic workers striving for decent wages, always beset by fascist employers.

The National Association of Manufacturers or the Chamber of Commerce would prefer the same period to be taught as showing conscientious employers victimized by a lazy, destructive, incompetent work force unwilling to understand the principles of productivity.

One of the reasons that curriculum issues become blown up into major public relations problems with the apparent suddenness of a solar flare is that educational managers who are responsible for curriculum do not recognize that *when* is almost as important in teaching as *what*.

Censorship is almost as great an anathema to teachers as it is to newspaper reporters. (Not editors. Editors are management and oppose censorship only when it goes against the corporate image.)

The Index of forbidden books of the Roman Catholic Church, a classic and enduring example of censorship, became less and less effective as a moral control as more and more Catholics came to realize that they had both the intelligence and, indeed the duty, to take personal responsibility for the morality of their reading.

Censorship, in short, is traditionally thought of as un-American. I agree, both as a former newspaperman and a former teacher.

But let us substitute another word for "censorship." Let us try "judgment" instead.

Now it is not my intention to slip the camel of censorship into the classroom tent, and justify it by calling the camel a mouse. We have seen too much of that type of word play and inexactitude in public education already and the public relations problems which have resulted are fearsome indeed.

But "censorship" is a negative word to most of us. "Judgment" is a positive one. Two-bit dictators impose censorship; solons exercise judgment.

Yet in the classroom, the two can be the same—sometimes.

Dr. Max Rafferty, the former California Superintendent of Public Instruction, was a man who could—and whose very name still can—drive the liberals of public education into fits, jerks, and foamings of the mouth. My personal opinion is that Dr. Rafferty did this with delight, in the same way that a raucous, but intelligent boy, will pester the neighborhood sissy in an attempt to make a man of him.

In Seattle in the mid-1960s Dr. Rafferty had just finished a heated debate with the chairman of his own board of education at a meeting of the Education Writers Association. Fortunately (for Dr. Rafferty) the position of State Superintendent of Public Instruction in California was—and is—an elected one, for by the time Dr. Rafferty had finished, his board chairman, Tom Braden (now a syndicated coumnist) was livid. (There is some reason to believe they were debating in Seattle not just by invitation, but because California was sick of listening to them, but that's another story.)

Ultimately, however, the issue of censorship came up. The use of labels is always misleading, but it would probably be fair to say that Dr. Rafferty was *perceived* as a conservative and Braden *perceived* as a liberal. Are you, someone asked of Dr. Rafferty, in favor of censorship?

"No," he replied quickly. "I am in favor of judgment." What Dr. Rafferty had to say by way of elaboration goes straight to the heart of the public relations problem which involves parents most deeply: what is being used to teach their children. Dr. Rafferty continued:

> All school people censor things all the time. We are speaking about educational censorship and, of course, in education we don't call it censorship, we call it screening. This is one of the things we professional school men get paid for, and if we didn't do it, we'd be out of a job. We don't give Gibbon's *Decline and Fall* to second graders (and) we don't give "Dick and Jane" to high school seniors . . .
>
> (Then there) is the question of political censorship. Should certain books, such as the *Communist Manifesto, Das Kapital, Mein Kampf* and so on, be eliminated from the school shelves because of pressure from one group or another on either end of the political spectrum. Well, obviously, you wouldn't have these books in elementary school because no one could read them and understand them. Obviously, just as obviously, you would have them in college and in many high schools where students, particularly the junior and senior year . . . I should say certainly that all types of materials of this sort should be made available as research material. I don't think it is appropriate to use them as a text, because a textbook, by the very nature of it, must present a broad point of view and a whole gamut of the spectrum.

Here is an example of how this sort of thing works, UNESCO. UNESCO material has been used in every school that I have ever associated with as a high school instructor or an administrator. But, we use it on the library shelves as a part of research material. We did not use it as it has been used in some school districts as classroom text, textual material on the United Nations. The reason as we saw it, was a very simple one. This material is valuable. This material gives an insight into the workings of this organization. But the material is very largely, if not almost exclusively, written by people who are directly connected and bound up and in many cases, in the pay of the United Nations itself. I would have the same objection to using a text or using this material as a text material, as I would have to using a high school American history class a book on the American revolution written by King George III and his Tory cabinet. It is simply an inappropriate textbook, although there would certainly be value to portray one point of view. But it constitutes special pleading.

Now, in summarizing, what have we said here? Simply this, that censoring is of the very nature of school work. Every time we put a book into a classroom and every time we say take another one out, we are in this popular sense, censoring, although we in education do not call it this. We will continue to do this as long as schools are in existence, because what are good and right and proper for children to learn in one stage of their development are not equally good and right and proper in another.[14]

The petty level to which the schools can be reduced in their reactions to what they *think* might make parents unhappy can also be a problem, although this admittedly is more one of ethics than public relations. Many years ago, while a high school student, I enjoyed reading Francis Hopkinson's "Battle of the Kegs," a poem written during the Revolution which satirized the British occupation of Philadelphia and their jumpy imaginations which convinced them American troops were hiding everywhere (including in some kegs seen floating down the river).

Recently, while thumbing through a high school literature book, I saw Hopkinson's poem listed and turned to it for a few minutes' enjoyment only to find that the poem had been "sanitized." It once had read:

Sir William, he, snug as a flea
Lay all this time a-snoring
Nor dreamed of harm
As he lay warm
In bed with Mrs. Loring

In the modern edition, the last line had been replaced with "His dreams of victory soaring." I'm sure Sir William would have resented the change as much as I did.

[14] From a tape transcribed and distributed to members of the conference by the Education Writers Association.

CHAPTER **9**

Bus as a Four-Letter Word

> *What all the wise men promised has not hap-*
> *pened and what all the damn fools predicted*
> *has come to pass.*
> —Lord Melbourne (William Lamb)
> 1770–1849

So much has been written and said about busing in American public education that the outsider would think this is a phenomenon that has *directly* affected every school system in the nation.

That, of course, is not so. But busing, or the transporting of children to schools outside their neighborhoods for purposes of racial desegregation, has spread, and with its spread has come considerably greater agitation concerning it.

During the years immediately following the Supreme Court's landmark 1954 school decision *Brown v. Board of Education,* which outlawed segregation based on race, most of the nation looked with approval and pleasure as the courts and the government began moving to force the racist, recalcitrant South, at whom the thrust of the decision was aimed, to end its segregation in the schools. In so-called *Brown II* (1955), the court expanded its anti-segregation order, and directed segregated systems, "to effectuate a transition to a racially non-discriminatory school system—with all deliberate speed."

Facing the Failure

The period from 1954 to 1967 was marked by sporadic violence in the South, such as that which led President Eisenhower to federalize the

National Guard to implement a desegregation order in Little Rock, Arkansas; a carefully orchestrated "massive resistance" by Virginia, which led to such things as the closing for a period of several years of all public schools in Prince Edward County; the growth of private schools as a means of avoiding desegregation, where such took place; and the requirement for desegregation being placed on blacks to continue to avail themselves, as individuals, of the legal right to attend white schools in widespread and continuing lawsuits.

Most significantly, however, this period was marked by the fact that almost all efforts at desegregation were aimed at the *South,* where segregation of the races in the schools and elsewhere had been *de jure,* or required by law.

The response in the South was a grudging compliance in those districts where blacks made up a substantial part of the school population. Placement boards were established, "freedom of choice" plans were implemented, each of which continued to place upon blacks the *initiative* to seek attendance at a desegregated school.

This changed when the Supreme Court speaking in *Green v. New Kent County School Board* 391 U.S. 430 (1968), effectively outlawed freedom of choice because it did not work to disestablish the segregated system. The burden was thus placed on the school board to come up with a workable plan, and to do so at once.

The second major decision which effectively ended segregation in the South where even vestiges may have remained was *Swann v. Charlotte-Mecklenburg Board of Education* 402 U.S. 1 (1971) which is considered to have established the court's authority to order busing, where necessary, to effectively eliminate segregated schools.

The issue of busing, indeed of remedial action to eliminate de facto segregation in other parts of the country, was joined in *Keyes v. School District No. 1, Denver, Colorado* 413 U.S. 189 (1973). In ordering the defendants there to desegregate, the court expanded desegregation law to states which never had *de jure* segregation, as in the south. Further, the court said in the Denver case that the effective practice of segregation, in the assignment of pupils and teachers, in *one portion* of the district, justified *district-wide* steps to eliminate segregation. The scope of school desegregation moved from the South into the Northeast and Midwest as black plaintiffs were able to prove that, despite the absence of *de jure* segregation, or "Jim Crow" laws in these states, the deliberate actions of local governments and school boards had had the same effect of segregating blacks and thus entitled them to the same types of judicial relief that had been made available to their black brethren in the South.[1]

---

[1] Fifteen years after so-called *Brown I,* the U.S. Civil Rights Commission reported (February, 1979) that racial segregation in southern schools had all but disappeared, but that half of all minority students in the United States were still in segregated schools—almost all of them in the North.

This trend was viewed with not a little grim irony, and occasional humor by Southerners who had suffered through earlier efforts at desegregation while other white Americans has taken pompous, holier-than-thou attitudes about the sanctity of their own schools' racial practices.[2]

As Louis Lucas, a veteran NAACP lawyer said to me, "When desegregation was occurring in Memphis, Mobile, and Birmingham, it had seemed very simple to Northern people. When desegregation came (to them) people found the issue difficult and complex, relating to the very fabric of society."

Yet even as busing spread to such places as Boston and Los Angeles, it was not a first-hand problem for the majority of school districts. The majority of such districts, of course, have not had large numbers of minorities to deal with, once one goes outside the South and the border states and the large cities of the nation. Problems of busing and integration are as alien to rural Iowa and Nevada and similar regions as they are to the moon, primarily because there either are no racial minorities or the few that do exist have long since been assimilated into the schools.

Is busing, then, a genuine public relations problem? Absolutely. Busing affects millions of pupils in the large systems, and, of equal importance, it speaks to the emotions and encourages those who do not believe that the American system of public education can, or should, survive in a given area if it is overwhelmed by groups that are national minorities. Sad though it is, we must face the fact of this

KEY CONCERN FOR SCHOOL PR: *In our society, busing will always fail unless or until exceptional steps are taken to ensure that the academic, social, and behavioral values of the middle class are preserved and protected in any school to which middle-class children are assigned.*

In city after city, plans for racial desegregation, whether court-ordered or not, have failed not only to integrate the schools, but have worsened the problem of declining enrollment. There have been ambitious, voluntary plans, such as that in Berkeley, California. There has been grudging compliance without the final order of a court, such as that in Alexandria, Virginia. There have been city-suburban mergers, as in Charlotte, North Carolina and Louisville, Kentucky. And then there has been Boston, "the sort of city," according to novelist Jim Harrison, "where much of the population strangles cats."[3] In the mid-70s, they seemed more interested in strangling the federal judge who ordered the busing.

---

[2] *School Desegregation: Making It Work,* College of Urban Development, Michigan State University, 1976, p. 36.
[3] *Wolf* by Jim Harrison, Manor Books, 1973.

None of this is to say that there have not been isolated instances of individual acceptance; and, thank God, the levels of violence associated with the Little Rocks of the 1950s have, with isolated exceptions such as Boston, been reduced, at least on community-wide bases.

But still, integration as a national policy in education, has generally failed despite all efforts at "clustering," "pairing," "magnet schools," "consolidation," or what have you. The literature shows no stable, enduring success. The fact remains: the so-called "tipping point," the point at which the percentage of black students becomes unacceptable to whites, can be specifically identified in school after school and in community after community. The figures sometimes vary: 25 percent black here, 33 there. But in almost no instance do the figures reveal a case in which racial "balance" has stabilized once the black enrollment reaches and exceeds 50 percent."[4]

Boston will serve as an example. In 1973, the year before busing began, Boston enrolled almost 94,000 students, 62 percent white. In 1978, the enrollment was 72,000, of which 41 percent was white. Why?

Many reasons have been offered, most of which have at least some degree of validity: a higher incidence of personal disorder in schools with high black enrollments; movement of whites with school-age children away from declining cities with their high tax rates; curriculum changes unacceptable to whites; and increasing social integration which many whites find unacceptable.

In a broadcast September 17, 1978 of the highly popular television program "Sixty Minutes," a woman being interviewed by Mike Wallace observed: "If you want something good, tune out the bad."

The woman interviewed was talking about how to improve television programming. But what she said could have been said with equal impact as a reflection of how the white middle class overwhelmingly has perceived the effects of large scale desegregation. Rightly or wrongly, where busing takes place, those whites who can do so will vote with their feet, taking their children and their financial and political support either to the suburbs or to the private schools.

Does this mean that all whites who opt for this choice are racists? Absolutely not, although efforts to convince blacks of this have no success nor are they likely to do so. The fact that the pattern is so inviolate, however, reinforces erroneous black contentions that all of white America is racist. As of this writing, there has been *not a single example of successful integration of any school system in America over a period of five years where the black minority exceeded one-third* when desegregation was first ordered. Whites simply are not going to allow their culture and their values to be submerged in such circumstances, and the facts show it. Busing in particu-

---

[4] In Hammond, Indiana, for example, the school board went so far as proposing that up to $6,000 be paid to each student who voluntarily spent his entire career in a desegregated school (*Los Angeles Times,* November 10, 1978).

lar has no chance at all when the education at the end of the bus ride not only does not equal, but is inferior to, what was left behind.[5]

The public relations problems are genuinely grim, and the issue facing school managers who must implement massive desegregation plans is substantial. It is not a case of how to "win," but of how to keep losses as low as possible. One of the saddest little books which unwittingly testifies to the truth of this statement was published in 1976 by the College of Urban Development at Michigan State University. Entitled *School Desegregation: Making It Work*, the book runs for 115 pages, examines many programs, areas, and platitudes, talks about board members, politics, the law, the media, and *is unable to cite* a single instance in which desegregation has "worked."[6]

What must be remembered, if we are not to fool ourselves and make the situation worse, is that desegregation and integration have entirely different meanings. For a period of one to five years, desegregation can be made to "work," if by "working" one means black and white pupils can be forcibly assigned to a single school. This lasts until the whites who can afford it—and many black members of the middle class as well—leave the schools. An *integrated* system is something else entirely.

A key to even a passable acceptance of desegregation is that the middle class is far more willing to accept desegregation if its children remain in neighborhood schools. If neighborhood schools cannot be preserved, due to racial imbalances, housing patterns, outright discrimination, or whatever, the chances for even a modicum of success practically disappear, because busing as a remedy to segregation is antithetical to the neighborhood school concept.

The statistics of white flight from the cities of the United States make a sad study in public education and public relations. They are statistics which should be studied and understood by educational managers. Here are some of them:

In 1978, the U.S. Department of Health, Education, and Welfare, using data in some cases a year or more old identified the ten major cities with the largest percentages of minority enrollment. Although in some cases, minority meant Hispanic, in most it meant black. The cities and their percentages: Washington, 97; Newark, 89; Atlanta, 85; San Antonio, 83; New Orleans, 81; Oakland, 80; Richmond, 76; Detroit, 74; Baltimore, 73; Chicago, and San Francisco, 72 each.

It is worth noting that busing, or other effective or threatened legal actions, were or had been present in each of these cities. Further, each city has a financial situation ranging from serious to critical insofar as tax support

---

[5] That a survey of the literature shows no success in stabilized desegregation (integration), given the conditions of this paragraph, is painful though oft-ignored evidence that the problems of public school integration in this nation are far from resolved.

[6] *School Desegregation: Making It Work.*

is concerned. And in each, the whites who do remain are generally from the lower socio-economic classes who do not have the option of escape.

Thus, another

KEY CONCERN FOR SCHOOL PR: *How can the schools fulfill their responsibility to reflect the racial and cultural mix of the United States if, increasingly, there is no one left to mix with?*

They can't, of course. This has led to one of two courses of action. In Detroit, Richmond, and Wilmington, Delaware, it has led to attempts to merge the black urban schools and their declining tax base with those of the mostly white, more affluent suburbs. In Richmond and Detroit the courts did not permit this relief. In Wilmington they did, although the verdict on whether it will stabilize racial enrollment there, when such a stability has not been achieved elsewhere, is not yet in.

The other course of action is almost as rare as the attempt to spread desegregation efforts beyond the bounds of the school district, city, or county where the problem originated. That course has been to win judicial approval for dropping busing as a means for desegregation because it has become counter-productive. In one of the few instances where this has occurred, the Inglewood, California City Schools won State Superior Court approval in 1975 to abandon busing because there were not enough white children left to integrate.[7]

It should be a matter of considerable interest that the same judge who ordered the busing in Inglewood in 1970 rescinded it in 1975. But of even more interest is the fact that, when busing was ordered in 1970, 62 percent of the city's school children were white; by 1975 that had dropped to 19.5 percent, a decline surely aggravated by busing. The result was that black children were being bused from 80 percent black to other schools also 80 percent black at considerable financial cost. This situation, sadly, was not restricted to Inglewood, California. The same thing, in the same percentages, was occurring at the same time in Richmond, Virginia, where a court order remained in effect.

Despite the evidence in the case of Inglewood, and other cities where white flight has occurred in response to busing, researchers are still arguing over whether there is such a thing as white flight. The question is rather like arguing over whether a human being, held on the bottom of a swimming pool for twenty minutes, and then brought to the top can be said to have drowned or to have suffocated.

Certainly, the educational manager in the urban area should be aware that the migration of whites from the inner city is a trend that in many areas pre-dates any desegregation effort, and he should not try to pin the white

[7] As reported by United Press International, May 11, 1975.

flight tail on the donkey of desegregation alone. However, any analysis of the statistics seems to indicate clearly that busing, or any similar desegregation plan, exacerbates or institutes white flight even under the best of conditions.

In Prince Georges County, Maryland, a once affluent suburb of Washington, D.C., for example, an annual average loss of 3 to 4 percent of whites jumped to 14 percent after busing began in January 1973 and has grown even higher, according to a Rand Corporation study.[8]

The Rand study, which looked at fifty-four school districts in 1978, provided objective data for something journalists and other observers of the national desegregation scene have been saying all along: that full desegregation, or busing, has no chance when the non-white minority involved is one-third or more. Actually, the Rand study indicated that when the minority population is 20 percent or more, the overall impact on attempting to establish *stable* integrated schools through busing or other mass changes in assignments is likely to fail.

Another factor pointed out by Rand was that integration orders in cities were likely to fail where whites had access to the suburbs.

Based on its study, therefore, Rand indicated that Los Angeles, where massive busing got underway in the fall of 1978, should be prepared for massive white flight in return.[9]

The semantics of this issue are such that the educational manager can find himself wrapped up in hair-pulling contests worthy of a Saturday night televised wrestling special. Researchers and sociologists are still arguing over what constitutes white flight, and why, and have come up with hundreds of studies and thousands of charts. The accusation "journalist," which is really the lowest form of verbal blow in the rarified world of educational research, is even being hurled at one group by another whose conclusions do not agree with the first, at least that has been the experience of some who have become involved in the academic aspects of the issue.

For the educational manager, the case is simpler. White flight from urban areas becomes a reality when massive desegregation is ordered, and no number of statistics can ultimately change that fact.

Quality and Desegregation: A Valid Question

Regardless of the obvious legal requirement to correct the history of racial segregation in the schools and to see that it does not recur, if possible,

---

[8] As presented to the American Sociological Association in San Francisco, September 7, 1978.

[9] They got it. According to *The New York Times* (November 7, 1978), enrollment in September 1978 dropped a record 4.8 percent to 555,755 in the Los Angeles Public Schools.

a question remains: Does quality education for a black child require that he or she attend a desegregated school?

Heavy subjective evidence suggests that it does. It is not meant here that attending school with whites will automatically bring up the generally poor academic performance of blacks, for evidence shows that these scores remain low. Rather, speaking subjectively, it seems important that any minority be exposed to majority kinds of education so that it will be able to function cooperatively with, and independently of, the majority throughout life to the self-interest of the minority. Probably no greater example of this type of subjective survival and functioning can be found in North America than the Jews, who have participated integrally in American life, and made substantial contributions thereto, while at the same time retaining, by choice, their own cultural privacy and identity.

It should be remembered also, that as Sowell and other educators of unquestioned integrity and credentials have pointed out, the *objective* academic performance of blacks is far more likely to be effected by the quality of teachers and the expectation and support from the home than by any other factor, including facilities, equipment, and the presence of white faces. (See Sowell on the outstanding history and performance of all-black Dunbar High School in Washington, D.C., Chapter 3.) It is important to recognize, therefore, that the educational manager needs to understand that the academic success or failure of the school need not rest automatically or simply on its racial composition. There is no guarantee that an all-white school with poor teachers, disinterested students, and little parental support will turn out students who anywhere approach those cited by Sowell from the all-black school. That this excellence and achievement on the part of blacks in all-black schools is still possible is one of the few hopes urban areas have of establishing and stabilizing public education to any degree where the return of whites can even vaguely be hoped for.

In the long run, unless blacks can stabilize the schools and systems they inherit during and following white flight, then it is black children who are being hurt the most. The promise that desegregation would be a panacea for blacks, and give them an automatic increase in academic performance, has proved as specious and untrue as common sense should have shown it to be. Now, as blacks become increasingly isolated—at least those who remain in urban schools—they have to turn to themselves and their own resources for their school solutions. Too often, this has meant an overemphasis on athletics as the way up and out, despite the fact that less than one black athlete in every thousand makes a successful career in the major leagues of professional sport.

The solution, of course, is the same as it is for whites, and indeed always has been for all students—now that discrimination in education, housing, and employment is officially outlawed—an adequate preparation for a vocational or technical skill or entry into college.

Yet a frequent cry, and one that is echoed without thought by many parts of the white establishment, is that black youth do not want to prepare themselves for jobs because there are no jobs for them. This cacophony continues despite the fact that in the very same cities where these cries are the loudest, the newspapers are full of appeals for workers. Most of these jobs are for the unskilled and are at minimum wage level, it is true, and many are in the fast food restaurants or in other transient and statusless businesses. Yet whites, particularly those of college years, flock to these jobs, particularly during the summers and at holidays. Why then this problem?

It is attitudinal, and it is this type of attitude that public relations conscious administrators, particularly in urban schools, must seek to change. For as Professor Walter Williams of Temple University, a black economist, points out, "as late as 1948, black youths had a *lower* rate of unemployment than whites." Yet segregation, *de facto* if not *de jure*, was far more common then, and certainly there were fewer jobs for blacks in 1948 than there are today.[10]

How can this attitude be changed, particularly in urban schools? The first step is to recognize a particularly painful

KEY CONCERN FOR SCHOOL PR: *Except in isolated instances, white leadership in black schools and communities is bankrupt. If the attitudes and performances of black students are to be upgraded, this will have to be done by black leadership, whose first priority must be to convince black youth that white society cannot be blamed for all their problems.*

The literature of sociology, social psychology, education, minority affairs, and the like is replete with articles which attempt to contend that whites lack the sensitivity and the ability to administer black schools or teach black children. This is an often mentioned concern where desegregation is to be implemented.

Such an attitude, of course, makes the public relations role of the education manager far more difficult, be the manager black or white. If he is black and holds to objective teaching, measurable accomplishment, and middle-class goals and values, he must be prepared to be accused by other blacks of being an "Uncle Tom," a "handkerchief head," an "Oreo," or other racial epithet to indicate that he has sold out, or become subservient to, the white community and/or power structure. A white who holds and attempts to defend and implement the same positive objectives will be perceived   by

[10] As quoted by syndicated columnist Michael Novak, November 22, 1977.

blacks in school and community as a "traditionalist" or "conservative," both code words among blacks for one who is segregationist at heart.

Of course, these perceptions are untrue as generalizations, but overcoming them is all the challenge any educational manager could ever need. The diminution of the meritocracy in the schools has simply made the matter worse. Fulsome reasons for double standards, and excuses for poor performance and lack of effort can always be found. For years, segregationist whites contended that blacks were unable or unwilling to do serious academic work that would lead them to the professions. Now, sadly, it is large segments of the black community which, in effect, are saying the same thing by demanding exemption from rigorous academic work while continuing to insist with equal stridency that they are entitled to admission to the professions and programs for which they have not prepared. Such attitudes led to the Baake[11] case in California, to a separate national Merit Scholarship Program for black children so they would not have to compete intellectually or academically against whites and other minorities, and to various financial assistance programs based on race or class which have served simply to infuriate those portions of the national community who have to continue to perform and to pay their own way to gain access to the professions, the trades, or other aspects of national life.

Factors such as these have brought about the tardy recognition on the part of some proponents of artificial integration, such as busing, that the goal is a whole lot tougher to implement in real life than it is in the insulated world of academia, or as a research project in social and educational theory.

The admission by James S. Coleman, the University of Chicago sociologist, that he was wrong in projecting automatic educational gains for blacks who were massively desegregated is probably the most disturbing and depressing. Coleman, who made his admissions in a formal paper in April, 1978, is widely regarded as the father of the busing concept which was seized upon by the courts, following Coleman's publication of it in 1966. What once appeared to be fact is now known to be fiction, Coleman has admitted.[12]

Given all this hodgepodge of conclusions, the chaos, pandemonium, violence, disorder, white flight, and racial hatred that have been engendered by busing and by massive desegregation, there is still public relations and administrative perspective that the educational manager must find. Points which he must not lose sight of are:

[11] *Baake v. Regents* (S.C. of the U.S., 76-811).
[12] James C. Coleman, "Equal Educational Opportunity: A Review," Paper presented at the University of Chicago, April 1978.

1. Racially integrated education is both legally and ethically desirable, and is a proper and appropriate goal and extension of the American public school.
2. Racial integration cannot be achieved by a diminution of the quality of the educational program to satisfy any group, class, or race.
3. Parents must have absolute evidence that the quality and security of the education in an integrated school is compatible with the goals they have set for themselves and their children.
4. Achieving a stable, integrated school system where more than 25 percent of the students are black, and where whites have any way to opt out, is probably the single most difficult job in public education leadership today and one which so far has proved virtually impossible.

As Coleman finally discovered, busing does not exist in a microcosm. Real people with real lives, goals, and aspirations are affected.

It should be remembered that the public relations problems of busing are essentially insoluble for the schools, and the only thing that can be done is to minimize the disruption of school programs for all children, their families and for teaching staffs. The destruction of continuity and security that quality education can provide, whether it is academic or vocational, is one of the invariable results of busing, and must be minimized wherever possible.

Whenever busing is accomplished by a change to black control of schools, the new black leadership can save itself much grief by *not* following the real or imagined discrimination which may have been practiced at some time in the distant past by white administrations. It is axiomatic that the acquisition of power breeds the desire to exercise it.

Still, black power in American public education does itself no favor by an overnight expulsion of the white technocracy which makes the schools run. But sadly, this is the practice, just as one after another, emerging African nations have thrown out the only administrators and technicians who knew how to run the utilities, operate the airfields and the copper mines, keep the books and otherwise contribute to a stable operation and assist the new regime, just because those administrators were white.

Further, even when black power gains control of the schools, and even of the city councils, economic power frequently remains with the white establishment, the cooperation and support of which is necessary for the progressive survival of the schools. In city after city, in varying degree, from Richmond to Philadelphia to Atlanta, this situation has occurred.

One of the interesting public relations problems which is likely to occur as blacks gain complete control of more and more school districts, either as a result of busing or because of other causes, is the perceptions which the *black* community has of the quality of the schools.

The 1978 Gallup Poll which reflects public attitudes toward the public schools showed that 86 percent of Northern whites and 85 percent of Southern whites felt that blacks and other minorities in their respective communities have the same educational opportunities as white children. Among blacks, 54 percent of the Southerners and only 21 percent of the Northerners felt that their children had the same educational opportunities as whites. Yet in many cases, the children of these black parents were attending the same schools as the whites who were in the minority.

In all likelihood, as districts become more black, the lack of educational opportunity for the black children who remain—whether this is real or imagined—will be blamed by black school managers on lack of money; in other words, contending that the white community should continue to be held responsible even though the school system may be black in population and black in control. Only an exceptionally courageous black school leadership seems able to make its public understand that money alone is neither the cause of quality education and high pupil performance nor the cure for their absence.

The issue of busing, therefore, cannot be ignored just because it does not affect thousands of school districts directly. Busing, whether in Richmond, Boston, Louisville, or Los Angeles, raises the passions of people. It causes headlines; makes news. Most importantly, the questions it raises about the effectiveness of education, about social, cultural, racial, economic and instructional issues in one district, are easily transferred to other districts where busing itself may not exist. The small city district, or the rural district in a state or region where busing is an issue in some metropolitan area should watch the storm clouds on the horizon and realize that only through operating the most efficient, most satisfactory district of high quality can they insure that the virus of educational discontent which busing breeds will not spread to them in some other form.

CHAPTER 10

Safety in the Schools: A Must for Public Success

It has been the better part of a decade since Wayne Phillips turned sixteen and looked forward to two things: the start of baseball season and getting his driver's license. But Wayne didn't make the team that year, and he didn't get his driver's license either. Instead, he was gunned down in the hall of his public high school one February day and went to his grave, the victim of a mindless confrontation between two other students who had sought to kill each other over a teenage girl.

The death of young Phillips, a white youth killed during a confrontation between two blacks, carried with it the added poignancy of making him something of a martyr to people who had never known him. To them, Wayne Phillips was a victim of judicial murder, sent to his death in a school seven miles from his home under a geographical gerrymandering designed to put white students into black schools. It was the application of such a court order that put Wayne Phillips from one end of Richmond, Virginia into Armstrong High School at the other end and thus into position to receive a .38 caliber slug in his chest as he scrambled for safety along a corridor wall.

Is the death of Wayne Phillips typical of the American schoolhouse today? Fortunately, no. Murder and manslaughter in the public schools still involve fewer than 100 tragedies per year, but other serious crimes are much more frequent. Take these statistics from the 1977 study "Safety in the Schools" compiled by the National Institute of Education (NIE) at a cost of three years and $200.4 million:[1]

- 5,200 secondary school teachers physically attacked each month by students; 6,000 are robbed at school.
- 232,000 secondary school students are attacked in a typical month.
- 2.4 million secondary students have something stolen from them each month.
- The risk of being robbed or attacked in school is five times greater than it is on the street.
- There is really no accurate statistic as to the total of crime and violence in the public schools because school boards and administrators do not report or record all incidents.

The NIE report, unfortunately, does not represent an isolated pattern, for it reflects much the same trend as did a 1973 study released by the office of Congressman Birch Bayh. At the same time, the annual Gallup Poll of public attitudes toward education continues to show a priority concern among taxpayers over misconduct, criminality, or some variation of discipline.[2]

It is an issue with everyone; its evidence is everywhere. William Saroyan was not an educator; he was a California native of Armenian extraction whose books, plays, and stories brought him considerable fame and much fortune. He may never have read the NIE report, the Bayh report, or the Gallup Poll. What he had to say about people will no doubt set on edge the teeth of all psychologists, some educators, most social workers. But it is a statement to which many other adults, including quite a few parents, can nod their heads to and pat their collective feet:

> Nobody is willing to suggest that a large part of American youth is just plain stupid; and that they are encouraged in this unnatural condition by adults . . . who achieve hysterical drama by demonstrating that a fifteen-year-old moist-eyed sniveling monster . . . beats old women because (his) mother didn't embrace him every morning . . . , or his brilliant father didn't share his interest in hot rods, rock 'n' roll, and marijuana.[3]

---

[1] The unfortunate thing about government studies such as these—and similar studies that are conducted as a public relations measure by local school districts—is that they leave the impression that action will result because of the dramatic nature of the findings.

[2] "The Tenth Annual Gallup Poll of the Public's Attitudes Toward the Public Schools," by George H. Gallup, 1978.

[3] *I Used to Believe I Had Forever Now I'm Not So Sure,* by William Saroyan, Cowles, New York, 1968.

And if this were not enough, the headlines tell the story their way:

Student Shot
Teacher Raped
Principal Assaulted
Counselor Mugged

Ho, hum, the school manager is tempted to say, that's not *my* school system. And he turns over to his next project in school PR—getting the bond issue passed, wondering if the newspaper will really send a photographer to Miss Smith's demonstration of third grade finger painting, or preparing another brochure.

Painful Planning: Anticipating Trouble

Well, friends, the time to think about the PR aspects of school violence is before it strikes—if this is a luxury your school can afford. School managers who don't recognize this simple fact may be pricing themselves out of the successful bond issue, losing any newspaper support for Miss Smith and her finger-painters, and helping cut their own throats at a time when the public at large is becoming increasingly willing to do it for them.

The public schools have lost too many friends already. And when as distinguished a Christian humanist as Malcolm Muggeridge says public education today "is the greatest enemy that human enlightenment has ever had," the prognosis for our course is not good.[4]

The fact is that poll after poll has shown that the incidence of school crime, lack of classroom discipline, call it what you will is THE major parental concern about public schools. It is all the more puzzling, therefore, that so many school systems still seem to think this is something that can't or won't happen to them. And when it does, the answer too often is a mad dash to hire security guards, install metal detectors for every door, or mass suspensions of the unruly.

These measures, however, are reactions, not actions. The best time to look at the public relations implications of school violence, to admit that it can happen in your school system, and to start thinking negatively in order to do something positive about it, is before the first major incident takes place.

PR planning for school violence recognizes that the ideal would be to determine the causes and find immediate solutions. The pursuit of these solutions is admirable and to be encouraged. Specifying causes is manda-

---

[4] As quoted by Tom Ascik of the *Washington Star*, February 20, 1975.

tory, be they racial, economic, social, or the natural outgrowth of public education's masochistic tendency to be welfare agency, public health service, social psychologist, probation worker, soup kitchen, and—occasionally—imparter of skills and heritages. Current trends seem to indicate that lasting solutions to school violence will not emerge, however, until society demands them even more stridently. But in the meantime, the implications and the problems have to be faced by those who must try eternally to live between a suspicious, restless public and non-communicative educators who see the schools as their personal possessions and their "expertise" as exempt from public challenge.

So, what do you do?

Plan.

This does not mean appointing another broad-based, blue-ribbon, democratically devised, selected, and controlled committee to bring forth another report like a baby burping up a mouthful of mush that was practically pre-digested before he ever swallowed it.

It *is* proper to check with other school systems of comparable size and composition to see what, if anything, they are doing to handle the PR aspects of school violence. Some systems are active in this area and some have found things that work. So, pick some brains. Ask for help, particularly if you are a school PR director or even a superintendent facing a recalcitrant and terrified board.

If you are in educational PR you must wrestle with that age-old problem: everything your district does or does not do has PR implications, but not all of these actions or inactions come under your authority. If you are a school PR director, get your facts together and talk frankly with your superintendent. Remind him of the need for a contingency plan, one you hope will never be used. Get his support, personally, for involving the area directors, and, most of all, the principals.

Be prepared for some empty answers when working with principals. Try it. Ask one what he'd do if a student got knifed. Don't be surprised if the answer deals solely with calling an ambulance and ignores the news media, public response, and parental concern entirely.

Remember that a serious school incident can seldom be successfully covered up in today's climate. The sooner your administrators, principals particularly, understand this, the more receptive they will be to proper planning and the easier it will be for a perceptive school manager to help them deal with disaster when it comes.

Now that you've talked to your own people and gotten them to cooperate, do something too many districts overlook: talk with the police candidly and fairly. Ask their help. This is a badly overlooked area because, it seems, educators spend too much time looking down their professional noses at the tradespeople of law enforcement.

Nothing could be less smart. Many cities and counties have ride-along programs where citizens may accompany police on their patrols. If a few principals, teachers, and, Lord knows, some of those guidance counselors, could be persuaded to ride an evening or midnight tour with the police in the neighborhoods from where their children come, some eyes would be opened. It is sadly true that the cop on patrol may know more about some of our children—their positive sides and their human needs—than the counselors, teachers, and principals who are now being paid not only to know the same thing, but to act on that knowledge.

So, don't be too proud to talk to cops. Cops don't want to take over education. They have enough problems. But they are willing to help. They will make security checks of school buildings to point out unsafe areas. They probably know a good bit about who is pushing or using hard or soft drugs and where. Get their advice. Establish your communications with them before the needs of crisis arrive. Have a high-ranking contact in the police department so you can decide who will make what statement to whom after the incident happens. But do not expect the police to ignore their jobs, or to violate their oaths. School managers must expect to cooperate with police even if it means prosecuting staff or students. Indeed, failure of a school manager to report overt criminal activity may make him an accessory, and although prosecution of the manager is unlikely, such a cover-up attitude does nothing to help public relations.

The degree to which police are involved depends on a variety of factors; the size of the school or school district and the seriousness of the problem.

Between 1974 and 1976 for example, the Chicago Police Department made more than 560 school-related felony drug arrests.[5] These were based primarily on the use of youthful looking male and female police officers in undercover roles as students. One case involved seizure of two pounds of PCP (phencyclidine, an animal tranquilizer which can be used by humans as an hallucinogen), which was the largest such seizure made in the United States up until that time. The street value of the drug in that case was $2 million.

It is obvious that this program alone has not made the Chicago schools totally secure, nor has it restored to that school system a positive posture in the minds of the public. Yet it should be obvious that an untold number of children have been spared a deleterious experience with drugs because of the arrests made by police in cooperation with school officials.

Conversely, raid after raid made with general public support as a police effort to break up promiscuous use of marijuana in the affluent bedroom community of Montgomery County, Maryland in the winter of 1978–79 led to frequent street confrontations in proximity of the schools between police and students. A subjective analysis indicated that this stemmed partly from the fact that school officials did not vigorously support the police and that students had become so accustomed to using marijuana

---

[5] Annual reports, Chicago Police Department, 1974–76.

whenever and wherever they wished that they felt such practice did not warrant arrest.

A study by W. G. Katsenmeyer and James E. Surratt (*Phi Delta Kappan*, November 1975) gave some idea of the scope of the issue: nearly 28 percent of school districts with over 10,000 students in enrollment were using undercover agents for police work, and 8 percent were even using watchdogs for building security at night.[6]

The study concludes that, while police services in general have been beneficial in the opinion of both superintendents of schools and chiefs of police responding to the survey, only one-fourth of both groups feel police patrols in the halls of schools are desirable—an apparent indication that neither group wants to become actively engaged in the work of the other except under the most extreme circumstances.

Common Sense Procedures

Other steps should be underway at this stage of planning and, although they all have PR implications, few are apt to be under direct PR control. (Name tags for all employees? Sign-in requirements for all visitors to school property? Sensitivity training for teachers AND pupils if desegregation orders or other social revisions are likely which may lead to or exacerbate problems of crime and discipline.)

It is now time to do two relatively ticklish things in the planning process: moving quietly to involve appropriate parent groups—if this has not already been done—and establishing your ground rules with the news media.

The boards or executive committees of your district-wide parents' organizations should be kept informed that you are making contingency plans. Emphasis should be on keeping a low profile, but parents should be reminded that the primary responsibility for the attitude a child brings to school comes from the home.

Principals, in messages to the parent, should stress at the individual school level parental responsibility for attitudes and actions by pupils. Suspension and expulsion rules should be reviewed internally for conformance with the latest court decisions and both parents and pupils should be informed of these.

Media Responsibility: Yours and Theirs

Media contacts should be made above the reportorial level. Most news personnel will appreciate your candor and work with you. They will

---

[6] Katzenmeyer was professor of education and associate dean, graduate school, Duke University and Surratt was superintendent of schools in Goldsboro, North Carolina.

recognize that your planning is an effort to be fair to everyone. Your contact should be at the level of city editor, news editor, or the like, because, when your incident happens, the reporter assigned probably won't be your friendly neighborhood education writer. What you and your principals are apt to encounter is a hard-nosed police reporter who does not know you, your principals, or anyone else in the educational establishment. That's why you need an advance understanding at the management level. Your contacts should be in several areas.

Radio is your first priority. A radio station that broadcasts a spurious report of racial disorder, a shooting, or a knifing at a school can touch off parental panic. Conversely, there are times, a bus accident, for example, when you will want to get to the radio as rapidly as possible with the number of the bus involved and the school to which it was traveling. This may further alarm parents who have children on that bus, but it will put at ease the thousands of other parents whose children are also traveling on buses.

You must remember, however, that for radio and, to a lesser extent, for television, there is a deadline every minute. The arrangement which has worked best in the author's experience has been this: radio reporters who receive a citizen's call, or who pick up a police call to a school which they think involves violence, called the director of public information for the schools immediately. An obvious prerequisite was that the director had to be always available, or at least reachable, within a matter of minutes.

Upon contact, the director had ten to twenty minutes in which to confirm or deny the incident, or gain enough facts to put it in perspective. If a denial is warranted the radio stations do not broadcast the spurious incident report that they have received. If an incident has occurred, however, everything possible has to be done to see that the stations, and other media, get rapid, accurate information. Frequently this process determines that what has been reported as a major incident is in reality a routine student fight and the media quickly lose interest.

Never let a radio station down on this agreement.

For the print media, the same level of discussion and the same candor are necessary. Here are some points all parties need to understand:

1. An incident in a school will probably involve a violation of law. The police are in charge of crime scenes and crime sites. Statements involving evidence or potential testimony should be cleared through the police. Photographers should not be allowed to a crime scene without prior police agreement, but the media need to know the proper school manager will help them get photos of some type just as soon as possible.

2. Educational personnel who have knowledge of an incident should be told that they do not have to make a statement individually or collectively to the media unless they wish to do so.

3. Reporters should not be allowed to interview pupils on school property about an incident, particularly when the pupils are very young. Conversely, school managers must not attempt to interfere with news media attempts to interview anyone, pupil or otherwise, once they have left the control and responsibility of the school.

4. Make sure all school personnel understand that information in a pupil's cumulative record is not available to the press or to anyone else without the knowledge and consent of the parent or guardian or that of the pupil himself if he is eighteen or older. Most school districts can safely take this to mean, however, that basic information on a record card can be made available (name, address, grade in which enrolled, and age).

5. *Do not* release any information about an individual pupil's injury or death to the media until the parents or guardians have been notified.

Leave speculation about arrests to the cops. Let the hospitals give out information on the condition of victims.

And, above all, *make sure the director of public information gets the word as soon as an incident occurs.* There is no way the director can serve either the schools or the media if he is the last to know (or even the twentieth, tenth, or fifth, for that matter).

Although all this preparation, and the publicity which results from a major incident, may make it appear the press is out to get the schools in this area, it just isn't so. In one school system of personal acquaintance which felt itself assaulted by the media a study showed that fewer than 2 percent of the 750 calls to schools answered by police in a single year were ever reported by the media.[7]

Survival is not Security

O.K., your district has survived its first incident (shooting, mugging, armed robbery) with a public impact that varies with the size of the district and the media which serve it.

Now is no time to let up. Immediately, go over what took place and how school managers responded to it.

Did the principal remember to see that the director of public information was the first or second person notified, either before or after the superintendent? Were board members called immediately if warranted so they would not have to get their first report from the radio? What informa-

---

[7] As reported by Jack Fulton, director of public safety, Richmond, Virginia, in remarks to a meeting of the schools' department of instructional support services, 1976.

tion was released? When? Too soon for the rights of the individuals and the schools or too late for the rights of the media?

Could the incident have been prevented? And once it has occurred, what can be salvaged from it? Increased parental support? Better security? Here are two actual examples; one in which an incident was prevented, another in which something was salvaged.

One of the most important things to remember in the PR planning for school violence is that school management will never know the things good planning may have prevented. And because this is true, critics of planning for negative events may feel the whole thing was unnecessary, just because of this success. Here's one to prove them wrong.

Early in the 1974–75 school year, several incidents of rape and attempted rape against pupils and staff took place in a medium-sized urban school district. Some occurred during lunch hours, but others took place after school.

A security director at a neighboring college, concerned over what he had read about these incidents, volunteered to prepare a security manual which we ultimately distributed to all our personnel.[8]

Only a few days later, two female teachers at a high school were working after school in a classroom. One left to go to the office for more materials. She had just entered the office and, following the new security instructions, she switched on the office intercom to listen in on the classroom she had just left. The intercom had barely warmed up, when she heard a cry and sounds of a struggle. Other teachers were alerted, ran to the classroom and an armed, would-be rapist was captured.

What could have been another tragic event was turned into a narrow escape and an apprehension, because (1) there had been planning and (2) the information got to the people who needed it. The publicity was considerably more favorable than if the rapist had succeeded.

The second example of an act of violence was one from which something positive was salvaged—recognition, widely disseminated by the media, that children do care about one another and so do many adults.

Laurie Corbin was a white child bused from an area of strong resistance to busing into an 80 percent black school in all black neighborhood. She and her classmates were going out to play on the school ground one afternoon when she was struck in the head by a .22 caliber bullet fired by a black teenager from a home a short distance away.

The assailant claimed that he had been firing at pigeons, but the critical injury to Laurie Corbin was perceived by the majority of whites as

---

[8] "A Manual of Guidelines for Safe and Secure Living in the Richmond Public Schools," by Hulon L. Willis, Jr. of Virginia State College, 1975 (photocopied; uncopyrighted).

the disastrous result of sending their children into a high-crime, black neighborhood.

Media coverage of the incident was extensive, but generally accurate. Laurie was hospitalized for weeks but recovered almost completely from her wound. As the school year neared its end, she expressed the wish to return to visit her class.

After much soul-searching, the school managers involved decided to notify the media of the visit, but only on the day it was to occur. Laurie and her family had previously proved receptive to the media and had granted several interviews. It was felt (1) that her visit would be found out, even if it was after the fact, although (2) notification to the media too far in advance might turn the visit into a circus.

The resulting photographs, the tears, compassion, and concern which were reflected in the coverage of Laurie's return to the classroom at least took some of the edge off the tragedy.

It is never pleasant to have to think on and plan for the negatives in life. But to an increasing degree schools have lost their special isolation in the community. On balance, much of this is good. Yet when the society of which we are so much a part tolerates violence—when it does not openly condone it—the schools cannot escape forever.

Many of the factors which have contributed to the rising level of minor misbehavior and major crime in the public schools, however, have *not* come just from forces outside the school which are beyond the ability and the responsibility of school managers to control. The tactic of blaming student discipline problems on others is one which may be naturally attractive to the harassed school administrator; in sum, however, it just doesn't wash, at least not all the time.

One of the contributions to major problems is simply *size*. Approximately twenty years ago, many educators, particularly those in urban areas, became enamored with something called the educational park. Simply stated, the idea was to have schools in clusters in proximity. Size was considered advantageous and, in a sense, it was. The more students who could be packaged into a unit or a "park," the greater the savings. There would be one high school science department of adequate size to serve a high school of three thousand or more. Far easier, went the reasoning, to do it this way than to have three or maybe six high schools in each of which there was demand for the major sciences and perhaps some of the minor ones as well.

The trouble was, of course, that the personal attention that adolescents not only demand, when they recognize it, but require whether they know it or not, was lost in all this educational euphoria. Generations of teachers and principals have survived, and in the process helped not only their schools but individual children as well, by looking at an incoming roster and recognizing a new arrival as a sibling of a dear departed student whose purpose in education was to raise happy hell in minor moments; refine his skills of robbery, theft, mugging, or worse at other times.

Of course, some will cry, this is guilt by association; this singling out of one name, one child, for special surveillance and/or attention simply because of the misbegotten behavior and talents of an elder sibling. Not necessarily.

It is a wise homeowner who watches a new puppy in the cynical, time-and-experience-proven belief that new puppies will pee on the rug. There are exceptions. A few puppies seem to be born toilet-trained. But it is an essence of puppies, just as it is an essence of certain children from other families, that until contained and controlled, they cannot fulfill their own potential and are unable or unwilling to allow others to do so either.

Such attention is not apt to take place as well in large schools (elementaries with over 500 pupils or secondaries with more than 1,000), at least not right from the start of the school year. And children, like puppies, can become justifiably confused if they are punished in October for conduct that was ignored or not even perceived the month before.

Prevent Your Troubles Now

So far, our discussion has dealt in statistics and in case histories. Yet in the moments between incidents and crises, part of the planning which must be made should still emphasize the aspect of prevention. In this regard, the school manager with an intense awareness and concern for the public relations effects of school violence must see his or her posture with considerable realism. For example, no reputable surgeon likes to inflict a mastectomy on a woman. But under certain circumstances where cancer is invasive, the surgeon may feel that he has no choice but to act in a professional, but radical manner to save the body of the patient at the expense of a diseased appendage. Yet even while he cuts, he should have a committed hope that a less radical cure for the disease may be found or that, ideally, prevention may keep the unwanted incursion from ever becoming a reality.

Educational managers who hold tenaciously to the hallucination that there is no such thing as a bad child, or that any form of behavior or "acting out," as it is sometimes ridiculously called, is justified as a form of self-expression or individual rights are digging a public relations pit from which neither they nor their schools can expect to emerge.

It must be recognized that minority children in particular and those from urban areas where a high degree of mobility discourages the establishment of positive, directive guidance and relationship with worthy authority are prime causal factors in school disorder. Yet even while excluding these young people, when that becomes necessary to prevent a full-scale criminal outbreak, the educational manager cannot afford to become hopelessly prejudiced or convinced that study of the problem can never lead to a resolution. Many of the children who are most prone to serious discipline problems or criminal misconduct are products of homes and environments that breed, condition, and/or reinforce the negative behavior they bring to school. The radical conservative would like to think this is so much social worker sop. Nevertheless, it is true. School managers must continue their struggle to establish a safe, positive learning environment even while knowing all the work they do with a child during the day may be undone at night in the home or in the community. In that sense, they are not unlike a physician who treats a patient with bacterial pneumonia with a penicillin regimen each day all the while knowing that the patient will be sleeping on the wet ground each night. It is difficult to continue in the face of such odds and such behavior, and sometimes the only consolation is the hope that, if the patient under treatment is lost, another will at least see what was attempted and try to take a cooperative attitude toward his own resolution.

This condition just outlined is most difficult and, perhaps, insoluble under current social conditions. Our society has flirted with such things as mandatory sterilization for the prolific, unmarried welfare mother whose children are without question a drain on social resources and a non-productive burden to the schools. Yet the idea of compulsory sterilization is anathema not just to certain religious groups but to those who fear out of a humanistic and libertarian concern that the concentration of such power in the judiciary, or the medical, or governmental bureaucracy may lead to a greater personal and social horror.

There may, of course, be some merit in an Americanized form of the "kibbutz," where children from the crib on into school age are fed, loved, and cared for in such a way as to free their parents to work and also to minimize some of the criminal, or negative social and parental forces and effects to which they would otherwise be exposed. Such a role on the part of legitimate day-care centers and churches which seek to practice the positive discipline of Christian love rather than the parochial preaching of the proselyte may represent the best compromise.

At the same time, educational managers who wrestle with the problem of serious delinquency and crime among their pupils must further recognize that the overt crime which their constituencies practice is just as socially acceptable in certain parts of the American social structure as ripping off the insurance company, padding the expense account, or cheating on taxes is in other segments. Something is indeed wrong with a value system that sends a person to jail for stealing, or even for robbery, of a few thousand dollars worth of substance when governmental officials, businesses, and industries may kill, cripple, or extort the public in the name of free enterprise, price fixing, shoddy merchandise, or other practices which have the effect of stealing even more in value and in life than the welfare thug who sticks up the mom and pop grocery with a Saturday night special.

It is sad but true that in the United States stealing is socially accepted as long as it does not constitute outright robbery or burglary, and that killing via air, water, or food pollution can be tolerated in the name of the profit motive. There is a socially accepted way to do almost anything in the United States, killing and stealing included, and this is not lost upon those segments of the public school problem who cause the most disruption and discipline problems and bring their overt violence into the corridors and the classrooms. While such behavior cannot, and must not, be tolerated in the slightest degree, its elimination will not solve the problem of criminal misbehavior in the United States. Such behavior is not something the young learn all by themselves.

And whereas many of the welfare families who exist in generation unto generation may not be aware of it, the welfare mentality is not their exclusive territory. The newspaper monopolies which receive favored postal rates to move their bulky editions; industries with protective tariffs; farmers with crop supports and subsidies for not planting needed foodstuffs are just as much tied to the welfare payout of the tax dollar as any unwed mother with a brood of urchins in some housing project. The difference is that the wealthy who get welfare do not like it called by its proper name, and, while the mother in the housing project may not be able to see further than her own condition, many of her class know perfectly well that in today's United States the group or individual which isn't drawing some form of welfare is the true minority.

Thus it should not be surprising that those who learn criminal misbehavior in our society learn it from their elders as well as their peers, whether it be corporate chicanery, boosting a stolen car, or shaking down the weak and the young in a high school bathroom. Even more regrettably, however, the school child in the United States is exposed to misbehavior, misconduct, or improper lifestyles not just in the community and in the home, but from their teachers and administrators.

The school manager who turns this head to the alcoholic teacher, or the chronic abuser of sick leave, or who accepts favors from vendors in return for steering the purchasing department toward certain wares does not operate in a vacuum. Children and their parents are astute; in the case of the children, sadly and prematurely so. The double standard of adult behavior is not lost on the child.

It may seem old-fashioned, archaic, even anachronistic or, as this generation says, whatever, but the teacher who comes to school with an obvious hangover does little to encourage children not to abuse drugs. Even in such things as dress and lifestyle, a teacher can still have an influence not just on the attitudes, but on the behaviors of his children. This is one instance in which small children may be more immune than the larger ones, for aberrations in dress and lifestyle may not be immediately apparent to them.

Teachers who dress as if they have no respect for themselves, their positions, or their responsibility provide little in the way of example for the child to do otherwise. Teachers who live constantly beyond their means (and this is no advocacy of penury or poverty for teachers) encourage a lack of fiscal responsibility and self-discipline in the child.

The element of instant gratification—of "I want" and "I want now"—can contribute much to the atmosphere that any type of behavior, including the criminal, is acceptable as long as two criteria result: (1) the gratification is met and (2) you don't get caught.

It is not herein proposed that the educational manager can eliminate all misbehavior or crime from his school by adopting an asceticism, no matter how valid. Nor is it proposed that a type of religiosity be imposed on the schools. But children are susceptible to example. And as obvious as that statement may seem, school management seems to have forgotten the degree to which it can create a climate in which anything goes or at least wherein the student feels subjected to a double standard if certain types of behavior are forbidden to him.

Of course, in many school districts, particularly those of a small or rural nature, teachers do not have the whim to behave in any manner they choose. However, there does seem to be a relaxation of the requirements for at least an adequate, if not a superior, lifestyle, the reasons for which will be explored briefly in just a bit.

Yet, in personal experience, some tragic examples have been observed which surely contributed to a deterioration of behavior. In one instance, the writer was the recipient of a call from a parent who charged that an employee of the school system in which the writer was then working was a major pusher of narcotics. Investigation personally conducted determined that the employee was indeed involved with children, and that he had recently been arrested in New York City and charged with possession and attempted delivery of a large supply of cocaine. Admittedly, none of the information provided would stand up in court as it was received. Yet the matter was never investigated at a level which could have determined at least the facts of the arrest and the employee remained on the job, working with children, until he chose to resign.

In another instance, a radio reporter disclosed that a heroin user of her acquaintance had been employed with a group of emotionally disturbed youths. Again, hearsay and libel were potentially involved, but an investigation that would have protected the rights of the accused could have been conducted that would also have protected the welfare of children. None was, and the accused remained an employee until he too resigned.

The concern for the rights of defendants, as well as the militancy of unions and the fear of educational managers that their own indiscretions might be disclosed as far as protection of pupils is concerned all encourages the lack of proper action in cases such as these. We thus come to another example of how schools have damaged not only their public relations, but their effectiveness, in their concern over the rosiness of their image as opposed to the difficult and demanding task of discharging reality.

This glibness, this blurring of the line between what is, what might be, and what is perceived, causes the schools endless amounts of trouble and is, in this judgment, a major part of the undisclosed problems of pupil behavior. It also contributes more directly and specifically in that a teacher can hardly be dismissed any longer for what once was (and still is, in the eyes of some) clearly a case of moral turpitude, such as the open admission of homosexuality. Yet, as the California referendum of 1978 showed (Proposition 6), most voters do not consider homosexuality grounds for disqualification of teachers. Such an attitude must surely be confusing not just to parents, but to their children as well.

This confusion is represented, as Dr. Chester Nolte, professor emeritus of education at the University of Denver, has declared, by the fact that out of school lifestyle, no matter how weird, bizarre, or even criminal, seldom leads to dismissal any longer or, even if it could, school boards and school managers are wearily concluding that the almost inevitable legal confrontation is hardly worth the effort, even if they should win.[9]

Adults and Majorities Have Rights Too

The problem of legalities as a contribution to the issue of pupil behavior is by no means a minimal one, however. The issue of busing for desegregation is classic. The admirable, laudable, and perfectly legal intent of righting the discriminatory wrongs of history against a new generation that, *post facto*, has not experienced them, may nevertheless make things worse for everyone.

In our society, as has been previously stated, pure democracy does not work, as indeed it should not, for that exercise, in its most basic form, tends to legitimize any insult or affront that a majority chooses to inflict on a minority. On the one hand, as the polls show, the public is clamoring for safety and sanity in the operation of their public schools. Given the facts uncovered by the National Institute of Education study previously cited— facts which certainly come as no surprise—the public has every right to want action. Conversely, a case can be made that most school managers have been intimidated by recent court decisions and by the apologists for pupil misbehavior under the guise of individual rights.

One of the best foundations, it would seem, is to try to begin from a basis of common sense. A school manager who takes this tack may be

---

[9] Remarks made while serving on a panel with the author, San Francisco conference of the National School Boards Association, November 1978.

surprised at the degree to which both the public and the courts support him or her. Here are some approaches:

1. From day one of a child's entry into school, school management should be reminding parents that the responsibility for the behavior of children lies first with the home.
2. While issuing such reminders, school managers must take care that the anarchy of the "open" classroom and a disorganized, nondirective curriculum does not create a climate for misbehavior at the school which the school contends it is trying to avoid. A teacher must show a child right from the start that *she loves the child enough* to refuse to allow him to behave in a way inimical to his welfare or that of others.
3. There is a legitimate role police can play in ensuring security at the schools.
4. The attitudes and practices of faculty can contribute to or detract from their own security and that of their children.
5. The exercise of individual rights by pupils—or staff—does not include the right to break the law. As simple as this seems, it is the practice of overlooking seemingly isolated and childish misdemeanors which helps create that climate in which serious misbehavior and felonious conduct can flourish.
6. Use an instinct for what is right, recognizing that prudent conduct, which courts tend to appreciate, does not permit the individual to trample on the rights of the majority any more than the majority has the right, in the guise of "democratic" conduct to overrun the constitutional guarantees of any minority.

The issue of discipline in the schools is by no means resolved, and school managers who sit back and wait for some court decision, action by the local council or the school board to clear the way for them are simply abdicating a major responsibility and ensuring that a grumbling public will soon be after them en masse. Each issue must be decided on its merits and those merits must be consistent with established, lawful policy equitably applied from one child to the next. It is when this is not done that a school manager stands the greatest chance of getting in legal trouble. The manager should recognize that many of the organizations which trumpet loudest in behalf of so-called rights of children are not acting illegally nor are they always in error. The American Civil Liberties Union, for example, has produced a handbook, *The Rights of Students* by Alan H. Levine and Eve Cary (Avon Books, 1977, Revised), which demonstrates this concern. Although it may very well encourage and protect types of student conduct which traditional school managers oppose and which, when exercised, make school management much more difficult, it is absolutely necessary that school management be familiar with the cases cited therein so as to understand—and defend—the role of the school manager in operating a lawful, stable school for the benefit of all.

Corporal Punishment?

One of the issues that has caused major public relations furors in the area of school discipline, and has attracted the attention of the American Civil Liberties Union and others of that persuasion, is the matter of corporal punishment.

That once-standard means of discipline, particularly among small children, has over the last thirty years or so drawn nervous frowns from the social worker-psychologist set which has infiltrated the school systems of North America under the guise of providing some of the many "supportive" services for children which have almost forced the schools into bankruptcy.

The use of such punishment is generally lawful, however, although any school district which does not have the practice established in writing with legal support would be unwise to encourage its use without appropriate guidelines. Where most school district employees get into trouble is in the use of *excessive* punishment of this nature. It should be remembered that, even where corporal punishment has judicial standing, there is no warrant extended for its excessive use. In others words, a teacher who may be safe under the law from conviction on an assault charge for the use of *reasonable* corporal punishment, may find himself subject to both criminal *and* civil action if his use of such punishment is judged excessive.

In point of experience and fact, corporal punishment seems of little practical value today, at least in the schools. Larger youth who may need it most are apt to react to attempts to administer it with a degree of physical violence that will make the confrontation worse. For small children who need it, the punishment is best administered by the home and the unacceptable behavior accompanied by changes in the home's attitude toward its responsibility to prepare the child. At either level, exclusion of the child from school—permanently in the case of older youth—may be a more sensible solution.

Such exclusion, whether in the form of suspension or expulsion, must follow prescribed forms of due process. And though this may be an aggravation, school managers must tolerate it until the courts restore a more reasonable use of their authority to them. In the case of permanent expulsion, however, school managers should remember that in most cases this authority is reserved to the school board and should not attempt to exercise it themselves lest they be subjected to a civil action brought on by their own ignorance or excess.

As a general rule in the matter of student discipline, school managers should be advised that the freedom of expression guaranteed in the First Amendment to the Constitution is a freedom that they are obligated to guarantee to their children unless the exercise thereof becomes demonstrably disruptive. Further, school managers should realize that attempts to legislate the dress or hair of pupils are generally illegal as well as unwise.

Other decisions which have an impact on disruptions of the school process, particularly where those disruptions are more perceived by the administrator than realities in the eyes of the law, concern such things as marriage of pupils (almost certainly permissible) and attempting to withold grades and diplomas as punishment (almost certainly impermissible as long as work has been done) and searches of students' persons or property (which varies depending on the circumstances).

Criminal conduct by and among pupils is a hideous cancer on the hide of public education. However, not everything the school manager perceives as misconduct, or even illegality, can withstand the test of the courts.

The clash of class and culture and race must be brought under control early in the school experience and never allowed to gain the upper hand again. Overt criminal behavior must be brought to a stop through aggressive police action if necessary and through the permanent expulsion of those who would endanger the lives, property, and education of others. A school manager should make no more excuse for taking these steps than a surgeon should apologize for eliminating from the operating room conditions which endanger the health of the patient, keeping in mind, of course, that the civil rights of students have not, as yet, been extended to bacteria.

Perhaps some day an organic cause can be found for more human criminality than those obvious few cases which have already been identified. Some work is being done in this area, but the evidence is far from conclusive, and attempts to link the exact science of biochemical conditions in the brain with the inexact sociology of behavior must go quite a ways yet before they can be included as yet another rationalization with which the harassed teacher and school administrator have to deal.

What school managers must remember is that fairness is their criterion and that tempering that criterion, because of class, culture, or poverty, real or imagined, must be done with great care. We have seen in the schools already the tragedy which results from trying to excuse the criminal conduct and misbehavior of segments of the current generation because of the condition of servitude in which their ancestors may have come to North America. It has been a tragic mistake to make this exemption, a tragedy which may have hurt the current minority generation most of all. This, of course, is not the sole solution to the problem of crime in the schools. Yet even given the increasing disrepute in which our legal system and our courts are sometimes held, the burden for operating a safe, sane system still rests primarily on the school managers and the fact that the rest of society has succumbed to an infatuation with criminality and generalized misbehavior does not relieve them of their ethical, moral, and legal responsibility to do what they can to impose discipline, while nurturing self-discipline, in the continuing interest of the children in their care and in the future of the United States.

CHAPTER 11

Things That Work and Things That Don't

Throughout this book places of particular peril in public relations for those who must manage today's public schools have been pointed out. Most of these points, however, have dealt with pitfalls that emerge from shoddy thinking or poor philosophy. The nuts-and-bolts of a sensible public relations program, however, involve *tactics* as well as strategy, and goes far beyond the relations with the news media that have been described.

Many of those tactics are basic, so much so that they are occasionally overlooked in the planning and implementing of a school public relations program. Most of the tactics which will be suggested have been used by the author with the results which are indicated. It should be noted that the tactics which are suggested are ways both school personnel and concerned laypeople can approach public relations for the schools. The practice of successful school public relations does not involve just the schools themselves, nor is that practice restricted to school people. Parents and other laypeople have a legitimate interest in school public relations and can make substantial contributions thereto. But they cannot do so unless they are informed and, although ideally the parents should take the trouble to inform themselves, in practice the problem descends on the schools themselves.

One of the ways parental groups can help is to assess the effectiveness of a school public relations program. For example, it is not inappropriate for the district-wide PTA or other laypeople's group to ask to be placed on the mailing list for such releases as the district's management is mailing to the media. Where errors in names, titles, dates, spelling, and grammar are common, it may be that a lay group can point out the failing more quickly and effectively than anyone else. (In reviewing releases from the community and governmental relations office of a very "image" oriented district, for example, at least 20 percent were found to have some type of error. The media is frequently suspicious of government-originated press releases in the first place, and is apt to distrust them all the more when they contain obvious errors. The result is a sort of guilt by association, which presumes that because the topic is erroneously presented, there is no news value in the topic itself. A positive prospect for school public relations often is missed as a result.) Where a school district is sending out good releases to the news media and to parent groups—and the releases are not being used—inquiries as to why are more effective if they come from the parents than from the schools. Reporters are tired of hearing public employees complain of lack of coverage. When the same complaint comes from informed citizens, however, it can bring better results.

What Are You Trying to Do?

Before any technique, device, or practice is put into effect in a school public relations program, a key question needs to be asked—and asked, and asked. That question is simple: What am I trying to achieve and from whom am I attempting to get action and support? Many, many school public relations programs bog down because this key question is never asked by those who are formulating a school PR approach.

Which brings us to American advertising—

There isn't very much that is good that can be said about the American advertising business, dedicated as it is to making consumers buy that which they do not want and do not need, frequently to the detriment of their health, welfare, economic condition, and simple sanity. But it must be said that the American advertising industry frequently knows how to succeed on behalf of its clients. The thinking behind this success needs to be examined by those who would engage in the successful practice of school public relations, but with a commitment that commercial advertising usually does not have: an awareness of ethical responsibility.

Some of the points which school public relations planning needs to understand, and which can hardly be stated better, come from John Caples, a successful advertising executive for more than fifty years. Writing in a series of advertisements designed to promote *The Wall Street Journal,* here's some of what he had to say:

Simple words are powerful words. Even the best educated people don't resent simple words. But they're the only words many people understand. Write to your barber or mechanic or elevator operator.[1]

Comment: But how often do school publications seem to be written only for those who speak a foreign language, that of the educationist. The barber, mechanic, and elevator operator are the people who pay school taxes, and who furnish the children for the public schools. They are not likely to be able to opt for private schools if they are dissatisfied with the public schools, so in that sense, they represent a foundation which will continue to furnish children to the public schools. At the same time, however, they are not likely to understand what is said to them in a vague sort of pedaguese, although they are almost certain to realize that they are being talked down to or patronized. And they are certain to resent that.

Caples:

Get to the point. . . . Don't stop by just telling people the benefits your product offers. Tell them what they'll miss if they don't buy it. If you have an important point to make, make it three times: in the beginning, the middle, the end. . . .

Comment: This is probably overlooked as much as any single thing in a failing program of school public relations. Yet it takes thought to answer the question directly and to determine what the point is. The question is simply this: What benefits do I as a taxpayer get for my children from the public schools and what would they miss if they didn't have them? As stated earlier, schools have become so confused as to what it is they should be doing that they may have allowed parents to lose sight of just what it is they are doing and how *specifically* this benefits the child. Remind them (although you may have to change your curriculum and your goals before you have anything worth reminding them about). Remind them again. And again.

Caples:

Be honest. Tell your client what works and what doesn't. Stop worrying about commissions. If your advertising works, your client will stay with you, and his budget will grow. Admit when the client is right. Be strong enough to fight with him when he is wrong. But don't argue to the point of making

---

[1] *The New York Times*, March 31, 1978. The mere fact that *The Wall Street Journal* would pay for an advertisement in another New York newspaper to tell its own story is an interesting use of the media and public relations consciousness.

an open break. The memory of the break lingers long after the reason for the argument has been forgotten. Be flexible enough to try it the client's way. He may just have an idea that'll make you a hero.

Comment: Make a few substitutions for certain words in this advice, and it fits right in with what a good school public relations program must have. It must begin with absolute honesty. Substitute *taxpayers* or *parents* for client and you have put the entire matter of school public relations into perspective as it should exist between the schools and the taxpayer. After all, school managers are to the taxpayer what the ad agency is to the client. The managers have been employed to use their particular training and expertise to do a particular job that the client (parent) wants and needs. Some school districts have lost sight of this, and it shows in the breakdown, or absence, of their public relations program.

From Negative to Positive

In adopting a successful school public relations program, educational management must recognize its responsibility to emphasize the positive but not to deny the negative. Sometimes, one can be used to offset the other.

I once was faced with convincing a group of middle-class parents that a high school in our system to which their children were being involuntarily assigned could do the job they wanted done. This group of parents was smart, and had done its homework, and because they had, they were not going to be put off with vague, non-specific answers.

These parents expected their children to go to college. Therefore, they wanted—and had a right to want—decent academic preparation. But the school to which their children were to be assigned sent only 25 percent of its graduates to college; the school which they otherwise would have attended sent 90 percent.

The parents were concerned, legitimately concerned. The answer was found in two ways: First, I checked to see what colleges the 25 percent were accepted by. In many cases, the colleges were the same and, overall, the caliber compared favorably with the caliber of the colleges attended by those students from the school that sent 90 percent of its graduates to college. That was one point.

The second point, and the most telling one, was the discovery that 99 percent of the students in the college preparatory program at the school that sent 25 percent of its graduates to college actually went on to college, *whereas* only 85 percent of those in the college preparatory program at the school that sent 90 percent of its graduates to college actually went to college.

Confusing? Let's put it this way, using round numbers. Ninety percent went to college from one graduating class. But 97 percent of the graduates of that school had been in the college prep program. Twenty-five percent went to college from the other graduating class, and practically 25 percent had been in the college prep program. Thus it was easy to show that the child who went to the school which sent 25 percent to college could get into the same colleges and, further, had a better chance of being prepared for her or his future. After all, what happened to the seven percent of the students in the 90 percent school who had been prepared for college, but who didn't go? The answer was obvious: they did not have a marketable skill and were thus faced with having to retrain through a vocational or business education to compete in the job market.

This statistical technique is very effective with the middle class, particularly in school systems where the percentage of students going on to college is not thought to be particularly high. A simple folder printed for only a few cents a copy can emphasize this approach. The cover should ask a question such as "Where are Last Year's Graduates of Our School System, Anyway?" Inside, the answer is given: "Here They Are"; then list by states the names of all the colleges and universities in the country where the graduates are enrolled. Even if there is only one graduate per institution, the number of colleges which can be legitimately and honestly listed is impressive, and the distribution of such a folder at PTA meetings, in neighborhood barber and beauty shops, and in speeches to civic organizations and church groups is a very effective technique. Brochures of this kind can even be sent out with utility bills in envelopes on which postage has to be paid anyway.

The outlets to which printed material such as this should be sent are substantial, and none should be overlooked. The inclusion of beauty parlors and barber shops is a must, because it is here that neighborhood information is most likely to be exchanged, and where opinions and impressions about the public schools harden into attitudes. Such printed material should also be included in kits of printed matter prepared for the community's real estate firms and chamber of commerce. Both get frequent inquiries from persons who will be moving into the area, and whose concern is apt to fall as much on the quality and offerings of the schools as it is on the availability of housing.

A particularly effective variation can be used if the cooperation of the chamber of commerce and the real estate agencies can be obtained. That involves obtaining names and addresses of prospective newcomers and sending them a personal invitation from the superintendent to visit in the school district, and to receive an escorted tour, should they so desire.

If this seems to be going quite a ways, it is nothing less than what a real estate firm itself would do in a competitive market to reach and sell a customer its wares. This indeed is a

KEY CONCERN FOR SCHOOL PR: *Public school districts are in a fight for survival in the face of declining enrollment. They cannot allow prospective "consumers" (parents with school age children) to pass up enrolling their children and choose a different district for want of accurate information and a sincere welcome.*

This key concern is particularly apt for township, small city, and urban school districts which are surrounded by suburbs which are automatically attractive to many new arrivals in the middle class. Obviously, the superintendent of schools may not be able to personally greet every prospective resident of his district, but he can ensure that someone from his staff can do so, even if it is the building principal (a person to whom any newcomer should be referred in any event so that the newcomer can see first hand the conditions and instruction extant in the school).

Make Principals Help Themselves

It is a good idea, in fact, to insist that all principals have a specific, on-going public relations program of their own. This program can be designed with consultative help from the central administration, but should be able to function independently nonetheless. Just as the superintendent does not expect to be called into the resolution of day-to-day administrative problems in any particular school, neither should he have to look over the principal's shoulder each day to make sure a public relations program is operating smoothly on the individual school level. At the very least, each school should have an economically produced handbook for pupils and parents giving major policies of the district and specific information about the specific school and its program.

Printed materials, as was stressed earlier, must be concise and correct. Newsletters, for example, must be reviewed carefully. Depending on the size of the school district, these can be produced by mimeograph, photocopying, or offset printing, and directed to various audiences. However, many of these which have been reviewed here seem to have been prepared without any awareness of time. Events which are listed in the future have already taken place. Programs which the recipient is urged to attend are over and gone. Here is how a typical newsletter might be devised:

Choose your audience. If it is district-wide, make sure the newsletter contains information that will have broad appeal, and not be restricted simply to parents. For example, the newsletter may need to contain an article on the adult education program, including the diverse types of people who enroll. (I was once able to capitalize on this by featuring in such a newsletter an article on a wealthy bank executive, a member of our school board, who was taking a course in small engine repair. He had decided to do so because he was outraged at what it cost to make simple repairs to his household tools and to his lawnmower. His only objection, he wryly admitted, was that his neighbors, all of whom were also executives, wanted to capitalize on his new-found learning to cut their own domestic repair bills.)

An article such as this one would have an appeal to the business, financial, and managerial segments of the community, those with decision-making influence, even though they may not have had children in school for many years.

KEY CONCERN FOR SCHOOL PR: *Any article in a newsletter of wide distribution which shows the readers how the schools are either saving or making money for them through education is bound to have a positive effect.*

Newsletters should include appropriate photographs; a message from the superintendent or board chairman which contains direct, specific, easily understood comments, and specific news of elementary, junior high, and high school achievements. There is nothing wrong in emphasizing problems in such newsletters, as long as the emphasis does not take the form of carping and complaint, but instead states facts simply, indicates what school management is doing to resolve the issue, and tells the public how it can reasonably be expected to help.

Some districts make a point of trying to produce their printed public relations material in printing classes of the industrial arts or technical education program. On the surface, this may seem sensible. In most instances, however, the teaching program cannot be built around production printing, and in most instances also, students are not at the proper stage of training to produce material needed in the quantity desired and still meet the deadlines the PR program requires. The best looking material has no value if it is not distributed on time and to the proper audience. Cosmetics in printing, as in curriculum, are not enough.

In an era of extreme cost-consciousness on the part of the public, any newsletter must provide a service (necessary information) the recipient would not otherwise receive. Extreme care must be taken that the cost of such a production can be justified. School districts that put more emphasis on glossy paper and multiple colors than on content will find that their publications programs boomerang on them in a hurry. One way in which this can happen is for the district—or the individual school—to send its publications by first class mail when they would qualify for bulk mail rates at less than one-fifth the cost of first class. Bulk mail, of course, must be sorted and bundled by zip code and meet other postal requirements, but the savings are substantial and so is the positive public relations effect.

One of the temptations which must be avoided in the publications arm of any school publications program is proliferation. While each school can and should have publications for its constituency in the form of newsletters, comments from the principal, and "glad cards" (notes to parents reporting some particular kindness or accomplishment by their child), a tight rein has to be kept on publications from central administration. As competition for the dollar inceases, each education office will fight harder and harder in an hysterical attempt for recognition, no matter how little justification there may be, until the central administration will appear as a Hydra at war with itself. Distributive education will be shrieking in print of its accomplishments; the arts and music folks will be doing the same; elementary education will be fighting a printing war with secondary to prove its financial needs are geater. The result can be the disruption of any concerted public relations campaign.

This type of behavior is a fairly standard practice in government, but is destructive when the public recognizes it and can destroy internal morale of employees who see a PR program being used for individual advancement or in other improper ways. (I once rejected a request from a supervisor for the printing and mailing at public expense of 1400 Christmas cards. The cards were subsequently ordered by a deputy superintendent of schools.)

Remember: Print Isn't Everything

There are, of course, many successful means for implementing a school public relations program other than the use of printed material. The most common of these is the use of the electronic media. Here are some suggestions, the implementation of which may vary depending on the size of the school district:

1. *Radio.* If the system permits it, schedule regular guests on radio talk shows to answer questions from callers or to discuss topics with the host.

Larger school districts will find that many radio stations welcome either tapes prepared to the station's specifications which can be broadcast as needed or else spot announcements (so-called PSAs or Public Service Announcements which all broadcast media are required by the Federal Communications Commission to include in their schedule). The tapes may feature an interview on an appropriate topic ("How the Budget Is Prepared;" "What Industrial Arts Does for Your Child;" "Adult Education and You"). The list is limited only by time, services, and the scope of your

district. Spot announcements such as those of school board meetings, reminders of parent conference days, or school closings can be pre-recorded
on a Code-A-Phone, or similar device, and may be picked up by radio
stations at their leisure simply by calling the Code-A-Phone number.

2. *Television.* The talk-show format of furnishing guests for interview
or discussion can be followed with television as well as with radio. If your
district's audiovisual department can provide support, your public relations program can furnish local television with PSAs in the form of graph-
ics and other still photos which can carry messages concerning pre-school
registration, or other announcements of appropriate community interest.
Taped PSAs featuring film, music, and other audio will also be used by local
television stations if your facilities can provide them to the station's technical specifications.

In working with either radio or television, however, one should be
aware of this

KEY CONCERN FOR SCHOOL PR: *As opposed to written communications to parents, radio and television messages are indeed "written on
the wind." If your audience does not get the message the first time, it has
no way of knowing when or if it will be repeated. This is the continuing
advantage written communication has over broadcast media.*[2]

---

3. *Slide-tape presentations.* Slide-tape presentations can be pre-
packaged by large districts for showings to civic clubs, PTAs, or other
groups. These are particularly effective when they stick to a single subject
of community interest and are accompanied by a competent speaker who
can answer questions and elaborate on the theme that has been presented.
It should be obvious that this is a valuable small-group technique when the
school district is launching a campaign for a budget.

4. *Speaker's bureaus.* These should be used, where possible, with
the slide-tape presentations mentioned above. A small brochure cross in-
dexed by speaker and topic can be prepared as part of the public relations
program and distributed to program chairs of all civic, fraternal, and religious groups in the community. The brochure will tell recipients how to
get a speaker of their choice on a subject of their choice. Considerable care
must be exercised, however, to make sure that those selected are com-

---

[2] Print has its own special problems too. Photocopying may be quick and handy,
but if more than a couple of hundred copies are needed, offset printing is likely to be
cheaper, particularly if you have a school-related printing facility. Over-runs in any
printing project seem to be a particular problem of government, the managers of whom
seem likely to believe that if 5,000 copies are good, 10,000 are twice as necessary—even if there aren't but 5,000 persons to whom the publication could possibly be
sent.

petent public speakers—a talent which is not found in all administrators. An incompetent description can damage even the most successful program.

Successful PR Is an Attitude, Too

Ultimately, of course, the best school PR is the kind that frequently takes place without appearing to *be* public relations. This involves an attitude and a personal approach, and is absolutely necessary for the small districts, and should be emulated by the large ones, where possible.

It is unrealistic to expect that the superintendent in even a modestly-sized district can personally talk with every patron, every citizen, particularly when the patron or citizen wants it. If the superintendent tries this, he or she will never get anything else done. This does not mean that the tactic has no place. Every superintendent should reserve part of each week for face to face contact with citizens and parents at the lowest level of his or her district's operation. Further, he or she should insist that each administrative member of his or her staff—and teachers too, if possible—do the same.

Prospective politicians know well the absolute necessity for personal contact, with the power brokers in private, and with the prospective voter in public. If they are to make names for themselves, their ideas and programs, they cannot count solely on the media, on their own advertising, brochures, or anything else to tell their story. They have to do it themselves, to the extent that it is physically possible to do so. This means they have to "press the flesh," shake the hands, establish their credibility, and listen and respond to the things people tell them are concerning them.

Politicians, of course, see their jobs as getting elected, building a power base, and letting the latter help take care of making sure that re-re-election follows. In a sense, this is true for the school superintendent as well. And just as the representative to the Congress is poorly advised to rely too greatly on the media or her or his monthly newsletter to maintain communications with her or his constituency, so too should the superintendent recognize this fact. The politicians' constituency is everyone over voting age. She or he establishes cliques of loyal supporters to make sure contact is maintained on a personal level even when she or he can't do so personally. The superintendent must do the same.

As part of any successful school public relations program, a superintendent must keep constantly in mind this

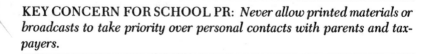

KEY CONCERN FOR SCHOOL PR: *Never allow printed materials or broadcasts to take priority over personal contacts with parents and taxpayers.*

Successful public relations in the realm of personal contact consists frequently of listening, rather than talking. It does not consist of making promises that any idiot knows cannot be fulfilled. However, the successful school manager will make sure he or she does promise specific goals, but only those which can be delivered.

Successful public relations is an attitude, an understanding, and a willingness to accept the responsibility for informed participation in telling the public school story to any individual at any time. The superintendent who makes time in his or her schedule to have coffee with a woman's club in the morning is taking a far more positive step to head off unenlightened cocktail party criticism of his or her schools that night than if he or she just made sure all members of the woman's club were on his or her mailing list.

The school manager thus must:

Have a simple, sound, and sensible program.
Make sure he or she knows where it is going and how.
Have a clear grasp of specific objectives.
Be able to describe those objectives simply and clearly.

Given such a foundation, the techniques of direct mail, speakers' bureaus, and effective use of the audiovisual media can capitalize on the successes of the schools and can marshal support for legitimate needs. Without such a foundation, no school public relations program in the world can succeed, no matter how flashy, how expensive, or how deviously devised.

Some years ago, the president of a dog food company called together all of his employees to try to find a reason for slumping sales. Manager after manager and salesman after salesman all tried to offer an explanation until at last the newest salesman raised his hand. "I know why the sales are down," he said. "People aren't going to buy what the dogs won't eat."

Given that condition, publications can't sell the public schools, either.

Misunderstanding from the Top

For all of the resources at their command, and for all of the responsibilities the public has delegated to them, most superintendents of schools and school boards have no understanding of the role a structured program of public relations can—and cannot—perform for their schools. Unless a particular board has a trained communicator on it, the board and the superintendent will flounder in organizing a public relations campaign and, more important, in understanding what will work and what won't. Most boards and administrators are unwilling to hire competent public relations help and follow its advice. The expectations of top management are thus unrealistic because they are unable to tell the difference between things that work and things that don't.

Alec Benn, who headed his own advertising agency in New York, makes this point quite clearly in his book, *The 27 Most Common Mistakes in Advertising* under the heading, "Most Advertising Fails":

> There is a great conspiracy participated in by advertising agencies, radio and television stations, and networks, advertising consultants, newspapers, magazines and others to mislead corporate management about the effects of advertising. Those who control the purse strings are not told about campaigns costing millions that fail to make any difference in company sales. There was, for example, little publicity about the results of some very entertaining commercials placed by Alka-Seltzer in the early 1970's. Only a few attentive professionals knew that Alka-Seltzer did not increase its share of the market. . . .
>
> The conspiracy could not succeed, however, without the willing cooperation of the corporate managers. Many chief executives get big ego boosts out of their company's advertising.[3]

This is precisely why public education has gotten itself into a public relations fix. Superintendents of schools are more concerned with ego-tripping on the image-making of their programs than with trying to do the two things most guaranteed to create positive public support in today's market: turn out better educated children and cut costs. And no matter how much most educational managers will deny it, this can be done. Most of them, moved into their positions without formal training in business administration, personnel management, public relations, or even the graduate school mastery of an academic discipline, are sadly unqualified to criticize.

Any school manager who can find a way to demonstrate skill in her or his program and cost-reduction without loss of quality or service has a built-in advantage in compiling a list of items out of which to make positive PR.

For example, stressing the fact that all administrators are essentially teachers (just as the Marines always stress that all members of the Corps are first of all riflemen) can have considerable positive public effect as well as raise morale among staff and students. Of course, this means that the administrators (including the superintendent) will have to take off a day a year and fill in in the classroom for a teacher.

Or perhaps a way has been found to cut down on teacher absenteeism, reduce the abuse of sick leave, institute a meritocracy, recycle materials (or retrain people). . . . Any manager who wants to make an effort can compile such a list of things he or she is doing or *should* be doing.

---

[3] Published by American Management Association (1978).

Saving money, retraining (or developing quality), providing *necessary* services, these are the things that work in school PR today.

But even with the crisis concentration on financial problems—a concentration without which most school districts are not going to survive for very long today—there must still be an ongoing commitment to the *proper* use of public relations strategies to deal with both new and old problems which face the schools.

It has become rather outmoded in some districts, for example, to have such an event as *Teacher Appreciation Day*. Done poorly, this smacks of paternalism, the kind a vigilant union is apt to see as something offered in lieu of a deserved pay raise. Done properly, it can improve relations with both public and staff. Such an event can take many forms. One might be to have parent volunteers to take over classes for a period so that the teachers might enjoy coffee and cake together. Such a tactic is almost certain to give the participating parents a more sympathetic understanding of what a teacher faces. And in all likelihood, the first such event of its kind in a community will attract both newspaper and television coverage.

Strategies for Survival

Here are some other examples and ways in which parental contact and involvement are either advantageous or mandatory to the success of a school program:

1. *Home visitation:* A once common phenomenon of behavior by good teachers, home visits have lost fashion as teachers and community live farther apart, as the cost of gasoline increases, as visits to ethnic neighborhoods become dangerous, and as teachers increasingly feel such visits are outside the scope of their contracts. However, particularly when a new school is being opened, or when massive student reassignments are indicated, such visitations, even when they may have to be paid for by the school district as a summer or Saturday event, can more than return the dollars invested.

2. *Use of surplus trailers:* With public school enrollment declining in many districts, some of which once had to meet enrollment problems with temporary facilities may find that they have surplus portable classrooms, or trailers. Having these moved into neighborhoods that will be affected by change, and staffing them with teachers, counselors, and others who can answer questions, can achieve some of the advantages of household visitation. For example, a neighborhood where high school children are to be reassigned might be served by having a trailer brought in to the neighborhood elementary school and staffed on weekends and evenings when parents can visit with appropriate school officials.

This tactic may have added advantage in a school district that is facing an influx of Spanish-speaking Americans, or other ethnics, who may have added suspicions over attending a school in a different neighborhood. It can form a basis that can help mean the difference between success and failure of a new PTA.

In planning PR programs for school districts with increasing numbers of Spanish-speaking, Asian, or other ethnic populations it is well to remember this

KEY CONCERN FOR SCHOOL PR: *In a time of declining enrollment, schools must build a base of survival by serving the objective academic needs of the new Americans. This is the historic role of public education in the United States, and one we cannot afford to neglect today.*

It is impossible to over-emphasize the fact that public schools in the United States no longer have the "captive audience" of participation and support that they may have enjoyed in the past. The revival of interest in religious education and the continued support for private schools, even in the face of horrendous inflation and expense, means public education cannot ignore the legitimate academic needs of the new ethnics. But it must make certain that the schools do not repeat past mistakes by becoming bogged down in social welfare programs that have damaged their credibility as educational institutions.[4]

3. *Use of student displays in public settings:* The display of student art and crafts in a shopping mall is a relatively easy public relations technique to master, since most such malls recognize at once that the display will help attract more visitors. A more modest variation of this technique is to provide student art on loan to individual commercial institutions, such as banks, which are belatedly trying to change some image problems of their own and make themselves seem more sympathetic and human to their customers.

4. *Recognizing teacher upgrading:* Teachers who receive graduate degrees should have that fact called to the attention of the community, something that is easier to accomplish in a small district than a large one. But even in the large one, an appropriate certificate signed by the super-

[4] Just how serious this loss of traditional groups on which the public schools have come to rely for pupils is indicated by a report in *The New York Times* (April 5, 1980) which cites the growth of predominantly black private schools. Affluent blacks have in recent years shown more and more drift toward traditionally *white* private schools, but the trend to enlarge and establish *black* private schools is new, and should be yet another warning to public education that it cannot count on automatic support and enrollment from any group.

intendent and the chairman of the board can be sent to each teacher and a tea or other quasi-social event can be held on a school by school or district-wide basis to extend further recognition.

A modification of this sort of recognition, and one that warrants consideration in this era of strained intra-educational relationships, would be to recognize the dean or other appropriate official of the college or university in which most teachers are pursuing their graduate degrees. Teacher training institutions are pretty well shell-shocked by now with the attacks on the competency of their instruction. If any way can be found in good conscience to give them credit for improving the training and quality of local school faculties, the wise school district manager will utilize it.

In the rush to recognize staff achievement, and call it to the attention of all, the temptation may be strong to cooperate too quickly and too freely with compilers of so-called teacher of the year yearbooks, which will list the teacher's name (along with those of thousands of others from across the nation) and charge the teacher twenty-five dollars or more for a copy. One such endeavor which came to my attention proved to be a gimmick for establishing a mailing list for cookbooks and magazine sales.

5. *Civic clubs:* Many of these organizations have, over the years, done considerable work in support of the schools; clubs such as Civitans, Lions, Rotary, Kiwanis, Ruritans, and many more. An easy technique for returning this favor is to have the school serve as the luncheon meeting site for one meeting each semester, with students waiting on the tables.

6. *Nice notes:* This technique can be used on any level, from the superintendent's office down. Someone in the superintendent's office, whether secretary or public information director, should read each day's paper carefully, and when positive news of an event in a staff member's family is noted, see that a clipping and a congratulatory note go out to the family over the superintendent's signature. The same tactic, perhaps for some type of positive school behavior by a pupil (courtesy in opening doors for adults; picking up waste paper without being told, etc.) can be included in a note sent home to parents by the principal.

7. *Energy:* Neighborhood energy surveys by classes in connection with science or social studies projects can gain positive publicity and give children, under supervision, a chance to meet members of the community who otherwise might not see some of them in a positive setting.

8. *Patriotism:* A long-overlooked means of positive public relations that may be enjoying a revival is to have students participate in poster contests, parades, musical performances, forensic contests, or other such activities as long as the activity does not interfere with their regular academic program or progress. Nothing sits better with older middle-class Americans than activities of this type when they can be engaged in without jingoism.

9. *Values education:* This is another increasingly popular area of interest in education. And though there are legitimate concerns more properly addressed in a book on curriclum, there are opportunities to use this trend positively. For example, students who can find a legitimate academic reason, or extracurricular one, for visiting retirement homes, conducting charity drives, tutoring smaller children, or serving as hospital volunteers demonstrate that American youth has indeed not all gone to hell, as some critics of the public schools would like to believe.

The items just cited are but a few examples that can serve as guidelines for school districts large and small. It should be remembered, however, that successful public relations in education begins with doing the job of basic education properly. With that achievement, few public relations programs can fail; without it, none will succeed for long, no matter how much money, time, and effort is spent on PR. Successful public relations is also an attitude. It consists of examining what is being done well, so that it can be called to the attention of those who would be (or need to be) impressed. It consists of recognizing that which is not being done well, so that support for corrective answers can be enlisted before the crisis occurs. No matter what the size of the district, successful public relations depends first on having something worth publicizing, second on common sense and only at the third level on committees, brochures, banners, and the type of "hands-on" activities which are so popular in many school districts today.

Time and time again, school district PR programs, some of them involving hundreds of thousands of dollars, have failed to deliver the support that was promised by the practitioner and desired by the administration. A sound evaluation, in most instances, will show that these programs were not realistically conceived, were based on perceived achievements of the schools, rather than realistic ones, and were designed to persuade, rather than inform; to cover up, rather than enlighten. To be credible in its public relations efforts, the American school must first be credible in its performance. Without that foundation, no public relations program can succeed.

There is a lesson here, and that lesson is best expressed in this

---

KEY CONCERN FOR SCHOOL PR: *It is important to know when a PR campaign can change the minds of the public, and when an attempt will only cause further alienation.*

Successful Crisis Management

What follows is an actual case of providing information instead of propaganda. The technique can be modified for use no matter what the continuing crisis that faces a school system.

Under the director of public information, a fact center was established, which citizens could call for factual information about what various court orders did—and did not—say; for information about racial percentages in various schools and communities, and for school assignments for pupils in respective neighborhoods. The center, with four phone lines, answered as many as 800 calls a day.

The operation of the fact center exposed those responsible for its operation to calls of all kinds, some of which were obscene; almost all of which were irate. Yet this type of operation cannot be recommended too highly in those instances when a school district is faced with substantial change which will affect the lives of almost all parents and pupils.

For one thing, it gives the school district a direct contact with the reaction of its citizenry. For another, it gives the district's educational managers an opportuniy to diffuse some of the greatest animosity and to correct the types of rumor and deliberate distortions which always spring up whenever a busing plan or other major reorganization of the schools is to be implemented.

It is important, of course, to see that such a center is run by someone who has absolute access to accurate information about the status of plans and who can train a staff to handle the kinds of calls that will be received. This is an opportunity to use volunteers from the community, although these, if used, must be chosen with exceptional care for dependability and performance. It is probably better to hire carefully selected individuals who have a combination of stamina and judgment and who, as paid workers, can be subject to the normal routines of office discipline.

Those who advocate the fact center approach may be surprised to the degree to which some ranking educational managers, including board members, resist the idea in the mistaken belief that they can "stonewall" or otherwise achieve their goals by refusing to answer, or, more important, to seriously and conscientiously *listen*. A recommendation for stonewalling to some degree will come almost invariably from the board's lawyers on the mistaken grounds that they, and only they, are competent to provide information to the public. This is seldom, if ever, the case, and any information prepared by a lawyer is apt to be too late, or too ridiculous in its wording, to do anything other than antagonize further an already irritated public.

Those things which are a matter of public record, which have been filed with a court, which have been discussed at a board meeting, or which would otherwise be available to the public and the press are perfectly legitimate forms of information to be provided in circumstances such as these, and to be placed in a non-argumentative perspective.

The public by and large does not expect reasonable answers, because it knows, frequently, that its questions are unreasonable and impossible. What it frequently wants most of all is to reach someone in the educational establishment who will hear it out. Outrage can be sustained for only so long, after which the fact center worker is in an ideal position to provide those facts the caller may not know, or may not want to understand. At the same time, experience in the Richmond center showed that the public is willing to accept an answer of "I don't know" if it is accompanied by an explanation of *why* the answer is not known (the matter is still in litigation, a final report has not been drafted, etc.). However, the person receiving the call should always tell the caller when the decision is likely to be made if that can reasonably be projected.

Many of the calls received in this manner can be neutralized simply by the mature action of respectful listening and the furnishing of factual information. *No caller should ever be misled.* The answer "No one knows," or "No one can predict that and here's why" is always preferable.

In addition, most callers will exhibit exceptional confusion or total lack of understanding about the executive, legislative, and judicial branches of American government. Many, many callers will not understand, for example, how the courts came to be involved in school matters and will be honestly confused because they believe that an anti-busing referendum or other negative vote, either by the school board, the legislature, or Congress ought to be enough to put a stop to it.

For this reason, those who receive calls in a fact center must understand the lessons supposedly taught in twelfth grade government courses and be prepared to pass them along, particularly that lesson which explains that the civil rights of an individual or class are not subject to popular vote under our Constitution, and that this is the basis for most of the litigation which has led to busing. In effect, there is no purer democratic decision than that of nine wolves to eat a tenth. That is not a condition, however, which does much for the civil rights of the tenth wolf, and this is something entirely too many Americans do not seem to want to understand.

However, opponents to any lawful school plan, particularly those who oppose one that doesn't have the support of law, can quickly raise this

---

KEY CONCERN FOR SCHOOL PR: *Skill in using facts and public relations techniques can rest just as much with parents who oppose your programs as they do with you. School PR is not a secret, the mastery of which lies only with school employees.*

The truth of this concern should not be applied just to controversies such as busing. In attempting to sell a particular program of *any* kind, the wise school manager will realize that a skilled opposition with sufficient funds, or even none at all, can use many of the same techniques to undermine a program that she or he is using in an attempt to build it.

It is true that the educational manager may have access to more facts more quickly than the opposition. Yet in an era of so-called sunshine laws, which open public meetings and public records not just to the press, but to citizens at large, these facts are increasingly available to the opposition, be the issue busing, curriculum, pupil-teacher ratios, or any other educational issue.

In fact, time and skill can be just as important as money, if not more so. The media is usually receptive to reporting "another side" if there are those who know how to contact the media; indeed, radio and television are particularly sensitive to charges that they do not give both sides, because of the fairness doctrine implications which affect their federal licenses. A speakers' bureau is not difficult to organize. Despite their non-political disclaimers, churches and civic associations can frequently form a network for spreading information and opposition to school plans and programs.

The utilization of school public relations, therefore, is not an in-house monopoly. Like the secret of nuclear fission, it now belongs to many groups, and how they choose to use it is beyond the control of any single arm of government.

Understanding the Extent of Trauma

It is sometimes easy to overlook the many ways in which the reassignment of children to schools not of their choosing can traumatize the community. What can be said to a child who worked hard to pay for a class ring that will not reflect the school from which she must now graduate? How do you tell a parent that their star quarterback of a son must now go to a school which already has two star quarterbacks? What can be done to diffuse the rivalry over girls and turf which teenage gangs and groups feel they must go through? How do you reassure a mother whose five-year-old will now be at a strange school ten miles away? How do you explain to the child that she cannot go to the school across the street from her home where her older brothers and sisters went and may still go?

These are the questions, in human terms, which, when multiplied, cause heartache and distress to say nothing of disgust when busing or other massive reassignment comes to a school district.

CHAPTER 12

The Positive Value of No

> When the canary gets unhappy, utters plain-
> tive cries and collapses, it may be time for the
> miners to surface and think things over.
> —Walker Percy[1]

From my office high up in this monstrous new government building, I can see not just much of the city, but the river and the seasons as well. Public education is my concern, primarily what goes on in the schools, as well as the marvelously varied remainder which affects those schools and their future.

It is a wearying concern, however, and I wonder: What now? Where now? With the best of intentions, we have taken the unwanted, the uncared for, the unmotivated, and the unwilling, and tried to supply in the public schools what the home, the church, and the remainder of society have long since abandoned. But at what price and for what purpose? What and who have we neglected in rushing to fill the gap caused by the failure of other institutions and the concomitant expansion of our own?

---

[1] As quoted by Martin Luchesi in his outstanding biography, *Sovereign Way-farer: Walker Percy's Diagnosis of the Malaise*, Louisiana State University Press, Baton Rouge, 1972. Percy's analogy is to the misery of people in the midst of what history would declare to be an age of plenty. To Percy, this misery—the malaise—is the product of the failure of humanism, in which we have put such stock, and it is past time to listen to the canaries.

In a sense, therefore, educational managers can be considered to be sovereign wayfarers whose duty it is to see that the paths which are chosen are those which will genuinely and permanently benefit those who must follow them.

Percy, a non-practicing M.D. and a convert of many years to Roman Catholicism, lives and writes in Louisiana. Now in his sixties, he is primarily a novelist, whose works are considered by some to have the most promise of enduring among any novels written by Americans in the latter half of the twentieth century.

Whither then and whence? Where do we go in public education? What do I see from my window that offers hope, a sense of direction, a way out of the storm of public discontent that rages about the public schools, their performance, and their expense?

There is an answer there. I came across it indirectly one day several months ago, while listening to an assistant superintendent complain. He was complaining, as all educators do, of a lack of funds from Washington or the state capital. If we just had this. If we just had that. One more grant. One more program. One more project. One more change of direction. It would all work out.

But alas, "they" were insensitive to our needs. Washington would not provide. The state would not provide. There was really nothing to be done. "They" were too far away. "They" were unreachable.

Yes, I thought suddenly. There is much truth in what you say. Public education is in many ways underfunded. Yet I cannot help but feel that the problem of funds in public education today is not what "they" give us but what "we" do with it.

I went back to my office and looked out the window once again. Beneath me, stretching from northwest to southeast, lay a large river. I could see clearly the geological phenomenon known as the fall line: the place where tidal waters end, the rocks appear, where the long slow struggle of portages into the Piedmont faced the men who first came this way. It is a phenomenon which led Washington, Richmond, Raleigh, Augusta, and other cities to come into being along the rivers on which they lie. For it was there, at the falls in the river, that men first paused in their rush to the interior, paused, and took stock, and changed their ways of travel.

It was this visible geology upon which the early settlers acted, whether they encountered it on the James, the Savannah, the Neuse, the Rappahannock, or a dozen other rivers. They read the signs and they acted accordingly, and, because they did, they put down roots in something of substance and they prospered—for a while.

Yet this river, this restless, changing river, alternately swift and silent, filthy, roiling, polluted and beautiful, had but recently flooded. A Hundred Year Flood it had been called. And so it must have been, because that seal of importance, national television, came and took pictures. Once in a century could the river be expected to flood like that. There was damage. Much damage. But after that, no worry. A hundred years is a long time.

And then the river flooded again, a second Hundred Year Flood in the space of a few months. What madness was this? What betrayal by the forecasters? What an argument for the dikes the experts had said were unnecessary? The river, could it speak, would not, I believe, have wasted words or breath in answer.

But the river was telling me something. It was telling us all something.

"We" cannot control the rain that falls upstream. That is "their" doing.

"We" cannot guarantee that the river will not flood and attempt to leave its channel.

But what we can do, I submit, is to recognize that there are forces in the American condition that will divert us from our purpose, just like that river. They will make demands, strident demands, that the schools feed the hungry, clothe the naked, succor the sick. They will demand and demand until the day comes when we look about ourselves and realize that we have abandoned the high heritage for which schools and schools alone are best equipped:

- To teach language that will enable youth to communicate as adults.
- To master the basic math which will allow them to understand what trickery can be practiced by the merchant and the government, by apostles of both left and right.
- To provide children with a sense of self, an understanding of others, a recognition of where and what they are, whence they came, who and what they might yet become.

Dignity, respect, honor, and justice. These are some of our roles, some of our responsibilities. We cannot teach them if we abandon our own duty, our own heritage, our own responsibility to teach and to teach specific topics of proven value.

More than twenty years ago, Gilbert Highet wrote in one of his marvelous volumes, " 'But,' you will ask, 'do schools exist only to train geniuses?' No, but they do not exist only to train the average and to neglect or benumb the talented. They exist to make the best of both!"[2]

[2] *Man's Unconquerable Mind*, Columbia University Press, 1954. If Walker Percy denies that humanism alone can prevent the malaise, Profesor Highet emphasizes in superb fashion that people are hardly more than animals without it, religious convictions notwithstanding. This does not mean that either Percy or Highet is correct, or that both are wrong. It is more likely that both are correct.

I can think of no two contemporary authors whose writings could contribute more to the development of a sound perspective among educational managers. Yet I doubt that either is known by one school manager, practicing or potential, in 500. I find it consoling, however, that my introduction to Highet is a debt of more than twenty-five years' standing that is owed, appropriately, to a teacher, Dr. George Pasti.

Highet, in *The Art of Teaching* (Alfred A. Knopf, 1950) made some observations that are as shrewdly true today as they were thirty years ago: "But it seems to me that resistance (to learning) was not shown by *entire classes* of youths and girls, year after year, until education ceased to be a privilege sought after by the few and became a compulsion inflicted on everybody."

It may also help the few educational managers who are committed to schools that *teach* necessary subjects of proven value to know that their frustration is not necessarily unique. For, as Highet adds, "Montaigne, who was a mild enough man and devoted to kindness as an education ideal . . . (suggested) that if a boy refused to learn or proved quite incapable of it, his tutor should strangle him, if there are not witnesses, or else he should be apprenticed to a pastrycook in some good town."

Yes, the river will flood. But now is the time to build sound dikes and levees.

It is the "we" in public education who have lost our way, not just the "they" in the citizenry and the other branches of government which have lost faith in us.

To paraphrase the distinguished contemporary novelist Walker Percy, we should watch the public's reaction rather like coal miners used to watch the canary they once took in the shaft with them to test the air. The public school managers of today are those miners, whether they know it or not, and they ignore the reactions of their "canaries" at their own peril.

Public education was established to do certain things for children. An eight-year-old head is capable, essentially, of absorbing only so much in a six-hour day. And when we try to cram into that head desirable, but nonessential items; when we assume, glibly, that we can do for children what home and church and other branches of society are unwilling or unable to do, then "we" have brought on ourselves exactly what "we" deserve.

Instead of building dikes and levees to harness the forces which would destroy public education, instead of seeing our goals as realistic and simple, if at times very, very difficult, we turn away. Play is more fun than work. Children know it. They know it because we taught them.

There is a considerable question as to whether the current generation of school administrators can change their thinking to a sound realization that it is in quality, and placement of the dikes and levees, not just their quantity or their size, that the salvation of American education lies.

The British, the spiritual fathers of so much that is American, cannot understand our obsession with built-in obsolescence, the compulsion to tear down buildings and programs simply because they are mature and proven, in the name of the new and the innovative.

In our training programs for teachers and school administrators, we have become so obsessed with finding a place to go that we have lost sight of the advantages of pausing long enough to look *back* on the route we have travelled in such a rush to see just where we have gone astray. Speed is no asset when you have taken the wrong road, or when the goal toward which you are rushing has not been clearly thought out or sensibly decided upon.

Our efforts to turn school management into a science have obscured the need to remember that it is an art—and that art measures achievement just as much as science does. We are indeed educating for the future. In that sense, all educators are futurists; they must be futurists. But there is no evidence, not one whit, that common sense is going to lose its value as a commodity for today's youth and tomorrow's adults. Indeed, if anything, in a world of technological and economic chaos, it may just be the common sense of the traditional verities that allows us to survive, individually and collectively, as persons and as a society with a sense of purpose.

If we are to chart a sound path for public education, we must develop a greater supply of talent, of brains, and, yes, of genius, and draw it into school management. We must find men and women of sound education, of judgment, of perspective, who recognize that science and technolgy and innovation do not have all the answers for what the public wants and needs.

We have elevated everything to a science—or tried to: social science, political science, the science of education, the science of public relations.

But in so-doing we have made a discovery, or rather a rediscovery, and that is the need for art to give science, or pseudo-science, a meaning. We can look at the great stone faces of Easter Island and even the dullest among us is stunned, in awe, as we ponder how they came to be and what they must have meant to the civilization which created them, and the meanings they have for us. Will another generation, stumbling upon a computer printout for utility bills or clothing shipments feel the same awe? I rather doubt it.

Simply stated, science does not have all the answers. It never has and perhaps it never will. Yet science has been immensely beneficial to humanity—*thinking* humanity—to a humanity that has not lost sight of the fact that it is its *thinking* that makes science go, that gives directions and purpose. And to know which way to go, we must know from which directions we have come—and where we are now.

It is a stunning thing to realize that science has failed, that the irascible human element refuses to surrender to a mechanics that would computerize bus schedules, assigning pupils through the science of demographics, for example.

So enamored have we become with that which science has made possible that we have blundered into two false beliefs, both of which have had profound, negative affects on education. They are:

1. Through science, all things are possible.
2. That which is possible is good.

It *is* possible, of course, to so fragment the elementary school day that we can "expose" children to a hundred separate five minute courses as if each child was a bit of x-ray film and all those exposures would "take." The mini-course of which so many schools are so proud is certainly a step in this direction, and a mini-knowledge is all that has resulted.

Why?

Because the computer scientists of education understand schedules but not people. They schedule a new "subject," another "learning experience" every five minutes but the attention span of that one non-scientific variable, the child, remains remarkably the same, limited. It is frustrating to the scientist, but it does not change. The child will learn only so much and thus we must choose the human things the child needs most to know, those things that have made humanity unique on this planet and perhaps in this solar system: language, judgment, culture, values, a sense of history and origins, an ability to use tools *for a thinking* purpose; tools such as math and physics and, yes, even computers.

But the human-child also needs to know how to make wise choices from this plethora, this plastic Eden. She or he needs to recognize the difference between snakes and apples. She or he needs to be able to think and, having thought, possess the courage to say no. No to her- or himself, first of all. No to those for whom she or he is responsible, as a parent or teachers use their wisdom to say a loving no to children.

Because so much is possible in our time, through the magic of science which flashes images and ideas about the world without regard to their value, we see humanity divided increasingly into two groups. The larger, non-thinking hedonistic group answers all questions with, "Why not?"

The smaller group, the one in which our hope for stability, survival, and, yes, progress lies, asks, first, "Why?"

This is no attack against pure research even though science has no intrinsic value as such. Fleming's mold could have contained nothing of value. Instead it grew penicillin. We never know where a discovery, the pursuit of which seems at first to be the height of waste and foolishness may produce bonanzas undreamed of, benefits unglimpsed.

But science, unquestioned science, will never do this alone. So it behooves us to say, "Why?" What evidence do we have that spending billions to feed cucumber seeds to all first graders twice a day will cure cancer? There is no evidence, you say, only supposition; the supposition of an individual not so much interested in curing cancer as in finding, and funding, a program that will guarantee his sinecure.

Yet even to such a questionable proposal as this, a door need not be closed entirely. Proceed if you must, with a small group of volunteers and we will wish you well. It is not education's job to rule out any possibility for progress, no matter how questionable. It *is* the job of education not to rush the public schools pell-mell down the road unproven while allowing the highway of proven progress to go untravelled. Thus we who must be responsible for education, for the children of the tomorrows we will never see, must have the courage to say no to you and your nationwide commitment to cucumbers and be about our proper business: teaching children that which has long since been proved that they need so that one day they too will have the wisdom and courage to say no.

This stand does not represent a neo-Luddite posture in which all science, all technology, is to be resisted because it has the potential for change. There is no intention here to hold back a revolution in learning as the original Luddites sought to oppose the Industrial Revolution because it brought a change they found both fearsome and threatening. Not at all. Rather, this warning is against hoping foolishly for that for which evidence provides no hope, just as we must live in a mortal world for the foreseeable future, no matter how much we may hope for, and work toward, the option of earthly immortality.

There are so many hard and serious questions we in education should be asking ourselves, questions we shy from like children fearful of the dark. But it is not the unknown we fear, but rather the subconscious knowledge that the answers we pretend to seek are really there, that they are so simple, so objective, that there is no way we can justify the continuation of our current practices of education once we are forced to face them. For these are the answers which would compel us to say no to our fulsome nature, our frivolous selves, our non-productive educational practices which have turned the public against us and which breed a betrayal of children which, in turn, will lead all too soon to a demand for revenge.

Do we, for example, help a child more by talking to him about intelligently watching that scientific marvel, television, or by conditioning him not to watch it at all in favor of taking a walk, of remaining silent for five minutes without moving, of trying to put into a single simple sentence what is most important to him?

This is how we teach that most valuable of all questions, the most subjective and, therefore, the most antipathetic to unthinking technology: It is by asking, and continuing to ask, the noblest question of them all: Why?

Why are you watching television?

Why are you eating an overly expensive cereal filled with sugar?

Why? Why? It is the question that most separates the thinking human from non-thinking human: human who can *be* from the animal who lives only for the what and where and how. The child who does not learn the self-discipline which asking—and answering—the question "why" demands becomes the adult who does not do so either. He becomes the adult who uncritically adopts whatever fad he encounters and claims that cause for his own. Educational managers should know his kind well. No innovation brings lasting satisfaction and none is ever enough for these adults. The educational manager who tries to satisfy parents bred from such stock has an impossible task. Yet these are frequently the same adults who cannot balance a checkbook because they will not.

In this sense, the prophets of science are spiritual kin of the prophets of advertising. In the world of advertising, tomorrow will always be better. Each product must be "new, improved." How often have we seen those very words applied to deodorant, razor blades, toilet paper, washing powder. Here, here the advertising scientists clamor. You don't like this discovery? Then give us just another season; you'll love what we have for you tomorrow.

Others are also finding this to be true. Even some of the purest scientific practitioners seem to understand that there are proper, finite limits to what they can do successfully. Here is Robert Jastrow, the internationally known astronomer, and the conclusion he has reached:

> . . . but the barrier to further progress seems insurmountable. It is not a matter of another year, another decade of work, another measurement, or another theory; at this moment it seems as though science will never be able to raise the curtain on the mystery of creation. For the scientist who has lived by this faith in the power of reason, the story ends like a bad dream. He has scaled the mountains of ignorance; he is about to conquer the highest peak; as he pulls himself over the final rock, he is greeted by a band of theologians who have been sitting there for centuries.[3]

Jastrow's conclusions cannot, however, be used to suggest that the schools' problems in satisfying the public can be found in a return to some form of sectarian operation, much as that might be desired by fundamentalists of both Protestant and Catholic belief. The schools have their own gods already, and they have called forth much of the trouble which is now being faced. These are the gods of Freud, Dewey, and Piaget, each of whom is partly responsible for preaching a pseudo-scientific shortcut to the solution which public education must find.

Indeed, public education may be considered to have developed partly as a long overdue antithesis to the narrow, restrictive, and prejudiced practices of the religious schools. Still, the sectarian school did at least have firm objectives toward which it strove. Perhaps it is time for the public schools—not in a denial of their heritage of liberalism or in any endorsement of sectarianism—to set reasonable and proper limits on their goals, to opt for a sensible retention of substance and a dislodging of chaff. Just as in the Dark Ages, the monastaries of the Roman Catholic Church held an oasis of knowledge from the past, a foundation to pass on to the future, so perhaps that role should be assumed by the public schools today. It is a high calling, and a lonely one, to accept the responsibility for the preservation of knowledge and the establishment of a foundation on which future knowledge may be built, but it is a calling worthy of the public schools. What better way to raise their standing in the eyes of a jaundiced and suspicious public than to return to the discharge of the honorable duties and responsibilities which public education once assumed?

There is no better way, of course, and it can be achieved without penalizing thought or advances or technology, as long as goals are established and a reasoned measurement is provided to record progress—or the lack of it—toward those goals. Fifty years ago, for example, in the heyday of the so-called core curriculum, public educators trumpeted the prospect

---

[3] *God and the Astronomers,* W.W. Norton & Co., 1978.

that a socially centered "core curriculum" would civilize youth. It did no such thing, of course, for the attempts at teaching of all subjects from a social foundation, or with social goals in prospect overlooked one thing: social people, civilized people, have to have the skills before they can function fully and effectively in modern society. It is the skills that make people social and civilized, not some glib participation in democratic interaction, or committee-based decision making.

Does this mean the core curriculum is bad? Yes, in that it had the wrong thing at its core. No, in that a similar approach, using for the core skills mathematics and communication—plus the requirement of objective measurement to see who is making what progress—can still work today.

Yet while we fiddle and stumble in public education, looking desperately for some new guru with another answer, "'Yes, my son, this will work for you if only you carpet the classroom, give every child a camera, or teach only what children already know" things, as Yeats noted, will simply continue to fall apart.

Public education did not come to its position of fulsomeness by accident. In a sense, this has been a growing part of Western civilization, made part most recently by the appearance of wealth and the development of technology. Malachi Martin, whose particular interest is the Roman Catholic Church, its development, and its periodic exercises in self-torture, either toward the right or toward the left, offers this observation:

> But the nearer the West has come to realizing its ideal of materialist and humanist happiness . . . , the more obviously it has succeeded in transforming its world into a meaningless, spiritless place overshadowed, not by a sense of meaning and purpose and hope, but by the imminent danger of nuclear extinction.[4]

Martin may not be right about the nuclear extinction, but the description of much of the way the Western world looks, thinks, and feels, particularly that portion of it that lies in the United states, seems certainly fair. I cannot help but wonder to what degree our prevailing attitudes about how children should be educated in public schools have contributed to this malaise.

Time after time after time, in word after word after word, in place after place after place, the civilized world is calling for a sense of perspective, of purpose. But the guru they seek will not come to them from outside. The guru will come only from within their own toughness and self-discipline, the development of their own sense of purpose. This longing has been expressed so often, in so many ways. James Michener, the

---

[4] United Features Syndicate, December 3, 1978.

popular novelist, said it in one of his lesser known novels of more than thirty years ago:

> For this is the journey that men make: to find themselves. If they fail in this, it doesn't matter much what else they find. Money, position, fame, many loves, revenge, are all of little consequence, and when the tickets are collected at the end of the ride they are tossed into the bin marked FAILURE.
> But if a man happens to find himself—if he knows what he can be depended upon to do, the limits of his courage, the positions from which he will no longer retreat . . . the secret reservoirs of his determination, the extent of his dedication, the depth of his feeling for beauty, his honest and unpostured goals—then he has found a mansion which he can inhabit with dignity all the days of his life.[5]

These are ideals. They are subjective. But they are goals. They are legitimate goals. They are goals toward which any and all individuals and segments and organizations in a society should strive. Yet they are difficult and demanding and for that very reason they are properly the responsibility of the public schools, there to be cared for and fed and nurtured and kept alive and implanted in the hearts, souls, and heads of children from generation unto generation. To do this, however, to achieve these goals rationally schools must enable children to find a stability and the tools of language and objective academic accomplishment with which to build the secure foundation from which to embark on their subjective journey through life.

Ann Roiphe, the popular writer of the "liberated" late 1960s and early 1970s somehow seemed rather poignant in a longing for some sense of structure and some feeling that there are values which endure:

> Sentimentally speaking, I wish we could return to an earlier America when society surrounded its members with a tight sense of belonging, of being needed. Maybe it's better to be . . . tribal and ethnocentric than urbane and adrift. We are like jellyfish in the vast ocean, dropping our young into the waves and immediately losing them because we have all become merely transparent.[6]

As I read those lines I thought of the children from the "urbane . . . adrift" homes of America—they can be rich, middle-class, or poor—and how the answer of America's public schools is to put them into an "open" classroom where chaos and anarchy pass for learning and the security which they need to *learn* to function for their own ultimate independence has been taken away for their own "good." How much better for such a child were he to know that the fourth seat in the fifth row was his,

[5] *The Fires of Spring*, Random House, 1949.
[6] *The New York Times*, February 21, 1973.

and his alone; that it would be at that point each day when he came to school from a home and a community otherwise "urbane and adrift" and that the same teacher would be in *his or her* place, educated, intelligent, loving, compassionate, reasonably demanding, developing in the child a sense of pride that he could attack tasks of continuing purpose and increasing difficulty and perform them.

We are caught up in a mentality that if we just don't like something, we can change it with more money or more technology. Never should we have to learn to live with it, no matter how much we hate it. Dr. Francis Crick, the British biologist who shared the 1962 Nobel Prize for the discovery of the DNA molecule, even went so far as to wonder if Americans were not spending too much time and money on medical research. "Americans have a peculiar illusion that life is a disease that has to be cured," he said. "Everyone gets unpleasant diseases, and everyone dies at one time. I guess they are trying to make life safe for senility."[7]

Or is it our educational system that is attempting to make life safe for senility? Obviously, the good Dr. Crick is not suggesting an end to medical research, but rather is pointing out that life is to be lived, with purpose if at all possible, not "cured" as if it were a disease. Yet in education, as in medicine, we have the peculiar American obsession of slinging money against the wall, hoping that if you sling enough, some of it sticks and some good will result. Perhaps this is why in America the hospice, that loving, caring home for the dying, has been so slow to come by, while in Britain the hospice realistically will provide a little gin and heroin and honey on request to the dying and, lo, thereby make the quality of their last days worth something, if only because they recognize the inevitability of death.

Which, after all, is nature's way of saying "no" and, in the case of the suffering, must surely be considered a positive answer and a positive value.

As James Dickey, the poet, observed in his striking little book of prose, *Self-Interviews,* "The medical profession may save your life, but it can never make your life *worth* saving. It's in the realm of values, the things we set store by, that good teachers . . . operate."[8]

In his speech upon accepting the Nobel Prize for literature, the late William Faulkner confessed his belief that man will not only "endure, but prevail."[9] If he does, then his system of values, tied up as they are, incorporated in, and reflected by, schools will make the difference. Yet it seems so often that education, if it is even aware of the Faulknerian hope, goes plodding along head down, uncritically ingesting whatever educational beliefs and practices are laid before it, and occasionally threshing about in a fit of pedagogic colic. It does not seem to be much of a way to reach a goal.

[7] As quoted by the Associated Press, January 18, 1973.

[8] *Self-Interviews* was recorded and edited by Barbara and James Reiss, Doubleday & Company, Inc., 1970.

[9] Delivered in Stockholm, November 1950.

There is more to making something work than that. James Thurber, the famous American humorist, used to tell of his Aunt Florence and a balky cream separator on which she had been laboring, hour after hour, in the privacy of her kitchen. (How many of today's children—or adults—know what a cream separator looks like is another story.) The going was obviously slow and demanding, but the rest of the family went about its business as Florence labored over her cream separator, until finally, late in the day, they heard her scream, "Why doesn't somebody take this goddam thing away from me?"[10]

It is easy to sympathize with Florence. The repairs to public education are demanding and tedious and the conscientious educational manager, working so often alone and in isolation, may feel he has been so abandoned that some type of hideous symbiotic relationship has developed and he is about to be devoured by what he is trying to make right again.

It is well, therefore, to remember, that although our ideals should lie with Faulkner, our pragmatic realities must also understand the problems of Aunt Florence and the cream separator.

We are throwing so-called knowledge in the form of so-called mini-courses and learning experiences at children as if we were pitching manure without considered purpose or careful aim, never pausing to examine the quality of our acts, or their lasting value, but acting rather with a frantic hope that somehow children will grow into what they want and need to become. At the same time, however, in classroom after classroom I see closets filled with "teaching materials," books unused, papers, crayons, pencils, scissors, audiovisual equipment by the case and by the ton—and children who are not learning because they are not being taught. In a world of plenty, teachers cry for still more gadgets and equipment. Surrounded by beverages of all kind, the dying man proclaims his thirst because he has not learned to raise his arm to help himself—or to swallow.

Once upon a time a child was fortunate to have a school book of any kind, and the child therefore treasured it, and his parents treasured it, even when they didn't understand everything in it, because for all their ignorance they still knew that it was in this manner that knowledge could be passed on from generation to the next.

Or perhaps a child could hope for, look forward to, a field trip once during his school career to his state or national capital, and thus it became an event of high importance, worth preparing for and remembering for its value. Today, particularly in urban systems, children are hauled out of classrooms and given federal funds to go shopping at Christmas, or fishing at a pond in the spring, when all the while the skills and tools for a lifetime of self-entertainment and of learning lie neglected in their classrooms.

[10] *The Clocks of Columbus,* a biography, by Charles S. Holmes, Atheneum, 1972.

How many among us remember the first or perhaps the only major league baseball game we ever saw—or the first mountain—or the first time we saw the ocean, or the first Beethoven symphony, or Shakespearean play, or movie? Yet today our senses are so jaded that the marvels of the past become in our limited vision the mundaneness of today. We are besieged by what the novelist Walker Percy calls the malaise of every-dayness and so the schools try to outdo television and the Burger King; they imitate the New York Giants, and the San Francisco Giants, because experience, multiple, uncritical experience, has become the god, and become the goal, and the flickering fires of conscience that cry out for a pause, an evaluation; a respite from the sensory onslaught so that the palate of the mind may yet recover and function; these fires grow dimmer and dimmer until they die out at last, because we have been unable or unwilling to discipline ourselves and our children to appreciate the special moment and the demanding and wonderfully satisfying requirements of learning and of thought.

The icy wind of economic disaster is blowing with increasing force against the fabric and the institutions of American democracy, including the public schools. And unless educational managers demonstrate objective leadership that will restore public confidence and instill a self-discipline in pupils that today seems almost unknown, public education has little future.

Those of us who are educational managers have not only the duty but the responsibility to lead the schools out of this dilemma. But we can lead only by example. Until we demonstrate our own self-discipline, our stewardship, to use a word long out of fashion, then we are not only foolish but irresponsible when we bad-mouth a public that is increasingly skeptical of underwriting our vague and excessive schemes.

It is at the edge of disaster, however, that the greatest opportunities sometimes lie. Achieving the goal may be hard for pupils, but it is we who shy from the goal most of all because we know that it will be ever harder for us; for the educational managers who have lost the will and purpose and sense of The Positive Value of No.

The task for children is simply this: objective subjects of proven value which impart a sense of self and purpose, of community instead of chaos, of the disciplined mind and the disciplined life, of questions before content, and in the knowledge that for all gratifications, no matter how instant, someone somewhere at some time will have to pay a price not just in dollars but in waste of time and life and freedom and opportunity.

We cannot afford this. We cannot afford it for ourselves and we dare not inflict it on yet another generation.

Despite all the hell American public education has been catching—much of it deserved—I still believe that public education is the best hope of the nation. For we are a secular society. I say that without intending insult to religious faith or to the churches and synagogues and their contributions to the greatness and the welfare of the nation. But religion has, at times, stood in the way of the true and the just and the right—as public education has at times stood in the way of progress.

But public education can fulfill the destiny of all in a way that sectarian religion never can and perhaps never should. Public education is *the* unifying force for greatness in this nation. It gives *meaning* to equality. It gives hope, a chance, an opportunity, to those who might otherwise be closed out.

I believe that public education has stumbled and stumbled badly in carrying out its mission, serving its purpose, reaching its goal. The obstacles are many. Some of them may not be immediately and directly within our power to remove or control.

My plea is that those of us in public education, the managers and the staffs, recognize simply that we have the capacity to be, indeed, the history of being, our own worst enemies; of being the worst obstacle in our own paths and that we commit ourselves, in wisdom and in conscience, to making sure that we no longer will remain our own worst enemy.

And all the while, the river waits. We have not built our dikes and levees to protect the *continuity* of what we know in our hearts that children need. The fads and fancies and glittering baubles are endless—"movement education," "organic curriculum," "differentiated staffing," "visual literacy," each is an opiate which takes us from what we should be doing, what the public expects; what it has a right to expect. Each tempts us to lean on our shovels in the sun, believing that the river will never flood again.

For teaching is not easy. It never was. And neither is learning. The suspicion persists in the documents and materials I receive from teachers: children cannot read because teachers do not; they cannot figure because multiplication is mystery to those we've charged with teaching it. But this is the very substance of scholarship. It is not in calling for help from the "task specialist" or the "curriculum specialist" or the visiting consultant that we solve the problems of ignorance in children. It is in what teachers themselves bring to the classroom from the breadth and depth or paucity of their own preparation, their own continuing education.

You do not believe me? Try this. Offer a dollar to any public school teacher who can discuss one new book of lasting value he or she has read in or out of his or her teaching field in the last month.

You won't lose ten dollars in twenty-five classrooms. Try it with administrators, too. You won't lose any more; probably far less.

How, then, do we recover? Is it too late? Have the floods of fancy, the specious tides of silly things swept all sense and substance from public education?

There is hope. It is not too late. The answer to our problems is so simple that we reject it. We turn away from it because, like wrinkles in a morning's mirror, we do not wish to know the truth.

And the truth is in the positive use of the word, "No!"

I say:

No. We cannot take a child for whom the home has assumed no responsibility and automatically turn him into a lovable citizen, unless the home is willing to admit its failure, come forth, and join us. We do both child and public a disservice to presume otherwise.

No. We cannot remediate in education beyond a certain point. We have betrayed enough children by letting them think today's work could be done tomorrow and tomorrow's not at all. We must do what any businessperson knows is simple sense: install the item properly the first time, then we won't have to keep taking it out and trying to do it over again later.

These are just examples. Anyone with any recent exposure to public education can add to the list of areas in which a resounding, constructive *no* could have a positive effect. A beginning can be made anywhere, at any level. The smallest school in the smallest district can set this trend in motion and will find it indeed an idea whose time has come and for which there is already a huge body of support among parents.

Read, write, spell, add, and subtract. Understand self and culture and that of others. Appreciate the dignity of work, of beauty, of ethics, of justice, of thought and wisdom, and the fact that we are all but links between past and future. It is enough of a chore for anyone, and this includes the public schools.

Do these things, and the public clamor and discontent will subside. Do the job for which we were created. Do it with understanding and compassion. Do it honestly. And never, ever, be afraid to say no. No. No to ourselves when we are tempted to use one more fulsome phrase for one more silly enterprise; no to the public which has helped make us what we are; no to children who are travelling through the void of ignorance without loving, purposeful discipline.

Each no will be part of the dikes, part of the levees. It will preserve the sense and substance and purpose of education. It is our job, not "theirs," to do this and when the river begins to flood with enticement, or fancy, or outrage, the continuity of education's true contributions will remain secure.

Love. Compassion. Common sense. The ability to say no.

When public education learns to say this, public education will have begun its long road back to its rightful place, the position of service, which it and only it can occupy in a civilized community.

But as long as education makes promises it knows it cannot keep, or talks in ambiguities to a public pleading for simple sanity, the flood of discontent will rise and all that education once was and could be again stands fair to be washed away for good.